SCOTTISH V̶O̶I̶C̶E̶S̶ ̶1̶7̶4̶5̶–̶1̶9̶6̶0̶

PROFESSOR T.C. SMO͟... School and Clare Co͟... appointed to a Personal ͟... the University of Edinb͟... present position as Professor of Scottish History at the University of St Andrews in 1980. Two of his previous books, *A History of the Scottish People 1560–1830* and *A Century of the Scottish People 1830–1950*, were described as 'by far the most stimulating, the most instinctive, and the most readable account of Scots history that I have read' by Hugh Trevor-Roper in the *Sunday Times*.

SYDNEY WOOD has specialized in the study of local history, and has been instrumental in the formulation of the history curriculum for schools in Scotland. He has published many notable articles and books over the last twenty-five years, and he currently teaches at the Northern College of Education in Aberdeen.

OTHER WORKS BY T. C. SMOUT

Scottish Trade on the Eve of Union, 1660–1707
A History of the Scottish People, 1560–1830
A Century of the Scottish People 1830–1950
Scottish Population History from the Seventeenth Century
to the 1930s (with M. W. Flinn *et al.*)
The State of the Scottish Working Class in 1843
(with Ian Levitt)

OTHER WORKS BY SYDNEY WOOD

The Shaping of Nineteenth-century Aberdeenshire
History in the Grampian Landscape
(with A. J. Patrick)
Living in Victorian Times
Scottish Life 1750–1945
The British Welfare State
Changing Lives: Scotland and Britain from 1830s
to the present day

SCOTTISH VOICES

1745–1960

T.C. SMOUT
AND
SYDNEY WOOD

FontanaPress
An Imprint of HarperCollins*Publishers*

Fontana Press
An Imprint of HarperCollins*Publishers*
77–85 Fulham Palace Road,
Hammersmith, London W6 8JB

Published by Fontana Press 1991
3 5 7 9 8 6 4

First published in Great Britain by
William Collins Sons & Co. Ltd, 1990

Selection, arrangement and editorial matter
Copyright © T.C. Smout and Sydney Wood, 1990

ISBN 0 00 686216 0

Set in Janson

Printed in Great Britain by
HarperCollinsManufacturing Glasgow

ACKNOWLEDGEMENTS

We are grateful to the following for permission to use illustrations:

Aberdeen City Library: 2, 26
Aberdeen Journals: 3, 29, 30, 34
People's Palace Museum: 6
North East of Scotland Library Service: 10, 17, 18, 25
St Andrews University Library:
    Cowie Print Collection 7, 20, 33
    Adam Print Collection 11, 12, 13, 14, 15, 21, 27, 31, 32
Scottish National Portrait Gallery: 5
Shetland Museum: 19
Stephen Patterson: 27
Strathclyde Regional Archives: 8, 9
D. C. Thomson: 1, 4, 16, 22, 23, 28

We are greatly obliged to the following for permission to reproduce passages from the works cited in the references on pp. 319–22:

CHAPTER II
(Extract 3) Century Hutchinson Publishing Group; (5) *The Evening Express* [Aberdeen Journals]; (6) Molly Weir and Grafton Books; (7) Liz Lochhead

CHAPTER III
(1) David and Charles Publishers; (4) Roderick Grant and Triple Cat Publishing; (5) Dr the Honourable Sir Ewan Forbes, Bart.; (6) Maurice Lindsay

CHAPTER IV
(2) Routledge Ltd; (3) Liz Lochhead; (5) Janetta Bowie

CHAPTER V
(3) Harrap Publishing Group; (4) Aberdeen University Press and the Centre for Scottish Studies, University of Aberdeen; (5) Workers Educational Association, S.E. Scotland Division; (6) Macgibbon and Kee, Grafton Books

CHAPTER VI
(8) Catriona Proudfoot and the Leura Press

CHAPTER VII
(3) John Hume and Abertay Historical Society; (8) David Winter and Son, Ltd

CHAPTER VIII

(5) Executors of the estate of Eleanor Sillar; (6) Messrs William Collins; (9) Macgibbon and Kee, Grafton Books

CHAPTER IX

(3) Professor David Daiches; (4) Ralph Glasser and Chatto and Windus, Ltd; (5) Mainstream Publishing Ltd and Gavin Muir

CHAPTER X

(5) Mainstream Publishing Ltd and Gavin Muir; (6) Michael Grieve

CHAPTER XI

(3) Ayrshire Archaelogical and Natural History Society; (5) Molly Weir and Grafton Books; (6) Lawrence and Wishart Ltd; (7) Methuen and Co.

CHAPTER XII

(4) Macdonald Lindsay Pindar; (6) Professor David Daiches; (7) & (8) Dr Michael Thomson and Aberdeen University Press; (9) Mainstream Publishing Ltd

CHAPTER XIII

(5) Nigel Gray and Gower Publishing Group

CHAPTER XIV

(6) Molly Weir and Grafton Books; (7) & (8) Century Hutchinson Publishing Group

CHAPTER XV

(5) & (6) Canongate Publishing Ltd
(8) Ralph Glasser and Chatto and Windus, Ltd; (9) The *Observer*

CHAPTER XVI

(2) Alan Sutton Publishing, Ltd; (7) Professor David Daiches; (8) Molly Weir and Grafton Books; (9) Catriona Proudfoot and the Leura Press

CHAPTER XVII

(2) Scottish History Society; (5) Hodder and Stoughton Ltd

CHAPTER XVIII

(5) James Shaw Grant

Every effort has been made to trace owners of copyright and we apologise to any whom it has proved impossible to contact.

CONTENTS

ILLUSTRATIONS

GLOSSARY

airt	direction of wind
aise-backet	box made of wood for carrying ashes
ashets	large flat dishes
bear bread	bread made from barley
bear meal	meal made from barley
bere	a hardy variety of barley
the Broo	labour exchange, or unemployment office
but-and-ben	a small cottage divided into 2 rooms
carses	stretches of level fertile land, near a river
deece	a long wooden settee that could be used as a bed
feu	plot of land held from a 'feu superior' to whom duty had to be paid (as a relic of feudalism)
feuars	the occupant of a feu
fly cups	occasional cup of tea
greeting	weeping
sousy	happy, jolly, plump
spurtle	wooden stick or spoon
tattie-chapper	tool for mashing potatoes
topping	leading, most important
unco	unusual, uncommon, exceptional

CHAPTER I

CHANGING TIMES

Scotland at the end of the eighteenth century was a profoundly different country from the Scotland of today. Obviously it was materially very much poorer, though with a sense that enrichment – at least to the level of contemporary England – was coming within reach. It was very much more rural before the Industrial Revolution created the great manufacturing towns, though urban settlements were already growing more rapidly in Scotland at this time than anywhere else in Europe. The New Town of Edinburgh, the squares of Georgian Glasgow of the tobacco age, and the spread of Aberdeen, Dundee, Perth and many smaller provincial towns were testimony to this, but the innumerable Lowland farm towns and clustered Highland settlements were witness to an older and commoner form of habitation. There were fewer people to share the resources of land, trade and industry – only about one quarter of the number in Scotland today, and those distributed relatively more densely in the Highlands, the North-East and the Borders, much more thinly in the Central Belt. London was further away and mattered less. It was of course true that Scotland had lost her own Parliament in 1707, but the scope of parliamentary legislation was trifling compared to the present day; businesses of all sorts were run from within Scotland, and for most practical purposes the Scots were left to get on with their own affairs.

Our book tells the story of changing times from those days in the words of Scottish men and women themselves, tracing the alterations and the continuities of experience through the traumas and successes of the Victorian industrial age down to our own mixed and perplexing century. We have selected certain themes – work, love, celebration, religion, sickness, shopping, travel and so on – to illustrate the real history of ordinary people doing everyday things. But we begin with three accounts, two from the Lowlands in the eighteenth century, one from the Highlands in the nineteenth, which convey above all else a sense of an old, traditional and very poor world passing away. We all live in changing times, but Somerville, Ramsay and Osgood Mackenzie had a correct sense of being on a watershed between one kind of society and another much better off, but also more hastened and acquisitive. Reverend Thomas Somerville was the minister of Jedburgh, and his concern was mainly with altered manners. He cast his mind back to the Borders of his youth and considered the gentry and their friends.

Before the year 1760 none of the poor, or only a small proportion of them, wore stockings. Even in the houses of gentlemen of high rank, the maid-servants seldom used them in the earlier part of the day while employed in servile work. The celebrated Charles Townshend used to give a ludicrous description of his being received by a "female porter" without stockings or shoes, when he paid his respect to Lord President Craigie in the Lawnmarket, Edinburgh, in 1758 or 1759, and also of the practice, at that time general in the country, of the women treading their dirty linen, instead of washing it with their hands.

The dress both of men and women alike in the middle and higher ranks exhibited by turns the extremes of gaudy ostentation and disgusting slovenliness. Not only the hats, but the body clothes of gentlemen in full dress, were fringed with gold or silver lace. The hats were all then cocked. (Velvet caps, however, were worn by many of the gentlemen, and leather caps frequently by the farmers.) At an early period of my life a few of the country gentlemen of more advanced age wore swords when in full dress, and I knew aged persons who remembered swords being held as an indispensable article of fashionable costume. The discontinuance of this practice may be considered as in a moral view an important improvement on the fashions of our fathers. On the occasion of sudden quarrels, especially in drunken brawls, the ready command of a dangerous weapon was unfortunately the frequent cause of bloodshed. Several instances of this fatality had happened within the memory of persons with whom I was acquainted in early life, as that of Colonel Stewart of Stewartfield, who was mortally wounded by Sir Gilbert Elliot of Stobbs in a tavern at Jedburgh, in consequence of a party dispute at an election dinner; and Mr Halliburton of Muirhouse-law, found stabbed to death near Ancrum Bridge, and who was supposed to have fallen, in similar circumstances, by the hands of Rutherfurd, the laird of Fairnington. They had set out together from Jedburgh the previous night, both of them being excited by wine, and were overheard by persons whom they passed on the road engaged in angry altercation.

Ladies when visiting or receiving company, wore silk gowns, or riding habits with gold or gilded buttons and fringes. A silk plaid wrapped loosely about the head and body was the prevailing fashion at church. Patches on the face formed a part of the full dress of ladies, particularly of those further advanced in life. This fashion was beginning to wear out in my early life. I have not seen any instance of it for the last fifty or fifty-five years; but I recollect many persons who followed it before that time, and have seen the patch-boxes, which once made a part of the furniture of every ladies' dressing-closet.

The undress of both sexes was often coarse and slovenly beyond any example even among the lower orders in modern days. Gentlemen used to walk about all the morning in greasy night-caps and dirty night-gowns (dressing-gowns), or thread-bare coats. The elder ladies wore large linen caps called *toys*, encroaching on the face, and tied under the chin, with worsted short-gowns and aprons. The word toy is probably derived from the French *toque*, the hood worn by women of mean condition in France.

The clergy in my early life were not less slovenly than their neighbours. Many of them wore coloured clothes of very coarse materials. Blue was the common colour for full dress among persons of my own profession in Scotland at that time.

Most families, both in the higher and in the middle ranks, used tea at breakfast; but among the latter it was only recently introduced, or beginning to be introduced in the afternoon, and then exclusively on the occasion of receiving company. The tea "equipage" at breakfast was placed on the uncovered table, small linen napkins being handed to all the guests. Though wheaten bread was partly used, yet cakes, or "bannocks" of barley and pease-meal, and oat cakes, formed the principal household bread in gentlemen's families; and in those of the middle class, on ordinary occasions, no other bread was ever thought of. Potatoes made a part of the food of the common people, but were considered a luxury, being cultivated only in gardens and more costly than meal. I do not recollect any instance of potatoes being planted in the open field previous to the year 1760. Horticulture, indeed, was not much studied, and the culinary vegetables then raised were few in number, and inferior in quality to those which are now found in every gentleman's garden. "Open kail", cabbages, turnips, and carrots, were the only vegetables in general use.[1]

John Ramsay of Ochtertyre, in the valley of the Forth near Stirling, was a contemporary of Somerville and a landowner. He describes the life of the rural population of a humbler class – a thrifty, poor and, in his view at least, an unenterprising group of men. The historian, however, is inclined to give most of the credit for the agricultural revolution in Scotland to exactly the stratum of tenant he describes, once altering economic circumstances began to put the chance of profit in their way.

In this corner, and in most of the carses, the tenants' houses were mostly built with *fail* or *divot*, which in a few years had the appearance of a wall of clay. Yet, when properly thatched, they were warmer and freer from damp than what was built of stone and clay. Within my own remembrance the farmhouses of the Muir were all built with fail, the last of them being pulled down only a few years ago. The chief objection to this mode of building was its uncovering so much ground. It accorded, however, with the inclination our tenants showed to save upon every article. The same simplicity and parsimony appeared in other things, stable-doors being made of wattles, and there were seldom any locks upon the barn-doors.

The most rigid economy appeared in the dress and domestic expenses of tenants. The clothes of the family, and even of the servants, male and female, were for the most part spun and dyed at home; and thus, though hardly anything was made for sale, the wife's thrift in a numerous household turned to excellent account, as it saved her husband from going to market for a variety of necessaries. In the last age, the most substantial farmers seldom had anything better than a coat of grey or black *kelt*, spun by their wives. Twice or thrice in a lifetime, perhaps, they had occasion to buy a greatcoat of English cloth, as what was homespun would not keep out rain. *Harn* shirts were commonly worn, though upon holidays the country beaus appeared with linen necks and sleeves. Among no set of people was female vanity ever confined within narrower limits; even marriage apparel being mostly manufactured in the family, and their ordinary wear being only a few degrees coarser and plainer. The gowns of women, old and young, were made by country tailors, who never thought of changing or inflaming the fashions. In point of equipage they were equally primitive, few of the topping tenants having either boots or saddles fifty years ago. It was the custom for them and their wives to ride upon *sods*, over which, on occasions of ceremony, a plaid or bit of carpet was spread.

And now of the food of our tenants, which they ate in a truly primitive manner, at the same table with their servants. Oatmeal-pottage was once esteemed a luxury among that set of people, bearmeal being generally used. Pease or bear bread was a capital article with them, wheat-loaves being now more common in farmers' houses than oat-cakes were formerly. In times of scarcity recourse was had to inferior kinds, which are now happily forgotten – viz., *grey* meal – i.e., a species compounded of oatmeal and mill-dust; others made use of *egger* meal, consisting of equal portions of oat, pease, and bear meal. The latter took its rise from the beggars mixing different kinds in the same bag. To some palates it is said not to have been unpleasant.

In every family water-kail was a standing dish, being made without flesh, of greens and *grolls* – i.e., oats stripped of the husks in the mill. Without it they did not think they could dine to purpose. If tradition may be believed, the country people of old ate very little animal food, except perhaps a few old ewes that would not sell, and were likely to die through the winter.

Walter M'Killop in Blackdub is said to have been one of the first tenants in the country that killed a cow every Martinmas; and Robert Buchanan says his father was in his remembrance the only tenant in Ochtertyre who had a winter mart. But for the last sixty years almost every tenant in tolerable circumstances killed either one or two.

When there was no flesh, *kitchen* of one kind or other was given after the kail – that is, either butter, cheese, eggs, herrings, and sometimes raw onions, which were annually imported from Flanders. To supper they had *sowens*, or flummery, a cheap and healthy dish. In summer their drink consisted of whey or butter-milk, and in spring a little milk. But hardly any ale was brewed, except on extraordinary occasions. Indeed, the chief beverage of our country people has always been the pure element. Upon the whole, it may safely be affirmed that there hardly ever was a set of people who lived more poorly and penuriously, yet they were in general well pleased with their lot. Whatever might be their grievances, the meanness of their food and raiment seldom gave them a moment's disquietude.

Such were the labourers of the ground, and such their situation in former times, so far as we can collect from the conversation of the aged. They appear to have been warmly devoted to the persons of their masters, and entirely subservient to them in everything where their own purse was not affected. Though by no means deficient in industry which would make a speedy return, they laid their account that any extraordinary exertion or outlay on their part would, in the long-run, redound as much to their master's profit as their own, and they had no mind to work for him. They therefore had a sytem of their own, founded on long experience, and suited to small capitals and tacks for nineteen years. From this they were unwilling to deviate, unless for some self-evident advantage; and with all its defects, it is not easy to figure one by which the same quantity of grain could be raised for the same money.

Their aversion to enterprise and innovation was fortified by a principle which pervaded every part of their conduct – viz., the desire of saving and hoarding. Indeed, no set of men ever followed more invariably old Cato's rule, of being "*vendaces non emaces*" [sellers not buyers]. It is astonishing what sums of money the tenants of the last age had out at interest with the gentlemen of the country. They and the burghers were of old the moneyed men, who supplied the demands of the nobility and gentry that were engaged in any expensive pursuit.[2]

Changes to a more commercial way of life in the Highlands, or at least in the remoter areas such as Gairloch in Wester Ross, came later than in the Borders and Central Scotland. Osgood Mackenzie, probably best remembered now as the famous creator of the great garden at Inverewe, was a young man when the Highland famine of the 1840s showed up the weakness of an economy based on potatoes and herring. In this long passage he portrays, and laments, the passing of the good old days, when people met their own needs to a far greater degree than in the integrated world of modern transport and the Victorian industrial economy in which he was writing.

How different from nowadays many things were when I first remember Gairloch. Such a thing as a lamp I never saw in the Tigh Dige. Only candles were used; paraffin was quite unknown and had not even been heard of; and the black houses depended for light chiefly on the roaring fires in the centre of the room, with, perhaps, an old creel or barrel stuck in the roof to let out the smoke. For use in very exceptional cases the people had tiny tin lamps made by the tinkers and fed with oil made out of the livers of fish which were allowed to get rotten before they were boiled down. But the main lighting at night was done by having a big heap of carefully prepared bog-fir splinters full of resin all ready in a corner, and a small boy or girl did nothing else but keep these burning during the evening, so that the women could see to card and spin and the men to make their herring-nets by hand. I do not remember hemp being grown, as it was, I believe, at one time in special sorts of enclosures or gardens, and prepared and spun for the making of the herring-nets. But it was commonly done in the west. I do not think they grew flax to any great extent, but on the east coast they grew it quite extensively, and all the Tigh Dige sheets and damask napkins and tablecloths in lovely patterns were spun in Conon House, our east-coast home, and woven in Conon village.

I shall now quote from my uncle to show what a good housekeeper my grandmother was. He says: "I doubt if there ever was a much better housekeeper than my dear mother, or more busy and better servants than in those times. They cheerfully put hand to work, the very suggesting of which would startle the modern ladies and gentlemen who serve us. A common sight in the Conon kitchen after dinner was four or five women all the evening busy spinning and carding flax for napery, or putting wicks into metal candle moulds in frames holding, say, a dozen, and pouring the fearful-smelling tallow into the moulds. In those days I seldom saw any candles but of tallow anywhere, unless in chandeliers or against walls where they could not easily be snuffed; so my wise mother made heaps of as good candles as she could buy from the spare suet in the house. Then, where could a storeroom be seen like my mother's at Conon? The room was shelved all round with movable frames for holding planks, on which unimaginable quantities of dried preserved edibles reposed till called for. There were jam-pots by the hundred of every sort, shelves of preserved candied apricots and *Magnum Bonum* plums, that could not be surpassed in the world; other shelves with any amount of biscuits of all sorts of materials, once liquid enough to drop on sheets of paper, but in time dried to about two inches across and half an inch thick for dessert. Smoked sheep and deer tongues were also there, and from the roof hung strings of threaded artichoke bottoms, dried, I suppose, for putting into soups. In addition, there were endless curiosities of confectionery brought north by Kitty's talents from her Edinburgh cookery school, while quantities of dried fruit, ginger, orange-peel, citron, etc., from North Simpson and Graham of London must have made my dear mother safe-cased in armour against any unexpected and hungry invader. Then every year she made gooseberry and currant wines, balm ditto, raspberry vinegar, spruce and ginger beer. I remember they were celebrated, and liqueurs numberless included magnums of camomile flowers and orange-peel and gentian root bitters for old women with indigestion pains."

My dear old foreman of works, Seoras Ruairidh Cheannaiche (George of Rory Merchant), who was at the head of everything, and who did everything for me at Inverewe when I began there in 1862, used to tell me the difficulty there was in his grandfather's and even in his father's day in getting any kind of planking and nails for coffins. It was a common thing, he said, for a man going to Inverness on some great occasion to bring back a few nails for his own coffin, so that they might be in readiness whenever the last call came. In Loch Broom wooden pegs were often used for coffins.

The ordinary way of interment in the time of George's grandfather was to have the dead body swathed in blue home-spun, carried on an open bier to the graveyard, and slid down into the grave. His grandfather could remember when, if one lost a hook when trout-fishing, the only way of replacing it was to go to Ceard an Oirthire, the old tinker at Coast (a little hamlet on the bay of Gruinord) and to get him to make one, and to tell him to be sure to put a barb on it. And in the days of old Jane Charles, who was a sort of connection of the Gairloch family, there was only one looking-glass in the district other than in the Tigh Dige, and the girls had to arrange their hair for church or for a wedding by looking at their faces in a pail of water. I can quite well remember when not a sack made from jute was to be seen, and one saw the big sixteen or eighteen feet rowing-boats on fine winter days arriving from the outlying townships at the mills at Strath or Boor piled up with bags of oats and barley (or rather bere), all in sheep-skin bags, with a certain amount of wool still on their outsides to remind one of their origin. It was rare then to see such a thing as a hempen rope. Ropes for retaining the thatch on the cottages were called *seamanan fraoich* (heather ropes) and made of heather. Ropes to hold small boats were generally made of twisted birch twigs, while the very best ropes for all other purposes were made of the pounded fibre of bog-fir roots, and a really well-made *ball maith guithais* (a good fir rope) could hardly be beaten by the best modern ropes.

I never saw a wire riddle for riddling corn or meal in the old days; they were all made of stretched sheep-skins with holes perforated in them by a big red-hot needle. Trout lines were made of white or other horsehair, and when one stabled a pony at an inn, it always ran the risk of having its tail stolen. Also, the only spoons in the country were those the tinkers made from sheep and cow horns melted down. How one used to smell the burning horn at the tinker encampments after dark.

Knives and forks were hardly known in the crofter houses, and everything was eaten with fingers and thumbs. Even now I hear them say herrings and potatoes never taste right if eaten with a knife and fork. My mother was one day visiting some poor squatter families who in those days resided on Longa Island, and one woman was very anxious she should partake of something. My mother was hungry, for she never carried luncheon with her on her long daily expeditions from early morning to night, trusting to her chance of getting a bowl of milk and a bit of oatcake or barley scone from those she visited. Well, the poor woman confessed to having no meal in the house and consequently no bread; all she had was a pail of flounders just off the hooks, and she asked if the *bantighearna* (lady) would condescend to partake of one of them. My mother said she would, and a flounder was instantly put in a pot. When it was boiled the woman took it out, neatly broke it in two or three pieces, and placed them on a little table without plate or cloth, knife or fork. My mother set to it with her fingers, and afterwards declared it was the sweetest fish she ever tasted. When she finished the woman brought her a pail of water to wash her hands in.

When people chanced to have a bit of meat they could not make what we should call broth, because they had no pot barley and no turnips or carrots, onions or cabbage, to put in it; so they thickened the water in which the meat had been boiled with oatmeal, and this was called in Gaelic *eanaraich* (broth). It was placed in the middle of the table, and everyone helped themselves with their horn spoons.

Perhaps a few of my readers are aware that almost within my own recollection the blacksmiths on our west coast did all their own smithy work with peat charcoal. Coal was rarely imported before 1840, and all the oak had been cut down, turned into charcoal, and used by Sir George Hay in his small furnaces or bloomeries towards the end of the sixteenth and the early years of the seventeenth centuries, so there was nothing to fall back on but peat charcoal, which I have always been told was quite a good substitute. I can just recollect the Cobha Mor (the Big Blacksmith) at Poolewe. He was the last smith who used it, and with whom died the knowledge and skill required to make it.

I wonder also if it is known that on our west coast, before tar was imported from Archangel, the inhabitants produced their own tar. When the late Lord Elphinstone bought Coulin in Glen Torridon he used a great deal of the old native Scots fir in the building of the lodge. One day, after a large number of the trees had been cut down, he and I started counting the natural rings on the stems of the trees, and found that they averaged about two hundred and fifty years old. My attention was drawn by Lord Elphinstone to the fact that nearly every one of the trees had had a big auger-hole bored into it just above the ground-level. He was told by the old folk in the neighbourhood that these holes had been bored by the Loch Carron people to produce tar for their boats. We could see the marks of the auger-holes in numbers of the trees that were still standing, as well as in those that had been cut down.

What far happier times those good old days were than these we are living in now. Even the seasons seemed more "seasonable" and the summers far hotter. What an abundance of cherries there was at Gairloch even in my days in the 'forties and 'fifties, and these crops were supposed to be degenerate in comparison with the grand fruity years of the 'twenties. There were about four or five big trees of red early cherries and one of black late Guines, and never did they seem to fail. No amount of blackbirds, ring-ouzels, nor any number of boys and girls, seemed to have the slightest effect on them, and they never, in my recollection, failed to be laden. At long last, however, they had to give in to old age and were blown down one by one; but though my elder brother took great trouble to plant new ones of specially good varieties, there has never, I believe, been another cherry in the Baile Mor garden, the new kinds evidently failing to suit the soil or climate.[3]

Our three authors witnessed, between them, the end of old, rural Scotland, ruled by gentry families and living close to nature but in poverty. Most of those who speak in the following pages are closer to ourselves in experience, as they confront problems of work, pleasure and stress born, in the main, of an industrial society. Old people often exclaim, with Mackenzie, 'what far happier times those good old days were than these we are living in now', but if history has a lesson it is not that it repeats itself, but that there can be no turning back.

CHAPTER II

ORDINARY HOMES

The rapid growth of population in the late eighteenth and nineteenth centuries created immense problems in housing people in town and country. Remote rural-area accommodation continued to be constructed from immediately available materials; for urban areas this approach was wholly inadequate. Improved transport allowed building materials to be moved to where they were needed. Vast armies of workmen cut timber, laid bricks and stones and constructed roofs. Through the nineteenth century the large number of farmworkers meant that the countryside too contained accommodation problems.

In lowland areas, many male farmworkers lived together in accommodation that was often in the steading. The English traveller and journalist William Cobbett visited one of these 'bothies' near Edinburgh in 1832.

I went to the "boothie" between twelve and one o'clock, in order that I might find the men at home, and see what they had for their dinner. I found the "boothie" to be a shed, with a fire-place in it to burn coals in, with one doorway, and one little window. The floor was the ground. There were three wooden bedsteads, nailed together like the births in a barrack-room, with boards for the bottom of them. The bedding seemed to be very coarse sheeting with coarse woollen things at the top; and all seemed to be such as similar things must be where there is nobody but men to look after them. There were six men, all at home; one sitting upon a stool, four upon the sides of the births, and one standing talking to me. Though it was Monday, their beards, especially of two of them, appeared to be some days old. There were ten or twelve bushels of coals lying in a heap in one corner of the place, which was as nearly as I could guess, about sixteen or eighteen feet square. There was no back-door to the place, and no privy. There were some loose potatoes lying under one of the births.

Now, for the wages of these men. In the first place the average wages of these single farming men are about ten pounds a year, or not quite four shillings a week. Then they are found provisions in the following manner: each has allowed him two pecks of coarse oatmeal a week, and three "choppins" of milk a day, and a "choppin" is, I believe, equal to an English quart. They have to use this meal, which weighs about seventeen pounds, either by mixing it with cold water or with hot; they put some of it into a bowl, pour some boiling water upon it, then stir it about and eat it; and they call this BROSE; and you will be sure to remember that name. When they use milk with the meal they use it in the same way that they do the water. I saw some of the brose mixed up ready to eat; and this is by no means bad stuff, only there ought to be half-a-pound of good meat to eat along with it. The Americans make "brose" of the corn-meal; but then they make their brose with milk instead of water, and they send it down their throats in company with buttered beef-steaks. And if here was some bacon along with the brose, I should think the brose very proper; because, in this country, oats are more easily grown in some parts than wheat is. These men were not troubled with cooking utensils. They had a large iron saucepan and five or six brose-bowls; and they are never troubled with those clattering things, knives, forks, plates, vinegar-cruets, salt-cellars, pepper-boxes, mustard-pots, table-cloths or tables.[1]

Throughout the nineteenth century large numbers of farmworkers continued to be housed in farms and steadings; but in one respect there was a major change in rural accommodation. Early eighteenth-century Scotland contained a very limited number of villages. By the 1840s a transformation had taken place. Tiny townships had developed into villages and numerous entirely new settlements had been created. These communities housed craftsmen and farmworkers and provided shops, markets and services.

The following account is by an elderly resident of the planned village of New Pitsligo and provides a portrait of village life in the 1880s.

Nearly all the houses were identical – the main building comprising a but-and-ben, with the "oot-room" attached. Between every second feu ran a lane giving access to the back premises. There stood the barn and the byre, and beyond them was the garden, termed the "yard." The lanes connected the three streets and in some cases led to the village lands. Most of the houses were thatched. Some had garrets, with little headroom but plenty of space for a few beds. Front and back doors alike were made of plain deal boards, opened and shut with an iron sneck and secured at night by a wooden bar. In most cases the floors were earthen.

Large families were reared in the cramped quarters of those dwellings, and overcrowding was common. Sleeping "heid an' tail" was the rule among the younger members of a family. Peat was the universal fuel and fireplaces were open and wide, with raised "binks" at either side. Cooking utensils were hung on a crook suspended from the "rantle-tree," an iron frame that swung out and in. The crook hung on a chain with round links of a generous size and could be adjusted to any height desired. A common saying was "as black as the links o' the crook." Indispensable cooking utensils were the round-bottomed, three-legged kail pot, a smaller edition of the same for sowens, brochan and skirly, the broth pot, frypan, girdle for oatcakes, gridiron for oaten bannocks, and a kettle, all of castiron; the teapot and the brander. Fires were never allowed to die out. Last thing at night the goodwife raked the live embers (quiles) into a conical heap and covered them with ashes (aise). In the morning all that was required to get a blaze was a few dry peats and a puff of the bellows. The daily supply of peat was kept in the peat-neuk, a dark, narrow compartment in a corner of the kitchen.

Naturally the place was redolent of peat reek. On calm days the blue vapour hung like a cloud over the village, and the pungent odour was noticeable well beyond its outskirts. It permeated every nook and cranny of the house, and the villagers carried it about with them in their reek-drenched clothing.

The few more pretentious houses were occupied by the various professional men – the ministers, the doctor, schoolmasters, and the gentleman who combined the two offices of banker and factor. Then there were the reconstructed houses, two-storeyed and slated, occupied by a few master masons and by traders who had contrived to make a little money.

And in the whole village there was not a single bathroom. To get a thorough clean-up meant commandeering the wooden washtub or walking six miles to the shore at Aberdour. There was no sanitation as the word is understood to-day. Dry closets, mostly wooden structures, stood adjacent to the midden, which was emptied once a year and the contents carried to the fields. The closets were commonly termed privies, or, by the unco genteel, office houses.

Owing to their light weight the closets lent themselves readily to a common form of practical joking, of which one instance may be given. One evening a villager visiting a neighbour, on opening the door to leave was confronted by stygian darkness. "Dyod!" he exclaimed, "it's afu' dark; it wis a fine clear nicht fan I cam' in." On stepping out he had found himself inside a privy.

There were four churches, two schools, and a Public Hall reached by an unsafe stone stairway and lit by a few small windows. Underneath the Hall was the weavers' shop housing about a dozen looms. Six weavers worked in it, all very old men. At one time the village could boast of well on to a hundred weavers.

Built on a steep hillside the streets ran parallel at different altitudes; in some parts the occupiers of houses could see clearly over the roofs of their neighbours on the other side of the street. Steep grassy slopes rose from the roadway to those elevated dwellings. The pavements with their ups and downs were risky after dark, but nobody used them; the middle of the street was preferred by pedestrians even in daylight. After nightfall not one glimmer of light brightened way-farers' path, except for a few dimly lit shop windows.

Water pumps were spaced along the streets and in some of the lanes. Two pailfuls of water was called a "fraucht," and was usually carried within a square wooden frame made for the purpose. The pumps were ideal gossiping places for the wives. There were also several stone water troughs for cattle; they went by the name of "waterin's."

Materially the village was well catered for. There were half a dozen "general merchants" who sold anything from a pin to groceries and drapery. At least the pins were not sold – they were given away, a handful at a time, if the shopper bought a fair amount of other goods. A bagful of sweets was handed out on similar occasions. The grocer was a bit of an artist. With finger and thumb and a turn of the wrist he deftly rolled a scrap of paper into a cone-shaped container for your pins and sweets. All done in the twinkling of an eye! This, one imagines, must be regarded as a lost art.

All the shops stocked tobacco; bogie-roll cost 3d per oz. with a clay pipe to the bargain. Matches were the almost unbelievable price of 2d, sometimes even 1½d for a packet of twelve small boxes. Despite the low price of matches some of the older men still used the "flint an' fleerish" method to light their pipes. Cigarettes were unknown, but tobacco chewing was prevalent, mostly among the younger men.

Sugar could be bought at a little over 4/- per 28 lb., butter 6d per lb., eggs in spring and summer 4d per dozen, 3d if bought direct from the producer, oatmeal about 10/- per boll, and syrup 2d per lb. A few pennyworths of rice or other cereals went a very long way. Milk could be bought from those feuars who kept cows (there were many such then) at the rate of 6d or less per gallon. Salmon and corned beef were the only foods that could be bought in tins.

You could still have a pair of boots made in the village, but the factory-made article was begining to make headway. The tailors were more fortunate; ready-mades had not reached us yet – their day was to come. There were four tailoring shops, four shoemakers, two bakers, two butchers, two joiners and an ironmongery shop. The musical clangour of hammer and anvil rang out from two smiddies, a slater was trying to oust thatched roofs, but two old stob-thatchers were kept busy rethatching and repairing. A druggist made up the doctor's prescriptions, in addition to being the only newsagent in the place. A few "oot-rooms" were occupied by old women, who sold loaves, potted-head, biscuits and "penny-wabble," a very mild ale. Those modest establishments were known as "penny-rattlers."

All furniture was locally made – the box beds, chairs, tables, stools, the dresser and the deece, the bakeboards, tattie-chapper, spurtle and aise backet. And of course the cradle, which, on the principle that first things come first, ought to have headed the list. Everything was solidly made; living conditions were too onerous to admit of frills. A clock was indispensable. The wives took pride in keeping their house spick and span. Cooking utensils, chairs and tables were scoured with white sand. No tablecloths were used. Walls and firesides were whitewashed, the swye and crook blackleaded.

A few pictures adorned the walls, mostly calendars enclosed in home-made frames. Plates in the rack on the dresser reflected the light from fire and oil lamp. The mantel-shelf held a few china ornaments, while window sills were crowded with flower pots; fuchsias and geraniums were the popular blooms.

A gasworks stood in the lower part of the Den, but it was plainly on its last legs; the incandescent mantle came just too late to save it. Over its gateway an arched signboard proclaimed in faded Latin characters "Let there be light." Paraffin was the universal illuminant, but it had one serious drawback – lamp chimneys were all too easily broken and cost a whole twopence to replace. Twopence was twopence then!

The people lived soberly – they had no option. Brose or porridge was the common breakfast food; in a few households this might be supplemented by a cup of tea. But in many others tea was served only on Sunday mornings; indeed, Sunday was often referred to as "the day o' the lang lie an' the tay brakfast." For dinner there might be kail and kail brose, neeps and neep brose, peasesoup, potatoes dished up in various forms, skirly, milk broth, etc. Scotch broth and boiled beef was commonly the Sunday dinner. The main dish might be supplemented by a plate of rice or other cereal.

Fancy dishes such as trifle, jellies or ice cream were never seen or even heard of, and there were no fly cups after dinner or at any other time. Mention of ice cream brings to mind a rhyme the boys used to repeat:

> Hoky-poky, a penny the lump,
> The more you eat the more you jump.

They had heard that hoky-poky was something so cold that it made one jump, but what it was they had no idea. You had to go to Fraserburgh to get it.

A bowl of peasemeal brose or sowens was often the supper dish, but tea was beginning to supplant these. But in times of dire stress it was nothing uncommon for a family to have to scrape out what was left in the dinner kailpot.

Fisher wives laden with heavy creels came regularly and did a good trade. They were a cheery, garrulous lot and their fisher idiom was an entertainment in itself. During the herring fishing season a hawker named Whyte came from Fraserburgh daily in a spring cart laden to overflowing with herrings. He was very red-faced, wore a bowler hat on the back of his head, and had a stentorian voice . . .[2]

Even in the 1920s and 1930s rural life displayed many of the attributes of self-sufficiency more akin to a nineteenth-century existence than later twentieth-century life. Lavinia Derwent's Borders farm-home was grand enough to justify a servant. But farmworkers and their wives continued to live a harsh and bleak existence in these years.

The stone-flagged kitchen seemed a vast place to a child. The big dresser, where the lamps stood ready for lighting, contained all the dishes and platters needed for the household, as well as drawers full of cutlery. There were other odd drawers where aprons, dusters and dishcloths were kept, and where anything lost could be found. 'Look in the dresser drawer' was an everyday cry when a key was missing or someone was searching for scissors.

A great bin with a sloping lid held sacks of meal, flour, salt, and sugar, enough to see us through a snow-siege; and a long wooden table stood in the middle of the floor at which a dozen or more men could feed at clipping-time or threshing. Six could sit on the old gaol-stool which was shoved under the table when not in use. Where it came from I never knew; it was just part of the household, as familiar as Jessie herself.

Great hams hung from the ceiling and strings of onions from a hook on the wall. There was no other adornment except a calendar advertising sheep-dip. It had splendid coloured pictures for each month. The Blue Boy, Buckingham Palace, snow-scapes in the winter months, and seaside scenes for summer.

The back-kitchen was a utilitarian place, full of pots, pans and basins, a rough wooden table, and a sink at the window where the washing-up was done. The window looked out over the untidy back garden and away down the fields towards the shepherd's cottage. Many a time I stood there on tiptoe to peer out and see if the postie was coming. He left his bicycle at the road-end before traversing the fields and climbing the fences with his mail-bag bobbing up and down on his back. What a welcome sight he was, coming as he did from the big town and bringing with him not only newspapers and letters, but, better still, all the gossip of the countryside.

From the back kitchen a door opened into the dairy which Jessie called 'the milk-hoose'. It was a cool place with wire-mesh at the window which could be left open so that the air, but not the flies, could get in. Here the milk was sieved when it was brought in from the byre and poured into shallow dishes. When the cream gathered it was skimmed off into an earthenware crock, to await churning. Eggs, butter and cheese were also kept in the milk-hoose, and sometimes trifles and cold puddings. Little wonder the cat was always sniffing at the door.

'If ye leaves the milk-hoose door open, ye'll no' hae your sorrows to seek,' Jessie used to warn me.

The nearest thing we had to a refrigerator was the meat-safe which hung outside and was reached through the back kitchen window. Here the butcher-meat or sausages were kept and our own mutton if the herd had been killing a sheep.

We had never heard of deep-freezes or, indeed, of any of the mod. cons. taken for granted today. Jessie sprinkled tea-leaves on the carpet to lay the dust before starting to sweep with a besom. She went down on her knees to scrub the kitchen floor, and spent hours blackening the grate and polishing the fire-irons with emery-paper. Sometimes she used pipe-clay to make fancy patterns of whirls and whorls on the doorstep as a finishing touch . . .

Looking back, I wonder what the hinds' wives got out of their restricted lives, stuck in the wilds miles from anywhere. What if the women, living cheek by jowl with each other in adjoining cottages, hated the sight of each other? They had no one else to talk to while the men were working in the fields and never went anywhere except to church or maybe once in a long while to the local flower show.

True, it took them all day to get through their repetitive household tasks with no mod. cons. to lighten their loads. The women were forever carrying pails of water, feeding their hens and pig, black-leading the grate, rubbing and scrubbing, baking and cooking, mending and patching, pipe-claying their doorsteps or cleaning their windows. In their spare moments they knitted socks and jerseys for the men or long black stockings for themselves. Rarely did they take time to sit down and have a read at the paper or a look at the *People's Friend*.

Making meals, however simple, must have kept them occupied for hours. They baked floury scones, cooked rabbit pie, and made great clooty-dumplings filled with currants. They got their milk and butter from the farmhouse, grew their own vegetables, and relied on the vanman or Wat-the-baker – when they could get up the road – for the rest. They saved up enough eggs to exchange for syrup and sugar in order to eke out the few pennies in their purses, and managed their frugal affairs without ever getting into debt.

On Saturday evenings the men sometimes dressed themselves up and went cycling away to the town. Did the wives complain, I wondered, at being left behind? Or did they just cast on another sock? All of them must have had inner lives and secret longings. Surely it was not enough for them to be mere household drudges.[3]

The Scottish fishing industry's rapid expansion in the nineteenth century produced not only a rash of building in fisher towns and villages, but also serious accommodation problems for a vast travelling workforce. As herring shoals moved round the coasts, pursued by fishermen, an army of female fish-gutters and packers followed too.

Their numbers were beyond the capacity of communities to adequately house. In 1891 in Fraserburgh, for example, Georgina Robertson (who worked for the Church of Scotland) noted the squalor in which decent women were compelled to live.

As Deputy from the Church of Scotland to the fisher folks in Fraserburgh this season, I have frequently visited them in their lodgings, and as I am conversant with sanitation and the Laws of Health – being a Member and a Lecturer of the National Health Society of 53 Berners Street, London – I would respectfully call the attention of the Local Authorities to the comfortless and insanitary condition of the majority of these lodgings, many of the girls' rooms being unfit for human habitation – smoky, dirty, draughty, without cupboards or shelves and only one bedstead to every three girls. According to the Bye-Laws, the cubic space of 250 feet has been granted, but the girls have to live, cook, and wash as well as sleep, and the space in many cases is insufficient. The worst of these places are in Hunter's Lane; the Barracks in Shore Street, a place behind the Oak Tree Inn, Shore Street – Denmark, Barrasgate and Castle Street. But the most crying evil is the want of W.C.s or such conveniences, near the lodgings, and in the Curing Yards. In the latter there is generally one, but the girls decline and rightly too, to share it in common with the other sex, consequently the Beach and outskirts of the Town are in a disgusting condition. There have been many ailments among the fisher folks arising from the want of these conveniences, and the sick people are put to great straits, which of course has aggravated their diseases. Two extreme cases I can cite: No 10 Castle Terrace, small house at the back, and 25 Lance Lane. The complaints from the people were more urgent than ever I have heard before; they said they were treated like 'Beasts', although they came out of comfortable homes they had to put up with any sort of treatment, and pay high rents too. These high-rented rooms tend to overcrowding. Widows with married sons and daughters and lodgers, besides, all living and sleeping in one room, sometimes as many as 12. These matters in the interests of decency and morality, as well as the physical health of the people require to be remedied.[4]

Overcrowded privately rented homes were a feature of urban Scottish life in the 1900s. Over a fifth of the population lived three or more to a room and a further 23 per cent two or three people per room. People crowded into tenements, attics and basements. Though council house building programmes became common in the twentieth century, especially when acts of 1919 and 1924 provided local authorities with Treasury support, the provision of sufficient accommodation was a very slow process. Bert Murray was born in 1913 in Aberdeen.

We lived in the sunks, or basement in 2 rooms, plus a small boxroom or closet. Father, mother and 9 of a family, the only thing I recall about sleeping arrangements was a large wooden home-made bed which occupied most of the space in the closet. A mattress, filled with chaff, laid on wooden spars and a long wooden board to save us falling to the floor. 4 boys slept in that bed. Lighting was by gas, brackets jutting out from the wall, and when lit the closet one had a rather poor flame while the 2 larger were fitted with gas mantles and glass globes. Main room, parents' bedrooms and kitchen was all one room.

We were fortunate that Dad was in steady employment most of his lifetime so that we always had food of some sort – cooking was done in the fireplace or a gas ring. A large iron kettle and pot was the main source of hot water. Normal washing of hands and face was always done in cold water. Only when you were exceptionally dirty was hot water used. Having a bath, a large zinc bath was pulled from under the kitchen bed and placed near the fireplace. 2 young lads at a time washed, using carbolic soap and cloth. As we got older the baths stopped so we were sent with a penny, carbolic soap and hot towel, to Hanover Street Bath. Lavatories were rather primitive then – along a lobby, out the back door, down some steps, around the corner of the building to 3 outhouses, 1 for each of 3 tenants on each floor. Wooden boards with a hole cut out. Cistern and lead piping had to be protected with sacking material during the winter, also, during this season, extra clothing or an overcoat had to be worn when nature called.

Round the next corner and under the building the washhouse with large wooden tubs sat on a bench, a huge mangle and the washing boiler which had to be filled and emptied by hand, heated by a fire under it. Stairs and lobby were lit by small paraffin lamps. Bedcovers were made with crochet squares all joined together. Odd pieces of material stored in a rag bag were cut into strips an inch wide. With the aid of a special needle and a piece of sacking 'clootie' mats were made. If you owned a proper rug it was carefully preserved. Lots of newspaper or brown paper was the underlay of linoleum.

Most houses of the time had 1 or 2 shelves running almost the whole length of a wall in the kitchen. On these were displayed ashets, tureens, best china, ornaments, griddle for making oat-cakes, pancakes and scones, a large brass berry pan for making jam. Food was plain, for breakfast a bowl of porridge with milk, a thick slice of bread and syrup. Dinner (or lunch) broth or 'tattie' soup, enough to last 2 days, with sometimes a small amount of pudding. Quite often porridge again at teatime or occasionally own make of fishcakes, sometimes a sausage with tatties, bread, syrup and tea. On most Saturdays or Sundays Dad would make a clootie dumplin' with treacle, currant, raisins and so on . . .

Street lighting was done by gas, the lighting was carried out by a man, the lamplighter, or the 'leerie' as he was known locally, carrying a long pole with a small metal part at one end similar to a hook shape into which he fitted a match. This was pushed up through a small space in the bottom of the lamp, turning a gas tap, a quick flick lit the match and the mantle. He returned in the morning, putting out the lights.[5]

The tenement blocks in which many Scots lived made washing clothes and bedding a particularly heavy chore for housewives. The actress Molly Weir grew up in one in Glasgow in the inter-war years. Each tenement close of twelve families was provided with a wash-house; careful arrangements had to be made to avoid friction over whose turn it was to use the wash-house.

There was never the same fierce competition to use the wash-house at night as there was in the daytime. Some of the night washers were younger women, daughters of those too old to do their washing during the day. They had the time, those elderly mothers, but not the strength, so the daughters had to tackle the household washing when they'd finished their day's work in shop or factory. Other women preferred to do their washing in the evenings for their own private reasons. My mother tut-tutted over this, for she felt washings ought properly to be done during the day when there was some chance of clothes being hung out in the fresh air and the wind, to dry, and acquire a fine fresh smell. Grannie would purse her lips and shake her head at the thought of pulleys in the kitchen, laden with steaming clothes, flapping in folks' faces as they moved back and forward to get the kettle from the range or put some coal on the fire. 'I don't like a hoose fu' o' wet cloots,' she'd say. 'It canna be good for thae lassies efter bein' oot at their work a' day.'

My mother would say of a neighbour who could easily have done the washing during the day, 'Aye, she must be awfu' glad to get away from her man and her weans when she'd put up with the damp cold of that wash-house instead of sitting at her own fireside.' And then she'd soften when Grannie would reply, 'Och well, maybe she's better off at that, for her man's a surly blackguard and gey poor company.'

Grannie's use of the word blackguard, which she pronounced 'blaggard', always sent a shiver down my spine, and I thought she'd invented this damning description herself. I was astounded in later years when I came across the word again and again to describe the villains in the romances I devoured, and realized that Grannie's blackguard was a well-known character to many authors.

Far from sharing my mother's condemnation of the night washers, I used passionately to hope I could coax her to become one of them. There was a theatrical air about the whole scene which made a great appeal to me. The ordinary grey-stone wash-house of the daytime was transformed, as though at the wave of a magic wand, and I couldn't imagine that I had ever played shops on its window ledge, or jumped from its roof on to the wall which divided the back courts.

Guttering candles, stuck in the necks of bottles and ranged along the window-sill, provided the only illumination in what now seemed a vast cavern. Mysterious shadows flickered in the far corners, and the foaming suds in the tubs took on a romantic radiance. When the lid of the huge brick boiler was raised to see how the 'white things' were progressing (the 'white things' was our name for all the household linen), swirling steam filled the wash-house, the candles spat and flickered through illuminated clouds, and the scene became fearsome as pictures of hell. The washerwoman bending over her tub changed from her everyday self too. Hair curled round her ears with the damp, cheeks flushed with the heat and the work, and her eyes glowed in the candlelight, and she revealed a beauty I'd never noticed before.

Like animals attracted by the light, other women would drift from their tenements into the back court, and pause at the wash-house door. 'Are you nearly done noo?' was the usual greeting. The patient figure at the tubs, or 'bines' as we called them, would pause from her vigorous rubbing of the soiled clothes against the wash-board, charmed to be the centre of interest for once, and say cheerfully, 'Just aboot half-way through. I've juist the dungarees to dae, and then the white things will be ready for "sihnin" oot.' I once asked my teacher how to spell this word 'sihnin' which we used when we meant rinsing, but she'd never heard of it, for she was from the north, so I just had to make a guess at the spelling and hope it was right.

At the word 'dungarees' the women would groan in sympathy. Washing dungarees was a job they all hated, and as ours was a Railway district, most husbands or brothers or sons worked with dirty machinery, and came home with grease-laden dunga-rees, so this was a task they all had to face. Our tenement women all had raw fingers from using the slimy black soap and soda which was the only way they knew for ridding the filthy overalls of their accumulated grease and workshop dirt.

The women's eyes would lazily follow the washer's move-ments as she scrubbed and rinsed, and put clothes through the wringer ready for the house pulleys, or maybe for the ropes next morning, if the next woman using the wash-house could be coaxed to let her put out a rope for a couple of hours before her own were ready to be hung out. But the ropes were only put outside if it promised to be a fine day, and the women were expert weather forecasters, for everybody detested getting their nicely wrung clothes wet again. The ultimate in disaster was reached when the weight of sodden clothes on the ropes was too much for the supporting clothes pole, and the whole lot came crashing among the dirt of the back court, and had to be taken in and rinsed through all over again.

I loved when the white things were judged to be ready, for then came the scene I liked best of all. The heavy boiler lid was lifted off, and leaned carefully against the back wall of the wash-house. Clouds of steam rushed everywhere. Up the chim-ney, out of the open door, into every corner. The washer, a long pole held in both hands, bent over the seething mass in the boiler, fished out a load, expertly twirling the steaming clothes to keep them safely balanced, and then ran with the laden pole across to the tub of clean water. Quickly and neatly a twist of the pole shot the clothes into the rinsing water. Back and forth, back and forth she went, her figure ghost-like in the rushing steam, until the boiler was empty. I longed to be allowed to help in this exciting operation, but met with scandalized refusal. 'Do you want to burn yoursel' to the bone?' the washerwoman would say in answer to my coaxing. 'You'll have this job to dae soon enough, hen, and then you'll no' be so pleased. Run away hame to your bed, or I'll tell your grannie on you!' But the women were more amused than angry at my interest in their activities, and they made sure I went nowhere near the steam.

When this final rinsing stage was reached the watching

women lingering at the doors couldn't resist a bit of advice, especially if the washer was a younger unmarried woman. As the tub filled, they'd say, 'Take oot the plug, hen, and let the clean water run through the claes. You'll get rid o' a' the soap faur quicker that way.' Or, 'Jessie, you're just squeezin' the soap into them again – you'll hae' tae gi'e them another water. You're putting them through the wringer too soon.'

They were all experts. This was their world. And the young washerwoman would listen to them all, glad of their company and of their advice, for it was a great source of pride to have someone say, 'Aye, she hangs out a lovely washing.' And the most disparaging thing a tenement woman could say of another's wash-house efforts were the damning words, 'She's hangin' oot her grey things!'

Another glimpse of the world of washing-day could be caught at the 'steamy', when we went to the baths. These were tubs and apparatus hired by women who had no proper wash-house in their tenement back courts, or who preferred the community atmosphere of the 'steamy' to a solitary session in their own wash-house. I used to pause in the open doorway, on my way out to the street, and watch the women at their work. It was like a scene from a play. The rising clouds of steam, the bare arms rhythmically rising and falling, the stately tread to the drying cupboards, and the measured walk back, bearing their washing gracefully before them, ready for packing into their prams or bogies for the homeward journey. Again I had a great longing to penetrate these mysteries and take part in the ritual myself, but I never did so, and these tantalizing glimpses were all I ever knew of this enchanting side of the baths.[6]

By 1947, when Liz Lochhead was born, council houses had been built in great numbers.

We lived, my mother, my father and I, in a single upstairs room in my grandparents' house. My father's side. A big between-the-wars council five-apartment. Roughcast. Pebbledash. Six in the block. In the shadow of all the steelworks, Colvilles, Anderson Boyes, the Lanarkshire – number thirteen, the Broadway, Craifneuk, Wishaw. Whenever I heard on the radio the Lullaby of Broadway I thought they were singing about us.

The place was full of adoring grown-ups all easily charmed and exploited by a smartypants toddler. There was my Gran, my Grandad, my father's youngest unmarried sister and brother – my Auntie Jinnet who was engaged and my Uncle George who was Restless. He was considering emigrating to Corby with half the workforce of Anderson Boyes. My Grandad spent a lump of every afternoon lying on the bed under the top knitted blanket in the back bedroom, often with me burrowed in between him and the wall, prattling and pulling his hair. He had been a miner before the steelworks and he had a touch, more than a touch, of silicosis. His lungs weren't so good.

But he was good and loud in arguments. Round the tea-table I remember him, long before I could make head or tail of it, the arguing – especially on Sundays if the rest of the family were there, Bill and Jean who had two children and a prefab and Annie and John with my baby cousin. He had been a miner. He was a Unionist. He was angry at how his sons and daughters had come back from the Forces voting Labour. Said they'd sold old Churchill down the river. He blamed the war for a lot.

He had been a miner. He was a Unionist. In the early twenties, preying on fears aroused by the recent large influx of Irish Catholics to Glasgow and the industrial West of Scotland, the competition for jobs, the suspicions about cheap blackleg labour, the hard times a-coming, the Scottish Unionist Party successfully neatly split the working classes. I know that now. Divide and Rule. People have told me. Then I knew a father and his sons around a table. His white hair. My grandmother wheeshting and clucking. The words Catholic and Protestant. Raised voices.

He was not an Orangeman. He used to say he had nothing against anybody. He was a good churchgoer. Regular. He talked about Idolatry. And told me about Covenanters. There was a blue and white plate on the wall with a man-on-a-horse who was William of Orange. He was Dutch. Delft. They had brought it back from Holland when they had visited my Uncle Robert's Grave, my Gran and Grandad. After the war. He had been my

father's second-youngest brother. He was dead. There was a
picture of him in his uniform. I spent a lot of time looking at
this photograph to see if there was anything different about a
picture of somebody who was dead. It was easier with my Aunt
Edith. She had died aged seven of measles ten years, fifteen
years, a long time ago. It was possible to imagine, when I
squinted at the family group with her in front, something slight
and shifting and otherworldly about her sepia presence among
her lumpier solid brothers and sisters. They said I'd her Eyes.
My mother said nothing at the time, later up in the privacy of
our room said nothing of the sort. Mine were brown.

The room wasn't that big. There was my mother and father's
big high bed. And my brown-varnished cot squashed in at the
end of it. A green-top card table and chairs, big brown boxy
rexine chairs. There was the radio, no, it was only a speaker
really, it had one on-off switch, no tuner, it was attached to my
Grandparents' radio downstairs. We had to listen to whatever
they listened to, when they switched it off we'd had it. We
listened a lot though, plays, music-nights, Take It From Here.
In April 1948 over the speaker they heard Stafford Cripps'
Budget increase the price of cigarettes from two-and-four pence
to three-and-four pence and my forty-a-day father looked at his
sleeping or squalling four-month-old daughter, said well that's
that and gave up just like that, never smoked again. Another
piece of family mythology.

There were few ornaments. My mother and father's engagement photo, framed. Head and shoulders, printed in mono-
chrome then hand-tinted. Cherryblossom – brown hair, pink
cheeks, carmine lips. A sweet smile each and a youthful look.
And the wedding photograph. Full length. My father in his army
uniform, my mother in the A.T.S. She said she could stand it,
the Khaki, because she'd good colouring and anyway there just
weren't the coupons. She'd had nothing else to fit her because
the army food blew you up. She'd consoled herself with what
the teacher had told her away back when she'd had to wear the
brown fairy dress in 'Fairy-Leather-Apron' in the school concert
– that brown eyes like that could bring out the beauty. She said
the big excitement had been seeing if my father's leave got

cancelled and the whole thing was off for the time being. It had been touch and go, she said. But she'd got a lot out of the A.T.S., enjoyed it, met all sorts. She said the main thing was not to marry too young. She recommended waiting until you were twenty-four like her. It had been the ideal age.

She talked to me a lot, did my mother. All day when my father was away at work. Bits of her life became legends. Descriptions of dance dresses, what devils they'd been she and her sisters, stories of how my Auntie Elsie, fifteen and with soot on her eye-lashes, had brazenly stolen someone's officer. She says now I was great company as a kid. She was that bit plumper again than in the wedding photograph. Seems that every time something my grandmother said rankled her (it was my father's side remember) every time she had to just swallow it all or just start a row over some domestic division, every time they'd had yet another disappointment over some house they'd been after – she'd walk me in my go-chair, chewing in her misery a whole quarter of newly unrationed sweets.

For a while we tried the other set of grandparents. I don't suppose things were much happier or easier for my mother and father. They kept putting in for houses here and there, getting nowhere.

They didn't seem quite so deadly respectable, my Gran and Grandad Forrest. For instance he swore, up to the point of 'bloody' and 'wee bugger'. He had been in the Navy in the First World War, still sang songs my grandmother tutted at. He had a terrible voice. A groaner. Tone deaf. He sang me Sad Songs – 'The Drunkard's Raggit Wean' – and laughed and tickled me when I got a lump in my throat. My mother always said what a right good storyteller he was, had a way with words, embroidered things just enough.

My grandmother said poems. Long storytelling poems. At sixteen she'd been maid to one of the Misses Reid who'd been an elocutionist. And gave lessons. My grandmother had remembered by heart every word, every inflection, every arch or pointed gesture of the voice. I grew wide-eyed at Little Orphan Annie (and the goblins will get you/too/if/you/don't/watch/out), tearful at the melodrama about the little girl searching for her dead mother (And I'se looking for heaven/but I can't find the stair).

I absolutely loved them both. But it's easy to love your grandparents.

When I was four we Got A House. A brand-new council four-apartment in the small mining village of Newarthill. A couple of miners' rows, the school, the pub, the Tallies' Cafe, the Post Office and the Co-operative. Now the pits were dying and they were building two schemes around it. It was four miles from Motherwell, expanding industry.

I went with my mother to do the place up before we moved in. I could feel her excitement. Eight years married and a house at last. We approached along newly laid out paths. What would soon be careful turfed lawns and neat rose-borders were great banks and churns of clay. The rooms seemed big and empty and hollow-sounding. Full of space. Cream plasterboard walls. My mother said they could get the downstairs done but maybe if she stippled the upstairs rooms there would be no need to afford to paper right away. She measured and scrubbed and I looked out of the window at the signs of life, a parked pram, the colour of someone's curtains, elsewhere windows whitened for privacy. A girl quite a lot bigger than me was wheeling a small girl in a pushchair and dragging a small boy by the hand. My mother said I should go and make friends, that was the beauty of it, I'd have lots of boys and girls to play with. It would be great for me.[7]

During the nineteenth century, shops proliferated in town and country, including the Scottish Co-operative Stores (from 1868), big department stores (around 1900) and countless tiny establishments. Shopkeepers were characters whose importance loomed large in the lives of children sent on errands. George Davidson's father kept a village shop in the little Aberdeenshire village of Whiterashes.

A General Merchant's business in a country village from 1900 to 1930 was something precious to be remembered for the friendly and personal part it played in the lives of the folk round about. Many people are crazy about antiques today, and a description of such a business is practically an antique of a different kind. Such was my father's business at Whiterashes.

It was a hive of industry every day of the week except Sunday and half-day Tuesday. Hours were from 8am to 8pm, but quite often earlier or later. When one entered the front door of the shop, the drapery counter was at the right-hand side and the grocery on the left. The first thing that caught the eye was a large flat glass case about 8 inches deep on the top of the drapery counter. It contained spectacles costing one shilling (5p) a pair. Echo mouth-organs were sixpence (2½p), purses, watches five shillings (25p), cut-throat razors, pocket knives, scissors, alarm clocks and lots of other necessary things. A revolving post-card stand was next, with daily and weekly newspapers beside it. The counter tops were stained oak or mahogany and polished to make the rolls of drapery slide easily when measuring with a round yard-stick.

There was the usual space behind the counter for the assistants serving, and the shelves at the back contained rolls of flannel 30 inches wide, grey, white and pink and also rolls of dark wincey shirting, flannelette, winceyette and prints for ladies' aprons and dresses. There was also curtain material, table baize, and cheese cloth. Two sliding glass doors showed large hanks of fingering, wheeling and double knitting wools of all colours.

Flannel linders were worn next to the skin by most outdoor male workers, along with dark wincey shirts or sarks. In the winter time, a home knitted wool short sleeved garment called a sarkette was worn between the linder and the shirt and it was needed in very cold weather when the men and boys were exposed to the elements for long spells. Long knitted wheeling pants and socks were also worn.

A yard long brass strip showing the inches was screwed to the inside edge of the counter for measuring elastic, window cord and such like. At the far end was a display of gents' caps, mufflers, and in winter lugget bonnets; also ladies' hats and corsets. Ladies' and children's combinations were very popular and it was quite common for a lady customer to ask us to bring her a new dress or coat from Aberdeen.

1 boll cotton flour bags were eagerly bought by housewives

for about sixpence (2½p) each. They made lovely pillow cases after being bleached to take out the printing on them.

The counter across the back displayed all the usual iron-mongery, together with a selection of all kinds of paraffin lamps; also large and small bellows to blow up the fire, iron girdles for baking oatcakes, scones, etc. On the floor in front were spades, graips, scythes, stable and byre brushes, horse combs, curry combs, and dandy brushes. There were also sample rolls of wire netting, barbed wire, plain wire, coir yard and binder twine, stocks of which were kept elsewhere. For some reason, near these in season was a crate of oranges, a barrel of Almera green grapes and a large barrel or box of American or Canadian apples. Above the shop door was a shelf with all kinds of ropes for farm use, including plough reins. Nearby were hanging strings of clay pipe lids, leather boot laces and coloured string for tying up horses' manes and tails. For lack of space, things like baskets, paraffin flasks, brush heads and stable lanterns were hung on hooks from the roof. These lanterns were made in Inverurie.

The grocery counter on the left near the door had a glass case with sliding doors showing cheese, bacon, butter and such like, with no refrigerator in those days. The two sets of brass weighing scales had flat and bell shaped weights. The groceries were much the same as today except that instead of being in packets, they were all loose in boxes, glass jars etc. and had all to be put into bags by the assistants.

Wooden bins with lids, on the floor against the wall at the back of the counter contained flour, peasemeal, sugar, barley, split peas and so on. At eye level on the shelves were all the usual grocery things such as sweets and patent medicines like Zam Buk, Steedman's Powders, Beecham's Pills, Castor Oil and other things. All the counters had drawers full of smaller things like 2oz packets of Stephen Mitchell's XXX Bogie Roll. Two of the drawers had the Post Office stamps, postal orders, registered letters etc. The old age pension was five shillings a week (25p). Underneath the counter was a shelf containing hard fish. Also near there in boxes were smokers' clay pipes, pipe clay, Thorley's Food for animals, sulphur, cakes of boot blacking etc.

About 1920 gramophone records were a feature, like Beltona

and Zonophone and the music of a new record, say 'Bonnie Strathyre' or 'When It's Springtime in the Rockies', cheered things up. Everybody who had a gramophone had to hear a newly out record before purchasing. The prices of these was about 7½p and 12½p.

Reserve stocks of everything were kept in the back shop, the cellar, and upstairs, dishes, cream jars, milk plates etc.

Commercial travellers from Aberdeen, most of whom were good friends, kept us up to date while policemen from Newmachar, Udny, Oldmeldrum and Inverurie usually met in the shop and compared notes. The postmen coming back in with the mail they had collected, and of course most of all an exchange of local news among the customers all made shop life more shortsome. The main shop was lit by central draught lamps hung from the roof and in winter required filling twice a day, so that it was almost a full-time job for an assistant cleaning and filling all the lamps.[8]

Greater affluence and the vast expansion of motor transport have destroyed the livelihoods of many corner-shopkeepers. The chores of shopping, cooking, cleaning and washing no longer swamp housewives' lives with their endless drudgery. In some respects, at least, technological change has brought real benefits.

CHAPTER III

A COMFORTABLE LIFE

Increasing wealth and the confidence, after Culloden, that peace had at last arrived inside Scotland, encouraged the well-to-do to provide themselves with spacious new homes. Members of the Scottish gentry travelled in England and in Europe; there they saw housing designs, estate layouts and living styles they felt eager to emulate. Freed from the need, even on the Highland fringes, to construct dwellings designed for safety they felt able to spread themselves. In 1765 James Murray of Broughton, a wealthy Galloway landowner who, among other activities, directed the planning of the community of Gatehouse of Fleet, decided his lifestyle required a new dwelling. The following letter from Robert Mylne describes the proposed property. As the contents show, the letter originally had a plan attached to it.

I have sent a sketch of Mr Murray's house, which I am hopeful he will be so good as to think as the bad-digested principals that a house should be built upon, rather than a house that I say is fit for him . . . The situation is supposed to be on a small rising ground . . . an extended plan before, for prospect; and the hill rising behind to preserve it from cold winds. This house is divided into 4 storeys. The first is for the use of all servants who work in the house. It holds the kitchen and all the nauseous places that should not be seen or smelt by company. It is half sunk in the ground to keep it cool, and half above to give it light, and make a pedestal to the whole building. The entrance to it is by the private stair at one end to keep the front free of the drudgery servants. The second storey is entirely appropriated for the reception and entertainment of strangers . . . the third storey is all the bed chambers for the master, company and children of the house. The fourth storey is rooms for the principal servants, nursery, and a few rooms for more company. The garrets are for the lower servants who work in the house.

In the ground storey, 'A' is a hall which gives admittance to all the rooms on this level without going through one another. It is lighted from the stair and must be painted very white. 'B' is the larder which, as it should be cool, is turned to the north. 'C' is the servants' hall, placed in this corner that their noise may be out of hearing, . . . 'I' is the steward's counting room, it lies next to the private stair and entry and has a door from thence for to admit those people who have business with him. 'L' is the kitchen, which as it should be clean and cool, is turned to the morning sun and coolness of the north. It is placed under the library to keep its disagreeable smell from the rooms where the company are. 'M' is the coalhouse by the windows of which the coals may be thrown in from the carts.[1]

The comfortable life lived in large homes was made possible by vast armies of servants. Janet Story's upbringing, in Melville Street, Edinburgh, took place amid the constant attentions of servants. She was born in 1828.

The parlour maids of those days had many a weary stair journey, and the Edinburgh houses, many of them, had long and steep stairs, and servants were not as much considered as they are now-a-days; a lift was a thing unheard of, and coals, luggage, and all the paraphernalia of the various meals had to be conveyed to their destination by manual labour.

My father furnished No. 37 from the upholstering firm of Messrs Whytock & Co. No scamped work came out of their shop, and to this day the drawers run and the hinges work as if Japanese artificers had been employed on them. The furniture was nearly all rosewood and old Spanish mahogany, especially the many leaved dining tables, my mother's particular pride, which were always kept in a condition of the highest polish. You could see your face in them almost like a mirror. And all this was true "elbow grease," for no modern French polish was ever allowed to desecrate those sacred panels. In winter, when a day of persistent snow appeared to have set in, or at other seasons when equally steady rain was in view, and no social interruption seemed probable, the tables were hauled out of their corners, the leaves inserted, and the entire household set to work to polish them up, first rubbing them hard with a small square piece of cork, and then finishing with dry rubbing, with a piece of flannel or even an ordinary duster.

At the corner end of Melville Street stood two stalwart Highland porters, Robertson and Davidson. I see them now, big, handsome men, whose vocation in life was to minister to the varied needs of those householders in their immediate neighbourhood, running messages, carrying luggage up and down stairs, beating carpets and over and above all rubbing tables. Their great strength enabled them to polish much more efficiently than a woman could do, and on all special occasions, when any extra work was required, the two Highlanders were sent for, and most satisfactory results followed.

The dinners then were something to speak of, and were affairs that required much arrangement and forethought. The cook who was to assist on the occasion must first of all be secured, long before the guests were invited; for the ordinary kitchen performer of that day was a mortal of very ordinary attainments, and would have been quite over-weighted with the prospect of preparing a dinner for twenty-two, or even a larger number.

The cook secured, the next most important matter was the head waiter, a very superior functionary, who was answerable for the arrangement of the the table service and appointments, and for the ushering in and general superintendence of the company. Kemp, the head janitor of the Academy, was for many years at the head of the Edinburgh staff of waiters: a steady, very dignified individual, who knew his duties thoroughly, was as sober as a judge, and could be trusted perfectly to carry out an entertainment exactly as it should be done.

On the occasion of a large dinner party the children of a household were dressed in all their best and permitted to remain in the drawing-room till dinner was announced, the guests noticing them or ignoring them according to their amiability or inclination. In our family, and also in many others, they were again in evidence when dinner was over and dessert placed on the table; a most injudicious custom, which has now, mercifully, become almost obsolete. Kindly and foolish people then amused themselves in stuffing the youngsters with a variety of fruits and sweetmeats most injurious to little digestions at that late hour, the result being generally a needful dose of castor oil or senna tea, the latter a very common juvenile medicament in my nursery days.

The dinner itself must have been almost equally trying to the seniors. Mrs Clerihew, the female chef, and my mother between them always concocted a feast for the gods: no cheese-paring economy was ever practised in our house.

Two soups, and Mrs Clerihew was not niggardly in her stock, two large dishes of fish, and these were all placed on the dinner table, my father serving the one, my mother the other. We had two very handsome silver soup tureens, presented to my father by the grateful owners of a sailing ship which in his East Indian days he was the means of saving from impending destruction. One was always placed at the head of the table, the other at the foot; and they almost invariably were the ready means of starting a conversation on matters familiar to most of those present. For among the guests were pretty certain to be several members of the "Services," as a large gathering from our Eastern dependency formed then a marked feature of Edinburgh society; and with their polished manners and often highly culti-vated minds were an acquisition to the most refined circles.

In succession to the soup and to the fish, four massive entree dishes were placed heavily on the table to be "seen of all men"; and were then lightly removed and handed, one after the other, to the guests. One of them was invariably a curry, which though served out of its proper order, which, in India, is at the conclusion of the meal, was of an excellence so superior as very speedily to win great renown for my mother's recipe – and that fame has continued with me to the present day.

One would have thought that it might by this time have been nearly over, but this was very far from being the case. The silver entree dishes were removed, and a huge roast of beef or a leg of mutton was placed before the host: the opposite end of the table being graced by a gigantic turkey, roasted or boiled. While my father devoted his attention to the beef, the male guest of honour carved the turkey; and I remember one gallant colonel, who was a frequent guest in our house, publicly stating that he considered it incumbent on him to satisfy all the demands made on him from one side of the turkey's plump breast, leaving the other half quite intact for the family lunch the following day.

Half way down the table on each side was deposited another large dish containing a still further variety of solid viands – ducks, a ham or tongue, beefsteak pie – so that every guest might be safe to have his or her particular taste gratified.

Then came the sweet course. At the foot of the table there was usually a dish of macaroni and cheese, more especially for masculine tastes; while at the other end towered a magnificent erection of spun sugar and pastry, filled with luscious preserves, a perfect death trap for indigestion, especially after all that had gone before. Two side dishes, one occasionally a simple pudding, duly appeared; while four handsome cut crystal dishes took the place of the previous entrees, containing a white vanilla and a pink raspberry cream, a pale wine jelly, and one tinted crimson with drops of cochineal: very pretty and tempting they all looked.[2]

Whilst living in her parents' home Janet Story found the smooth running of life was something she could take for granted. Once she married and had to direct servants herself, life did not seem so easy.

We had an admirable cook, Betty by name; but unluckily her temper was as hot as her very superior curry; and between her and the housemaid was a feud of long standing, which every now and then developed extra energy. On this occasion the outburst had been unusually bad; the wretched housemaid had been dragged across the kitchen by her thick coil of hair, and stretched across the table, while the cook brandished over her a large carving knife, and threatened her in a manner that rendered the poor creature almost unconscious: the prompt intervention of the parlourmaid, who chanced to enter at the moment, being believed by her and by the victim to have just averted a bloody murder.

It was out of the question to put up with conduct like this, so I summoned the culprit to my presence, and informed her, that much as I regretted parting with her, she must go. She was very contrite, and very unwilling to leave our service, but the fact of the carving knife could not be overlooked; it was an enormity of which no respectable cook ought to have been capable. Poor Betty had to depart, bag and baggage, greatly regretted by us all. The housemaid feeling aggrieved by some remarks which I addressed to her, left also; and a friend of mine, a Mrs. Sprot, engaged them both to go to her. Not long after she had taken up her duties, Mr. Sprot, hearing from his wife that what she considered too large fires were being burnt in the kitchen, and that the cook paid no attention to her remonstrances, went downstairs one day to have a look for himself. The fire was large, and he began to venture on some observations, when he was promptly arrested by Betty seizing in her hand a large kitchen towel and flapping it violently on the table, exclaiming in a furious tone, "Oot o' ma kitchen! oot o' ma kitchen! I'll hae nae spyin' maisters here!" while her attitude and manner were so menacing that the much alarmed gentleman lost no time in retiring from the lower regions, with the loud refrain of "Oot o' ma kitchen," and the heavy flop of the cloth sounding stridently in his ears. No more remonstrances were attempted, but Betty and her boxes made a second and speedy exodus.[3]

The long hours, low pay and lack of freedom make the reminiscences of domestic servants seem a commentary on a largely unhappy existence. Agnes Black worked as a servant in a great house in the Highlands in the inter war years. Her comments show that, at the time, servants did not necessarily feel discontented.

The cook reigned supreme in her own kitchen. She was boss. Discipline was her first concern – then cleanliness. She was so obsessed by this that she even made sure her own staff were properly dressed before she'd allow them to go for their meals with the other household staff in our own dining room.

In the mornings, as a kitchen maid, I had to wear a pale green linen frock with a green apron, while the cook was dressed in a black frock and white apron with hat. Now, before I was able to go to the dining room to have my breakfast the cook would inspect me as if I was a soldier on parade, checking that my dress was clean and all looked neat and respectable. Of course the others were subjected to the same treatment. We never objected. Well we couldn't – could we? We'd have been out on our ears looking for another job if we had. And anyway it was just a part of that way of life. Something you expected to happen to you. All the same, I was only about twenty and thought it a bit of a laugh, but one of the other kitchen maids we had was in her mid-thirties. Later, when I left and got married I did wonder what she thought about having to line up like a schoolgirl to have her nails inspected and she a mature, adult person. But I never asked her at the time. In fact we rarely discussed such things – on duty or off.

We might moan among ourselves and grumble over petty inconveniences or when we thought some extra chore was something we shouldn't be doing. But the wider aspects of things – the life we led bound in service to others – well, we never saw anything wrong with it, so we never talked about it. It was a way of life – our way of life. It was all we knew. Life might be better on the other side of the wall, but then none of us had ever been there to see for ourselves. So we stayed put – in a world we knew. We were secure. We were happy. We were sad. At times we liked the job – at other times we hated it because of the monotony. But as far as I knew, other people's jobs were exactly the same – sometimes good, sometimes bad. Other folk had boring and happy times all rolled into one life. So had I. My idea was to do the job well – to work hard and do things as best I could. I wanted praise. I resented being told off – well, not resented it; it's truer to say I was disappointed whenever the cook found fault with my work. But when I stood there every morning in the kitchen after nearly three hours of hard work cleaning things and preparing the staff breakfast, I never once felt any real animosity about having the cook look me up and down to see if my uniform was clean. She had her job to do. I had mine. Anyway, I suppose I was dreaming of the day when I would be a cook like her and it would be me doing the inspecting and dishing-out the praise or the criticism. I expect this dream of mine prevented me from feeling any real resentment.

So, before breakfast every morning the cook would give us all the once-over to see we were presentable to the rest of the staff. She had no intention of letting the side down – of appearing in the dining hall in front of the other servants with the members of her own department not up to scratch. There was usually a deep rivalry between the kitchen and household staffs; not so much between the kitchen maids and the housemaids, but between housekeeper, butler and cook. More often than not it was just a professional affair, each one thinking that his or her own department was a cut above the others and more important in the scale of things within the house. They would act very formally and be completely aloof when talking to each other in front of the staff, but get them on their own and they'd be laughing and joking – completely friendly.

In our case, however, the cook and the butler did not see eye to eye. And their dislike of each other was no pretence. It was for real. Along the passage we would go to the breakfast table in time to be seated at eight o'clock and there in the hall would be gathered the rest of the staff – the head housemaid and three maids, the footman and the butler, the lady's-maid and the two laundry maids. We always entered the room as close to eight o'clock as possible so that everybody else would already be there. It was a sort of grand entrance. The cook liked it this way. You could see it in her face. She never varied the habit the whole time I was there. The butler sat at one end of the table and the cook sat at the other. It was obvious they wanted to be as far away from each other as possible. Whenever their eyes would meet they'd look daggers at each other which, as you can imagine, was not the most pleasant of atmospheres in which to eat a meal – especially the first meal of the day.

As a general rule there really was quite often a great deal of jealousy between butlers and cooks in country houses. The cook always felt that the butler might be on better terms with the laird and his wife than she was – and vice versa. And neither could bear it if they thought the other was getting favoured and they were losing out on something. It was a common occurrence – you expected to find this wee bit of friction, of hostility, between the butler and the cook wherever you might go to work. And on occasions it wasn't just a little bit of friction, but total all-out war.

When you think of it, it was stupid really because living in a closeknit community as we did, all under the same roof, sharing the same table, it was extremely important that everyone should get along well with each other. Such constant bickering sometimes put us all on edge, but in our case the cook and the butler took good care to do their quarrelling out of earshot of her ladyship or the laird. It was absolute nonsense for either of them to think the gentry thought more of one than the other. The butler was good at his job. So, too, was the cook. They'd no need to think of each other as rivals. Basically speaking, the lady of the house treated them in like fashion – with restrained courtesy. As for the laird – well, he talked to each of them in the same way, just as he did to all of us; with a bit of a joke; easily, not stuffy or aloof at all. He talked plainly. He had great charm. And yet, if the butler saw the cook having a conversation with either the laird or his wife he'd be needling at the cook for ages trying to discover what had been said. And she was just as bad. What a pair.

Lord, it's not as if the pair of them had nothing to do. Their day was just as busy as ours, in its own fashion. I suppose it was just another case of human nature at work. No doubt they disliked each other at first sight. So, out of pettiness and spite, each decided to make a misery of the other's life. And they succeeded. Oh yes, they certainly achieved their aim. And in a strange way it never seemed to make either of them downhearted or dispirited in any way. They seemed to enjoy it. To thrive on it. The pair of them. The trouble was, all of us maids were caught in the cross-fire. And we didn't like it – not one tiny bit.

The staff ate all their meals together; breakfast at 8 a.m., lunch at 11.45 a.m., and the evening meal, a sort of high tea, at 6 p.m. Our meals were different from those served upstairs, but if there had been anything left over from the previous day, part of a roast, a pie, this sort of thing, it came to the servants' table. But usually we were on stews and things, rabbits done in all sorts of different ways or hare – common stuff, I suppose some folks might think, but there was always plenty of it – and it was good. A darned sight better than the food many ordinary people were eating at the time. We got quite a lot of meat, really, which was something a great number of ordinary working people in the 1920s found it difficult to get hold of because, quite simply, they hadn't the money to buy it. We were lucky in this respect. We were never in danger of starving. There was always a stock pot on the range – for soups and stews, things of this kind. So we were all well catered for.

Mind you, with our last meal being at six o'clock in the evening we were sometimes pretty hungry by the time the gentry had finished their dinner and we had seen to all the washing and tidying-up and stacking of the plates. So we had a cup of tea or cocoa or even coffee, sometimes, with a sandwich or a biscuit – this would be around 10.30 p.m. But very often if there was a great deal to do it might be 11.30 or nearly midnight before we could put our feet up. Then, with the cocoa drunk and the sandwich eaten, it was time to get off to bed. And it's no exaggeration to say that we couldn't wait to get to bed. As soon as my head used to touch the pillow I'd be off to sleep. I never had any sleepless nights. They were never a part of my life. I was usually too tired. Dead-beat. And no wonder – having to rise every morning at 4.45.

Still, us underlings weren't the only ones up and about to all hours of the night. The cook's hours of work were just the same when it came to the evenings. She was always there, right up to the last, to see that everything was completed satisfactorily and all plates, pots and pans put away in a tidy fashion. And the butler, he was upstairs making sure that his silver was all stored away, properly cleaned and shining brightly. Oh yes, they were there too. So, to be fair, although I, and others like me, had to slave on all day, our superiors were every bit as tied to their jobs as we were. It was long hours for everybody. We may have been their inferiors, well down the scale of things in the jobs hierarchy, but at least in this respect we were their equals.[4]

For the gentry, at least, the golden age of relatively low taxes and a plentiful supply of willing servants drifted on into the thirties. Ewan Forbes' family enjoyed life in two quite different properties. In summer they moved from the comfort of Fintray House to live in their early seventeenth-century castle of Craigievar. (The very different circumstances of post-1939 Britain mean that Craigievar has been turned over to the National Trust.)

At the beginning of August every year, the whole household set out from Fintray in a carefully devised plan to arrive at Craigievar by an exciting and varied means of transport. In the vanguard went the head housemaid, 2 days in advance, on her bicycle. This would give her time to make up all the beds with the overseer's wife, who was caretaker of the Castle in winter. At 9 a.m. on 'D' day my mother, driving a shetland pony in a governess cart, and my sister driving another wee shalt in a flat cairtie and myself mounted on a riding pony set on our way. We always put in at the stables at House of Monymusk where the good coachman attended to our ponies while we had lunch with that most hospitable Lady, the wife of Sir Arthur Grant. After lunch we continued on our journey. Meantime, the milk cow with the cook and a certain amount of baggage, set off in a small hired cattle float. You might think the cook was riding shotgun, but the whole timing was calculated so that food could be prepared for the many who would arrive in due course. The cook undoubtedly was the most important individual there. Later in the day the chauffeur drove the large Siddeley-Deasy with all the rest of the staff except the butler, who risked his life, with my father driving an Essex bringing varied bits of table silver and the rest of the luggage. By 7.30 p.m. the whole move had been completed, thanks to the flair for planning possessed by my mother. I should not forget to add, that the milk cow was very well milked by the overseer's wife who had a great rapport with all animals.

During one of these glorious summer holidays my precious pony developed stifles, for which the vet prescribed a quart of linseed oil mixed half and half with treacle, twice a day. I held her head up while the overseer poured the mixture down her throat. Unfortunately he was frightened of horses, which my little mare realised after one dose. Next time I saw her rolling her eyes with a very wicked expression and as the poor man poured the dose down her throat, she closed her gullet and blew the lot over him. He seemed to be doomed to stickiness, as during the summer months, various swarms of bees chose their residences in the roof of the Castle. A trap door was made for access to the honey above a large space known as the long-room. Old hip baths, berry pans and basins were prepared to receive an enormous weight of honey. On one occasion the butler's bedroom ceiling, situated immediately below the square tower was weighed down and drooped in a very dangerous manner. He was hurried away to other quarters, as his bed was menaced by honey and bees. As soon as the family had flitted to the house at Fintray, the joiner cut the ceiling and the portly figure of the overseer, well covered in a straw hat and veils all around, made his entry through the aperture, and lo there came forth sweetness, which ran in a sticky cascade down his jacket, waist-coat and right down his breeks, until he could touch nothing without becoming cemented to the spot. His wife gave me a blood-curdling description of her adventures in removing his garments . . .

As a youngster I would rather do anything than get entangled with high-society people who came to kill time and landed conveniently at tea-time as my mother was well known for her remarkable ability of organizing teas for over 40 people when no-one was expected at all. I was thin enough to wriggle through the kitchen windows and make my escape.

When no strangers were about, I caught a number of bumble bees and put them in a match box, then going to the outside wall of the kitchen where a hole had been bored through the wall, opening into a cupboard, I called "Hoo Hoo", and blew the bumble bees down the pipe. I didn't get an oatcake piece for my pony or myself for 2 days.[5]

The expanding nineteenth-century economy enabled men to make their fortunes in trade and industry, and in the professions too. The suburbs of Scottish towns and cities provide plenty of visible evidence of the taste and the wealth of the growing middle class in the shape of numerous sizeable and solidly-built homes. Maurice Lindsay grew up in just such an environment. He was born in 1918, the son of a successful Glaswegian insurance manager.

I was born into the numerically tiny but then still influential privileged professional section of this urban interlock of nearly a million people. My father, an insurance manager, was, in his own words, "a self-made man". We were never allowed to forget how much his present position, and therefore ours, depended upon his early sacrifices and unremitting effort. At nineteen, he found himself the eldest of a parentless family of five brothers and sisters. During the last months of the Kaiser's war, part of his left jaw was shot away, and he was pronounced speechless for the rest of his days. A grafted bone from his hip and a technique of rigorously applied courage confounded the doctors. I was almost two years old when he returned from his hospitals to business life.

Having inherited nothing from his own father, he brought us up to accept that what he earned – and he was as successful with his investments as with building up the interests of the insurance company whose Scottish office he managed – would be employed in our upbringing and education. Thereafter, we would be on our own. He did not believe in inherited wealth and, until old age, felt that the arts, except for the plays of Shakespeare, were softening and effeminate, but by the time his sight had begun to fail, music had become his main solace. Given a maximum life-expectancy of fifty silent years, he lived to exceed a garrulous eighty-four. Although our relationship was always ambivalent, I admired his courage and his industry.

My mother had a gentler nature. Somewhere along her line there was an opera singer who died young in America. As my mother grew older, my father's constant preoccupation with business, the League of Nations, the Rotary Club and other public causes, together with his lifelong habit of golfing every

Saturday with male cronies, isolated her. Although we were a family of four, I came to suspect that there was probably never very much sexual warmth between them. To the disapproval of my father, my mother encouraged my passion for music. When it was clear that I did not mean to be deflected from making a career of it, she slipped me regular sums of money to go to concerts and theatres.

We lived in the West End of Glasgow; at first in the privately-owned Ashton Terrace, parts of which have since been demolished to make way for a road and University buildings, and then in Athole Gardens, an enclosed hilly U-shaped crescent in the high Victorian manner of the 1870s with a private central common garden and a tennis-court. The pink flambeaux of a mature horse-chestnut tree illuminated the front of the house in early summer. From my high-up bedroom window, the roofscape at the back of the house was distantly topped by shipyard cranes.

There was in these days a sense of community about our district of Hillhead. The shopkeeprs of Byres Road knew us all by name, and we them. There was Wilkie, the grocer, who sent round a crate of apples at Christmas in appreciation of our custom; the 'thirties equivalent, I suppose, of selling loss-leaders or giving away trading stamps. The three – or was it four? – Misses Horn kept the dairy with the cows at one time in a byre behind the shop, though I cannot recall this. They had hands as blue as the wall-tiles of their shop, due, I used to think, to so much scrubbing. Yet their hands were not as raw as those of the daughter of Andrews, the fishmonger, whose fingers were forever lifting moist fillets off chipped ice. Mr and Mrs Todd, the fruiterers, added their contribution to the Christmas scene with a gift of tangerines to all their 'regulars'. Tully, the ironmonger, and Bell of the toyshop featured less frequently, being on the more occasionally visited periphery of my childish world of things. Most exotic of all was Henderson's stable, from which issued forth the faded, musty-smelling horse-drawn cabs that conveyed us to children's parties. In time, the horses gave place to cumbersome-looking limousines. Cabs and limousines have been swept away for a supermarket, where well-wrapped things wait on their shelves without that warmth of human contact the older way of shopping provided. Yet I still have a childish liking for shopping, a liking celebrated in my poem "How Do You Do?"

During the absence of my father in hospital, a bachelor uncle of my mother's – John by name, though my childish lips could get no nearer to it than Doan, which he always remained – acted as a much loved substitute, a role he maintained until his own brief marriage late in life. A grain merchant, he kept his samples in heavy manilla envelopes from which he extracted the pulses on broad ivory samplers to show to shopkeepers. I enjoyed watching him check their freshness before each new week began.

Every Saturday, he would take me on an excursion. It might involve jolting the length of a tuppenny tram-ride to some distant and magically-named suburb such as Auchenshuggle; or sailing model yachts or steamboats, bought by him, on the pond in Victoria Park. Once, it was an illicit journey on a real tanker steam-engine from Hyndland depot. My uncle got a row from my mother when we arrived home furtively with tell-tale oil marks on my Sunday jacket.

Sometimes our excursions carried us far outside Glasgow. When I was about eight or nine, we took a bus ride into Lanarkshire. Suddenly, the bus was surrounded by shouting men who made us all get out. Sweating and swearing, they pushed the bus over on its side. For many months after, the long tinkle of falling glass which followed the crash as the bus rolled over, sounded through nightmares in which I was leered at by the contorted faces of the protesting miners, sweating to dislodge a bus's equilibrium. I did not understand how pushing over a bus could help to get anyone jobs. Doubtless an adult hatred of, and contempt for, violent protest movements and Trade Union bullying, were established on that long-ago Saturday afternoon.

As I grew up, I became increasingly aware of the dichotomies between which our way of life was balanced: affluence against poverty, a nominal Protestantism against Jewery and Catholicism. My father frequently reminded us of our good fortune, urging us to "Count our blessings, count them one by one". My mother and her friends, and even our three domestics, often let fall sharp comments about Catholics and the Jews. This puzzled me. The nanny employed to look after my younger brother and sisters seemed the mostly likely source of information. The Jews, she explained, killed Christ, and were too fond of making money. No greater accusation against the Catholics was levelled than they were 'left footers'. For some time after, I used surreptitiously to examine the walk of a Catholic schoolmaster to see how this peculiarity affected him.[6]

The services provided by hired helps have, in more recent years, been increasingly replaced by machinery. The need for female labour created during two world wars opened the eyes of many women to better paid lives in factories and offices. The great houses of the past now decay, are passed to the National Trust, or seek to lure in a paying public intrigued to examine the 'upstairs, downstairs' life of the past.

Although the well-to-do no longer have access to a large pool of cheap domestic labour, the inventions of the twentieth century that fill the modern home do much to ease the painful results of the loss of servant help. Housework is no longer the vastly time-consuming task that it once was.

CHAPTER IV

AT SCHOOL

The Scottish educational system of the early nineteenth century seemed, to many of its leaders, to be something in which to feel pride. The majority of the population were equipped with some ability to read and write.

The kirk had played a powerful part in this achievement. It vigorously supported the parish schools that spread across the country. It backed the expansion of education in the Gaelic-speaking Highland areas through charitable organizations such as the Scottish Society for the Propagation of Christian Knowledge. Even so its efforts failed to cater for large numbers. By 1818 twice as many children were going to privately run 'adventure' schools as were attending parish and burgh schools. The latter varied greatly. They were commonly supported by town funds and offered a wider range of subjects than rural institutions did. The stonemason and geologist Hugh Miller, who was born in Cromarty in 1802, recorded his move from a private to a grammar school.

I quitted the dam's school at the end of the first twelve-month after mastering that grand acquirement of my life – the art of holding converse with books – and was transferred straightforth to the grammar school of the parish, at which there attended at this time about a hundred and twenty boys, with a class of about thirty individuals more, much looked down upon by the others, and not deemed greatly worth the counting, seeing that it consisted of only lassies. The building in which we met was a low, long, straw-thatched cottage, open from gable to gable, with a mud floor below, and an unlathed roof above; and stretching along the naked rafters, which, when the master chanced to be absent for a few minutes, gave noble exercise in climbing, there used frequently to lie a helm, or oar, or boothook, or even a foresail – the spoil of some hapless peat-boat from the opposite side of the Firth. The Highland boatmen of Ross had carried on a trade in peat for ages with the Saxons of the town; and as every boat owed a long-derived perquisite of twenty peats to the grammar school, and as payment was at times foolishly refused, the party of boys commissioned by the master to exact it almost always succeeded, either by force or stratagem, in securing the bringing along with them, in behalf of the institution, some spar, or sail, or piece of rigging, which, until redeemed by special treaty, and the payment of the peats, was stowed up over the rafters. These peat-expeditions, which were intensely popular in the school, gave noble exercise to the faculties. It was always a great matter to see, just as the school met, some observant boy appear, cap in hand, before the master, and intimate the fact of an arrival at the shore, by the simple words, "Peat-boat, Sir." The master would then proceed to name a party, more or less numerous, according to the exigency; but it seemed to be matter of pretty correct calculation that, in the cases in which the peat claim was disputed, it required about twenty boys to bring home the twenty peats, or, lacking these, the compensatory sail or spar. There were certain ill-conditioned boatmen who almost always resisted.

In dealing with these recusants, we used ordinarily to divide our forces into two bodies, the larger portion of the party filling their pockets with stones, and ranging themselves on some point of vantage, such as the pier-head; and the smaller stealing down as near the boat as possible, and mixing themselves up with the purchasers of the peats. We then, after due warning, opened fire upon the boatmen; and, when the pebbles were hopping about them like hailstones, the boys below commonly succeeded in securing, under cover of the fire, the desired boathook or oar. And such were the ordinary circumstances and details of this piece of Spartan education; of which a townsman has told me he was strongly reminded when boarding, on one occasion, under cover of a well-sustained discharge of musketry, the vessel of an enemy.

The parish schoolmaster was a scholar and an honest man,

and if a boy really wished to learn, he certainly could teach him. In middle life, though a licentiate of the Church, he had settled down to be what he subsequently remained – the teacher of a parish school. There were usually a few grown-up lads under his tuition – careful sailors, that had stayed ashore during the winter quarter to study navigation as a science – or tall fellows, happy in the patronage of the great, who, in the hope of being made excisemen, had come to school to be initiated in the mysteries of gauging – or grown young men, who, on second thoughts, and somewhat late in the day, had recognised the Church as their proper vocation; and these used to speak of the master's acquirements and teaching ability in the very highest terms. He himself, too, could appeal to the fact that no teacher in the north had ever sent more students to college, and that his better scholars almost always got on well in life. But then, on the other hand, the pupils who wished to do nothing – a description of individuals that comprised fully two-thirds of all the younger ones – were not required to do much more than they wished; and parents and guardians were loud in their complaints that he was no suitable schoolmaster for them; though the boys themselves usually thought him quite suitable enough.

He was in the habit of advising the parents or relations of those he deemed his clever lads, to give them a classical education; and meeting one day with Uncle James, he urged that I should be put on Latin. I was a great reader, he said; and he found that when I missed a word in my English tasks, I almost always substituted a synonym in the place of it. And so, as Uncle James had arrived, on data on his own, at a similar conclusion, I was transferred from the English to the Latin form, and, with four other boys, fairly entered on the "Rudiments." I laboured with tolerable diligence for a day or two; but there was no one to tell me what the rules meant, or whether they really meant anything; and when I got on as far as *penna*, a pen, and saw how the changes were rung on one poor word, that did not seem to be of more importance in the old language than in the modern one, I began miserably to flag, and to long for my English reading, with its nice amusing stories, and its picture-like descriptions. The Rudiments was by far the dullest book I had ever seen. It embodied no thought that I could perceive – it certainly contained no narrative, – it was a perfect contrast to not only the "Life and Adventures of Sir William Wallace," but to even the Voyages of Cook and Anson. None of my class-fellows were by any means bright; they had been all set on Latin without advice of the master; and yet, when he learned, which he soon did, to distinguish and call us up to our tasks by the name of the "heavy class", I was, in most instances, to be found at its nether end. Shortly after, however, when we got a little farther on, it was seen that I had a decided turn for translation. The master, good simple man that he was, always read to us in English, as the school met, the piece of Latin given us as our task for the day; and as my memory was strong enough to carry away the whole translation in its order, I used to give him back in the evening, word for word, his own rendering, which satisfied him on most occasions tolerably well. There were none of us much looked after; and I soon learned to bring books of amuse-ment to the school with me, which, amid the Babel confusion of the place, I contrived to read undetected. Some of them, save in the language in which they were written, were identical with the books proper to the place. I remember perusing by stealth in this way, Dryden's "Virgil," and the "Ovid" of Dryden and his friends; while Ovid's own "Ovid," and Virgil's own "Virgil," lay beside me, sealed up in the fine old tongue, which I was thus throwing away my only chance of acquiring.

One morning, having the master's English rendering of the day's task well fixed in my memory, and no book of amusement to read, I began gossiping with my nearest class-fellow, a very tall boy, who ultimately shot up into a lad of six feet four, and who on most occasions sat beside me, as lowest in the form save one. I told him about the tall Wallace and his exploits; and so effectually succeeded in awakening his curiosity, that I had to communicate to him, from beginning to end, every adventure recorded by the blind minstrel. My story-telling vocation once fairly ascertained, there was, I found, no stopping in my course. I had to tell all the stories I ever heard or read; all my father's adventures, so far as I knew them, and all my Uncle Sandy's, –

with the story of Gulliver, and Philip Quarll, and Robinson
Crusoe, – of Sinbad, and Ulysses, and Mrs Radcliffe's heroine
Emily, with, of course, the love-passages left out; and at length,
after weeks and months of narrative, I found my available stock
of acquired fact and fiction fairly exhausted. The demand on the
part of my class-fellows was, however, as great and urgent as
ever; and, setting myself, in the extremity of the case, to try my
ability of original production, I began to dole out to them by
the hour and the diet, long extempore biographies, which proved
wonderfully popular and successful. My heroes were usually
warriors like Wallace, and voyagers like Gulliver, and dwellers
in desolate islands like Robinson Crusoe; and they had not
infrequently to seek shelter in huge deserted castles, abound-
ing in trap-doors and secret passages, like that of Udolpho.
And finally, after much destruction of giants and wild beasts,
and frightful encounters with magicians and savages, they
almost invariably succeeded in disentombing hidden treasures
to an enormous amount, or in laying open gold mines, and
then passed a luxurious old age, like that of Sinbad the Sailor,
at peace with all mankind, in the midst of confectionery and
fruits.[1]

The growing size of Scotland's population, especially in urban areas,
and the increasing complexity of life in an age of technology, led to
noisy debates about how Scottish education should be improved. In
1833 the Government declared itself ready to make grants of money
to the setting up of new schools. In the 1840s inspectors began to
visit classrooms to check on how efficiently state funds were being
used to support teachers' salaries and provide buildings. (For pupils,
the long-established principle of paying fees for schooling continued
unaltered.) In 1872 the state finally acted. Scotland was divided into
numerous districts, and each district elected a school board charged
with making provision for the education of all children in its area.
Parish schools formed the basis of this system, but many new
schools had to be built. Board schoolteachers struggled to educate a
population that did not always wish to be there and that still
frequently went absent during the school year.

From a glen off Royal Deeside come these pupil's-eye comments on schoolboard life. Amy Stewart Fraser's father was the minister of Glen Gairn parish: she, like the children of much poorer families, went to the local school in the 1890s and 1900s.

Our school was designated a public school, as opposed to the type of private schools which existed before the state began to take responsibility for education. It was stonebuilt, surrounded by a low wall enclosing two playgrounds which were separated by a wall too high to climb. It was a bare barn of a place; its unhygienic conditions would not be tolerated now. It was dusty, it was stuffy, it was cold. In winter we were permitted to group ourselves round the fire, but as soon as we withdrew to make room for others we shivered again. The teacher must herself have tended the fire, chopping wood, carrying coal, and removing ashes, for no help was provided. The unplaned floorboards were scrubbed only after a social gathering, by a woman engaged for the purpose and paid half-a-crown for her trouble.

Girls entered by one door through a porch with pegs for outdoor clothing; boys entered by a similar porch from their own side of the wall. That was the extent of their segregation.

The windows were placed high in the walls, presumably to discourage wandering attention on the part of the scholars. They were never opened, even in the height of summer. The walls were distempered that sickly green shade that is supposed to be kind to the eyes. Scholars sat in pairs on narrow deal benches facing scarred tops hardly worthy of the name of desks, as they sloped but slightly and had no lids, merely a shallow underspace in which to keep a couple of books. The fixed seats were clamped to a cast-iron support. At 'socials' it took strong men to move the desks to make room for dancing.

The building contained two rooms, the main one known as the School, in which we were taught; the smaller one, called the Classroom, used only for storing equipment, handicraft materials, paraffin-lamps, and the big boiling-urn.

All grades were taught by a single teacher, who somehow contrived to keep every child occupied. Each group stood in turn in a semi-circle round the teacher's chair and answered questions. Whoever answered quickly and correctly moved to the top of the class and remained there till displaced by somebody quicker off the mark.

The teacher used no desk, but a large table stood in the middle of the room and was called the big desk. It had a hinged top which, when raised, disclosed a recess in which were stored out-of-date textbooks, old copybooks, a set of Indian Clubs, and ... the tawse.

My first teacher had heavy family responsibilities, and I believe it was her perpetually worried state that led to her harsh treatment of the scholars. She used to tawse freely and unkindly, reducing even the biggest boys to tears as she lashed repeatedly round their bare legs and feet. (In summer all the loons went barefoot but at other times wore, like their fathers, strong boots shod with steel.)

The Three Rs ... Reading, 'Riting and 'Rithmetic, were hammered home by repetition and practice. They were the foundation of our education and we were plunged into all three without delay. After learning to identify the letters of the alphabet we proceeded to master three-letter words descriptive of the crude drawing on each page of our Primer, a small brown paperback. It contained no coloured pictures. On the first page was a drawing of a brindled cat seated on a recognizable mat ... the original 'cat on the mat' now quoted in derision of an antiquated method of teaching; but it was a straightforward method, and by the repetition of letters and words in a concerted chant, we did learn to read, and quickly, too. The Primer convoyed us from our ABCs up the thorny paths of knowledge through various 'Readers', which contained ballads and chapters of history and travel, until each was supposed to be turned out, The Compleat Scholar, in Standard Vi at the ripe age of fourteen.

We had pleasant reading-books in Cassell's 'Eyes and no Eyes' series, designed to interest children in country life. They awakened interest in nature study and gave new values to much we had hitherto taken for granted. From Nelson's 'Royal Osborne Readers', and similar textbooks, we received instruction in geography and history; these largely consisted of feats of memory ... the names of continents and countries, the population of cities, long lists of exports and imports, strings of dates of battles and sieges, the reigning years of monarchs, and Acts of Parliament up to the time of Queen Victoria's accession to the throne, and the repeal of the Corn Laws.

Our classwork was done on slates with slate-pencils that, when new, were an attractive grey colour, wrapped halfway in harlequin paper. The colour wore off with usage and so did the paper, leaving the functional dark-blue pencil squeaking its way across the slate. In theory, sums [and] writing were rubbed out with a wet rag; in practice, a saliva-moistened grubby handkerchief came handier. After learning to write on slates we were promoted to copybooks, pen and ink. First, between two parallel lines like railway lines, we had to make row upon row of pothooks, carefully formed as shown at the top of the page. In later books, between narrower lines, with fine upstrokes and broad downstrokes, dipping the pen in the inkwell sunk in the desk, we faithfully copied 'Honesty is the best Policy', 'A Stitch in Time Saves Nine' and other copybook maxims. By this system we learned to write really well, in spite of inky fingers and occasional blots. Lead pencils were issued for drawing-lessons, which entailed the copying of an object outlined on the opposite page. No crayons, coloured pencils, or water-colours were used in the school, nor did the teacher use coloured chalk on the blackboard . . .

Shiny old maps hung on the school walls, lowered by a pole when required. We gathered round to learn the mountain ranges, the source and course of every river and its tributaries, the situation of islands, lochs and promontories, towns and their industries, urban districts and their produce . . . wherever the pointer paused, the answer had to be forthcoming. The map of the world showed an immense area of pink. There was no British Commonwealth in those days; Empire was the word and it had a proud and satisfying sound. Maps were splashed with red to show the extent of that Empire. The red splashes had faded on our school map, but there was nothing faded about the Empire.

We had a weekly singing-lesson, learning by ear, for there was no piano, such songs as 'Jock O' Hazledean' and Tannahill's 'Bonnie Wood o' Craigielea'. A modulator was unfurled and draped over the blackboard and we intoned the scales of the tonic sol-fa from low doh to high doh and down again.

By folding small squares of glazed coloured paper into triangles, rhomboids, and octagons and pasting them in a book, we were expected to become familiar with geometrical figures.

Girls were also required to prepare samples of darning, hemming, and patching on squares of white cotton and red flannel, mounting them in a book for inspection.

We were taught a simple form of the ancient craft of basketry, soaking the cane in water to make it pliable. Our baskets were somewhat fragile, but we were dab-hands at making tea-pot stands.

We sewed the simplest of samplers, nothing so ambitious as the admirable achievements of our great-grandmothers, and spent hours weaving strips of coloured paper to make silly little mats and baskets; we also learned fretwork, patchwork, and clay-modelling . . .

Senior girls had lessons in domestic economy, reading from a textbook; senior boys had what they called 'agrie', a weekly lesson from a book on the principles of agriculture, and the fertilization of land, which technically was far removed from their experience of life close to the land cultivated by their fathers using the methods of their forebears.[2]

Scottish teachers had long coped with the large classes that confronted them by means of strict discipline and ready use of corporal punishment. Liz Lochhead went to school in the 1950s. By this date Education Acts, especially the Act of 1944, had reformed the system, separating off primary education, providing secondary schooling for all children and raising the leaving age to fifteen. But some aspects of school life still had a schoolboard feel to them.

Newarthill Primary School. A big black stone-built place with railings around it. Old, it had the date 1897 cut into stone between the Boys' Entrance and the entrance marked Girls. I was five. My mother took me to enrol and on the way back she said she hoped I'd stay on at school, go to University if I had it in me, she and my father would make every sacrifice. It was a great shame my father had never had the chance.

We were taught by Look and Say. Apple says ah. Miss Brown was not particularly pleased that I knew how to recite Ay Bee See Dee and recognise the characters, and said that Parents didn't know the damage they did. But I learned to read very quickly. Most of the class did. We learned by rote. Off by heart. Tables: nine sixes are fifty-four ten sixes are six-ty; Similes: as black as coal, as green as grass; Singulars and Plurals: hoof, hooves, sheep, sheep, fish, fish or fishes, spoonful, spoonsful. We chanted aloud like a prayer.

The school did seem to be staffed by a collection of remarkably similar mainly maiden ladies. The odd widow. Does my memory lie to me in showing me so many Miss Jean Brodies twenty years beyond their prime? Each time before you moved up a class you were afraid, had heard the shouting spill into the corridor, had heard the rumours of beltings for Nothing, knew that this was going to be the most terrifying class in the school. But it always turned out to be much the same. The teachers had their moods. The sums got harder.

Each day started off with the Lord's Prayer, half an hour or so of Bible. The Story of Joseph read, verse each, around the class, a chapter a day, missing out Chapter thirty-nine, being the spicy one where Potiphar's wife stages her seduction scene. But I was suspicious enough, had the sense to read it anyway. Or we had to repeat what we'd learned at home a verse a night, Isaiah 53, or the gibberish of a Scottish Paraphrase.

> Oh god of Be-ethel by hoosand
> thy pe-ople Still are fed
> Who through the Weary
> Wild-er-ness has stole our father's leg.

After the Bible then Reading, your homework piece, without a stammer. Aloud. Then Spelling. Every night you had to learn one group from the little red and white Schonell's Essential Spelling Book. Every day we wrote them down.

See	six	by
tree	fix	cry
been	box	try
sweet	fox	sky

More than two wrong got the belt. Hugh Hilmour and Jeannie
Nielson got the belt every day. For the Spelling and for other
things. Remember his pink flush, his orange hair, his gallus grin,
how cock of the walk he was when he swaggered back to his
seat. He kept count of his beltings, his boast was that he could
take it. Farm Jeannie Nielson was big and cow-dumb. Smelt of
the byre, carried it in on her shoes. Her eyelashes were matted
together with a sticky affliction called Sleep. She cried easy. Sat
alone at the front to see the board. When one of us nice girls
or clever boys was Bad we were moved down to sit beside her
as punishment. She cried easy. Still she was belted for her
Spelling Errors.

Can that be true? Can they have been so cruel, those dedi-
cated ladies with their flowery smocks to keep the chalk-dust
from their good dresses, with their churchy peppermint mothball
breaths?

They all played a club-footed piano, taught songs. Flow
gently Sweet Afton. On their autumn window-sills bulbs split
their sides in purple crocks, in spring milky frogspawn quickened
into wriggling punctuation marks. The weather chart was filled
in up to date. They taught us to tell a tree by its leaves. Once,
thanks to my teachers, I knew the difference between the Mute
and the Bewick's Swan. Nature study was the gentle ladies'
favourite subject. Once for weeks we had a snuffling hedgehog
in a cardboard box. They loved animals.

Everything was a competition.

Every Friday there was a reshuffle, you were moved in
descending order from the back row to the front, according to
your marks, according to your stars.

Every summer there was a week of Tests. From this was
decided the list of prizewinners. Black Beauty – for General
Excellence Elsie Lochhead has been awarded Third Prize
(Equal) in Class Primary V says this florid label, laurel leaves, a

garland. My mother thought this poor and to be honest I had not thought to sink so low. One place lower next year and it would be a mere Certificate of Merit. No book.[3]

Teachers in the eighteenth and early nineteenth centuries emerged from a variety of backgrounds. Some, like Hugh Miller's teacher, were university graduates.

Eighteenth-century Scotland contained five universities – one in St Andrews, Edinburgh and Glasgow, and two in Aberdeen. During the latter part of the century they expanded, opened new departments, attracted some able lecturers, and encouraged a flourishing array of student societies. University education cost far more than ordinary families could afford, though a number of bursaries helped some poorer students to sustain their studies. There was, too, an informality about university existence that was to vanish in Victorian times. As late as the 1830s most students began their studies at the age of fourteen. One such youthful student was Pryse Lockhard Gordon. He was born in 1752, the son of the minister at Ardesier in Nairnshire.

At 14 I had acquired a pretty competent knowledge of Latin and a smattering of Greek grammar. I wrote a good bold hand: I knew something of geography and arithmetic and was pronounced as being fully qualified to go to College. Fortunately one of my brothers had taken his degree so that I stepped into his shoes. There 'exhibitions', though only £9 for four sessions of 5 months each, are nearly sufficient to maintain a youth of prudence. The sons of the richer lairds, having the privilege of wearing a scarlet cape to their gowns, hold up their heads and look down on the poor bursars, who, in return, pelt them with snowballs and treat them with contempt to show how little they value these aristocrats.

Young men, in my opinion, are generally sent a year or two too soon to our Colleges and before they have acquired a sufficient knowledge of grammar. This was my case and the consequence was that I had not time during the short sessions to make any great progress either in Greek or Mathematics.

I kept a regular account by mother's desire of my disbursements during my absence of 6 months.

1776

Expenses of a journey on foot from Deskford to Aberdeen (50 miles) performed in 2 days	£0–2–4
College fees to the bellringer and sacrist	5–0
My share of coal and candles	17–6
Pens, ink and paper	6–6
Breakfast of bread and milk, 9d a week	19–6
Dinner at College table at 14/- a month	4–4–0
Bread, cheese, butter, smoked haddocks, small beer and other 'luxuries' for supper	1–4–0
Tea and sugar once or twice a week	12–0
Expenses at taverns and dancing halls	18–0
To Sweety Nell, an old woman who sold lolly pops	13–0
Washing	1–4–0
Expenses of College balls	8–0
To the bed master	8–0
To squinting Sandy for cleaning shoes	6–0
A pair of gloves at the graduation ball	1–6
Sweeties at various times	6–0
3 penknives (always losing them)	3–0
Shuttlecocks	1–4
Fines for being late at roll call	3–6
Fines for throwing Snowball at Sacrist	6
Fees to the Greek Professor	1–11–6
Fees to the Professor of Humanities	0–15–0
Charity in Church	0–1–1
Charity to the beggars	0–1–6
Paid for lessons in drawing	0–12–0
To a Highland Sergeant for lessons in the broadsword	0–6–0
Skates and cudgels	0–4–6
Expenses for returning home, partly in a back chaise	0–5–0
	17–4–3[+]

By 1872 Scotland possessed a well-established system of 'pupil teachers'. Children who wished to enter the profession, and who could achieve the necessary standards, worked with teachers and studied for examinations before eventually going to one of the teacher-training establishments founded in the major cities. Overseeing changes in teaching was the 'Scotch' Education Department (it changed its name to 'Scottish Education Department' in 1918). In 1905 the Department took control of formal teacher-training from the churches.

Not till 1939 was the SED finally persuaded to abandon its London offices and settle in Edinburgh. Janetta Bowie trained for teaching in Glasgow in the late twenties and early thirties. Her first experience of teaching practice brought her into contact with a teacher whose methods of keeping order were somewhat unusual.

'Put your hand up!' says he, taking his revolver from his pocket and laying it on his desk. 'Now – answer the question.'

And every hand shoots up.

The 'Brigadier' manages his class that way. It is rumoured that the hole at eye level through the aged classroom door had been made when he had shot at a reluctant Cowcaddens lout who had failed to raise his hand quickly enough. But it may just as well have been made by a knot in the wood falling out of the near-fossilized door. The door matches its contemporaries, the desks, where the knots and ridges stand up like veins on ancient hands – desks scored, stained, gouged and hacked by the raspings of fidgety youth.

This week I am a student in the 'Brigadier''s class at Primary 7 level, and I am enjoying it. Last week I suffered along with the pupils in Miss Broadbottom's class. The only ironic glimmer of humour about her is in her name, for, on the occasions when she would turn her back to the class to write on the blackboard, never had a leaner pair of buttocks presented themselves to any class.

The class itself has to have broad – and better upholstered bottoms – to withstand her indiscriminate strap. On the very first day their initial risibility at the sound of her name had soon gurgled away like sink water to a terrified silence. Then the class – and I – had sat as still as a row of cacti on a window-sill, and as dry in the throat.

I had trembled inside for the 'criticism' lesson I had to do for her. Then miracle! I was saved from it that day by a sudden crescendo of bells in chain reaction – a Fire Drill.

The 'Brigadier''s class is the one to get into. He is a hand-some man with a fierce moustache and side-burns, which could be regarded as being either highly Balaclava or highly avant-garde. The 'Brigadier' had come into the teaching profession as a 'mature' student, after the World War, in fact, with several medals and a determination to teach history as he had lived it. His gun is his fortune, of course, as far as his class is concerned. To the children in this part of the city of Glasgow a university degree means nothing. A gun is a better qualification, even if it is just for show.

We came into this school last week for the first time as students. We remain here all day. This will go on for three weeks, when we shall go back into the Training College for another three weeks to recharge the knowledge batteries in readiness for the next battle with reality in the schools.

The school that I have landed in is a dismal three-storey block with Glasgow soot and industrial grime smeared upon it, as if dirty fingers had wiped themselves on its outside. Inside, right up its middle like a twisted spine, are flights of stone stairs from one landing to the next. Chain-gangs of children move from one landing to the next when the bell rings – up, up, up, – and when the next bell rings – down, down, down.

The students, Peg, Meg and I, have been given a 'Room of our Own', students being of a lower order, as far as we can see. Each of us is trying to exist on a grant of £35 a year, and, since our parents are not well off, we can only afford the very cheapest tram and train fares. We have over twenty-five miles to travel every day. The rest of our daily subsistence is scarcely paté-de-foie. Today we bring corned-beef sandwiches, relieved by a banana. It has to be a dry lunch.

This is ironical, as the 'Room of our Own' is a dark but spacious WC. It is lit by a naked bulb of maybe ten watts. The electricity is the only sign of modernity in Midden St. The electric switch is naked also, as we discover at once. We take turns at sitting on the toilet seat. A prison-size skylight far above shows us that the electric bulb is there.

The afternoon school is surprisingly enlivened by a visit from our Master of Methods from the Training College, come to see if we have settled in comfortably. We have – in the way in which the word is used in hospitals.

The Methods Man, Teddy Thoms, is a dramatic figure, more like a conductor of an orchestra, having yellow-white hair, highly-coloured cheeks and sweeping gestures. He listens to my lesson on the Spanish Armada, complete with a model galleon and a set of bowls, cajoled from the keepers of the local museum and bowling-green respectively. Teddy sits at the back of the class among the pupils, and he keeps putting his hand up to give the answer. This is meant to disconcert me. I wish I could think of some questions which he wouldn't be able to answer. Not being as clever as this, I play up just taking his answer as casually as I can . . .

I begin today in the 'Penny Buff', the beloved name for the beginners' class. Tomorrow I go to the 'Tuppeny', and by the end of the week I shall have experienced the most of the first Sixpence of school life.

I discover the Infants Mistress has a weakness. You can catch her napping. This nap she takes in her private room, while I take a lesson on mice. It is strange how many teachers with students suggest that they should take lessons on mice. I imagine that these are the very ladies who will jump as high as the top of the black-board if they see a mouse so much as put a whisker out of a hole. Miss Patty asks me to take this lesson tomorrow.

This afternoon I remember that Teddy Thoms' code for the teacher is 'always to obtain the real thing, for it is far more effective than pictures.' I therefore go again by the now known route to the furnace room to interview the janitor. I ask him to consider the proposition. 'Any mice here?' I ask.

He looks rather affronted at my doubting it. 'Mice? Aye – lots o' them – but under control, of course, under good control. General Kitchener here will maybe catch you a nice specimen.'

And he picks up a gigantic tabby from behind a pile of coal. General Kitchener performs this service for the Education Committee for the sheer love of the job.

And, sure enough, today, there is the mouse. The gentle General has apparently only given it a temporary knock-out with his big paw, for it revives. I now have that rare adjunct to a nature lesson, a live exhibit. I carefully put it in a box punctured with holes.

And all would have been well, I am sure, but for the totally unexpected arrival of HM Inspector of Schools. HMI is spotted coming in by the gate. I learn later from Peg that there is a sort of native-drums signal when this danger looms. The intelligence is passed from teacher to teacher with as great expedition as the Fiery Cross.

Miss Broadbottom it was who had looked from her front-facing window and seen him. She had flown immediately to the door in the glass partition that pretends to divide her class from the activities of the one next door. Peg says that she heard Miss Broadbottom say with great excitement to Miss Sulley, 'Aitch-Em-Aye!'

Miss Sulley had flown to the next door and said to Miss Strong, 'Aitch-Em-Aye!' (Peg has been with Miss Strong.)

Miss Strong had resourcefully grabbed Jimmy McNeillage from the front seat in the class and said to him, 'Run up to Miss Vinegar and say, "Aitch-Em-Aye."'

'Aye,' said Jimmy and ran.

That, Peg says, was how it was done. Peg had been doing her lesson at the time, teaching the class Who's Afraid of the Big Bad Wolf?

That is how it is done. It is also how I am undone. For Miss Patty comes hurrying back to the classroom, nap abandoned, and rushes into the room to get here before the Inspector arrives. She rushes so much that she trips over my box with the mouse in it. The lid comes off and the mouse runs gratefully out.

Thus it is, when Aitch-Em-Aye comes into the room with the Headmaster, Miss Patty is already mounted on a desk holding her skirt coyly above her knees.[5]

Despite the curriculum upheavals of recent years, schooling in Scotland has retained the distinctive design of a broad-based structure reaching up through a wide range of Highers to four-year degree courses. Whether this system will survive current financial pressures and centralized direction is another matter.

CHAPTER V

STARTING WORK

The age at which children started work depended on the income of their parents and what occupation they hoped to follow. Even before the great changes of the nineteenth century, child labour had been essential to keep the fragile domestic economy of a farm servant's household viable to provide food, clothing and shelter for all. It was common for girls to help their mothers at spinning or winding flax or wool from the age of six or seven, and for boys to be sent out to work as herds for the farmer at the age of seven or eight. A little later, both sexes might find employment as field hands weeding or hoeing turnips. One of the great advantages from the parents' point of view was that the growing child was fed at the farmer's table.

With the coming of the industrial revolution, therefore, there was nothing new in child work. However, the harsh character of factory labour and the experience of frequent beatings by a stranger in place of correction by a parent, were now horrendously widespread features of growing up. Here James Myles reflects on his first days at a Dundee mill around 1815: his father, a shoemaker, had been sentenced to transportation for manslaughter and his mother had set out for the town to work in a mill:

Our support now depended on my mother's own energies, and, though she rose every morning by five o'clock, and toiled on until nine and ten at night, she could not earn above 6d or 7d per day, or on an average 3s 3d per week. Those accustomed to such labour will make a little more, but it being new to my mother, she could only gain this pittance by fifteen or sixteen hours close application. Every Monday morning she had to pay 11d for rent, which left her with about 2s 4d for our support. On this small sum, and a few shillings that remained of the money which she received for her labours, we lived four weeks.

On the beginning of the fifth week, I got work in a spinning mill at the Dens, which filled our hearts with joy, but so near starvation were we then, that my mother had only 4½d in the world. It was on a Tuesday morning in the month of "Lady June" that I first entered a spinning mill. The whole circumstances were strange to me. The dust, the din, the work, the hissing and roaring of one person to another, the obscene language uttered, even by the youngest, and the imperious commands harshly given by those "dressed in a little brief authority," struck my young country heart with awe and astonishment. At that time the Twelve Hours' Factory Act had not come into operation, and spinning mills were in their glory as huge instruments of demoralization and slavery. Mercenary manufacturers, to enable them to beat more upright employers in the markets, kept their machinery and hands active fifteen, and, in many cases, seventeen hours a-day, and, when tender children fell asleep under the prolonged infliction of "work! work! work," overseers roused them with the rod, or thongs of thick leather burned at the points. The lash of the slave driver was never more unsparingly used in Caroline on the unfortunate slaves than the canes and "whangs" of mill foremen were then used on helpless factory boys.

When I went to a spinning mill I was about seven years of age. I had to get out of bed every morning at five o'clock, commence work at half-past five, drop at nine for breakfast, begin again at half-past nine, work until two, which was the dinner hour, start again at half-past two, and continue until half-past seven at night. Such were the nominal hours; but in reality there were no regular hours, masters and managers did with us as they liked. The clocks at the factories were often put forward in the morning and back at night, and instead of being instruments for the measurement of time, they were used as *cloaks* for cheatery and oppression. Though this was known amongst the hands, all were afraid to speak, and a workman then was afraid to carry a watch, as it was no uncommon event to dismiss anyone who presumed to know too much about the science of horology.

In country mills, a more horrific despotism reigned than in Dundee. There, masters frequently bound the young by a regular contract which gave them a more complete control over their labour and liberties than taking them from week to week. In one establishment in the vicinity of Dundee, the proprietor, a coarse-minded man, who by accident had vaulted out of his natural element into the position of "vulgar rich" man, practised the contract system, and had bothies where he lodged all his male and female workers. They were allowed to cook, sleep, and live in any dog and cat manner they pleased, no moral superintendence whatever being exercised over them. His mill was kept going 17 and frequently 19 hours per day. To accomplish this all meal hours were almost dispensed with, and women were employed to boil potatoes and carry them in baskets to the different flats; and the children had to swallow a potato hastily in the interval of putting up "ends." On dinners cooked and eaten as I have described, they had to subsist till half-past nine, and frequently ten at night. When they returned to their bothies, brose, as it is a dish that can be quickly made, constituted their suppers, for they had no time to wait the preparation of a different meal. They then tumbled into bed; but balmy sleep had scarcely closed their urchin eyelids, and steeped their infant souls in blessed forgetfulness, when the thumping of the watch-men's staff on the door would rouse them from repose and the words "Get up: it's four o'clock" reminded them they were factory children, the unprotected victims of monotonous slavery.

At this mill and indeed all mills, boys and girls were often found sleeping in stairs and private places, and they have been seen walking about the flats in a deep sleep, with cans of "sliver" in their hands. When found in this state, they were caned or kicked according to the mood of their superiors. One poor boy, who is still alive and who, by force of mind, great persistency and activity rose to be a mercantile clerk in Dundee, and fills a responsible situation on one of the principal railways in England, was for some time in this factory. One day he was carrying an armful of bobbins from one flat to another. When ascending the stair, he sat down to rest himself, as his legs were sore and swollen by incessant standing. In a few moments he was fast asleep. Whilst enjoying this stolen repose, the master happened to pass. Without the least warning he gave him a violent slap on the side of the head, which stunned and stupefied him. In a half-sleeping state of stupefaction he ran to the roving frame, which he sometimes attended and five minutes had barely elapsed when his left hand got entangled with the machinery, and two of his fingers were crushed to a jelly, and had to be immediately amputated. His unfeeling taskmaster gave him no recompense – in fact never asked after him: he was left to starve or die, as Providence might direct. The reader will no doubt imagine that boys working 18 and 19 hours a-day would have nearly double wages to boys at the present time, who only work ten. I can only speak from experience, and what has come under the range of my own knowledge on this point. When I went to the mill, I was paid with 1s 6d per week, and my nominal hours, as already remarked, were 13 hours per day. When the Twelve Hours' Act was in operation, boys had from 3s up to 4s per week; and now since the Ten Hours' Act came into force, their wages vary from 3s 3d to 4s 3d. In short, as far as I can learn, their wages are as good under the Ten Hours' Act as they were under the Twelve Hours' Act. Of course the Act precludes such young boys as I was from working yet considering the hours, I was confined, and the wages I was paid with, the contrast is highly favourable to the humanity and wisdom of those good men who procured protection to factory children, and said to competition and capital, "Hitherto shalt thou come but no farther."[1]

This passage was written in 1850 at a time when Parliament had begun to restrict the hours worked by women and children in the factories.

The next author, Alexander Somerville, was the son of a farm labourer who decided, at the age of seventeen, to leave the country to look for better earnings in the building trades of Edinburgh, then in the last phase of the building of the New Town. Although work was scarce, he found employment through his brother, but town workers in these circumstances were none too friendly to incomers.

Walking in from Berwickshire, he stayed overnight with relations near Stenton in East Lothian:

Next morning, their father, who was a stonemason, and chiefly employed on Biel estate, went with me several miles on the road towards the town of Haddington. It was a hard frost, the ground covered with snow, from one to three feet deep. He wishes me to remain a day or two with them, until the snow melted, or was tracked down on the roads to make walking more easy; but I was too strongly bent upon reaching Edinburgh as soon as possible, to relax in my determination by a storm of snow. As he could not go out to do mason's work in such weather, he went the farther with me, and the farther he went the more good advice he gave; warning me of the dangers of Edinburgh, and cautioning me against continuing my journey, if the snow-storm increased.

We parted, and after a journey which was almost an over-match for me, of twenty-five miles in the soft snow, I reached Edinburgh. It was dark when I got within sight of the streets; and the lamps newly lighted, stretching out in long chains of fiery links, amazed me more than I can now tell. I was not long there until I heard complaints of bad trade; that 'everything was flat'; 'nothing was stirring', and so forth; to which I could not help saying, that I wondered what like the town must be when everything was 'brisk' and 'stirring'; for it seemed to me that the stir, the din, and bustle were excessive and never-ceasing.

But it was a dull time for trade. Edinburgh was then, had been for two years, and continued to be for years after, depressed beyond almost every other place, especially in the building branches of its trade, from the excessive extent of building speculations previous to the commercial crash of 1825.

I was kindly received by friends, some of whom I knew previously, some of whom I did not know. Most of them wondered why I should have left, what they, being town bred, believed to be a happy country life, to come and work in a saw-pit in a town. The sawyers objected greatly that my brother should at such a time of depression introduce a new hand and they were disposed to prevent me from working. They said little to him; but on several occasions they told me I might probably get my head broken, and would possibly be found by somebody dead in the Cowgate Burn. Had it been at a busy time, they would have struck and refused to work for my brother; but as it was otherwise, so many being out of employment and suffering dreadful privations, they were powerless. In the country where I had come from, men were without work; it was the difficulty of getting employment at anything which would yield me higher wages than I had received as a boy, and the certainty that there was not constant work at such wages, that had caused me to go to Edinburgh, to add one more to those who competed for a livelihood at sawing timber.

In the course of five or six weeks the sawyers became reconciled to me. One who had been readiest in secretly telling what I had to fear from some unknown enemy, intimated that this unknown person or persons and himself would protect me on certain conditions which were hinted at, though not explicitly named. A neighbouring publican came and explained the matter more fully; and I found that the chief article in the conditions of friendship and brotherhood which the sawyers wished to establish with me was whisky. A certain quantity of whisky was to initiate me into the mysteries of brotherhood, and to secure the good will of the whole body. This condition being complied with, I was allowed to work without hindrance or molestation.[2]

Between the status of labourer and craftsman there was an enormous gap, and no one could hope to enter the magic circle of such skilled work without serving an apprenticeship. But on the Clyde at the start of the present century apprentices were not taken on in most trades until the age of fourteen or fifteen, while children by then generally left school at twelve. They thus had to spend two or three years in dead-end jobs before being taken on in the engineering shops. Davie Kirkwood describes it:

It was the ambition of my father and mother that I should be a tradesman. They knew what it was to live on a labourer's wage of about eighteen shillings a week. The crafts were looked upon as the aristocracy of labour and, at that time, when engineering was beginning to become a great industry, the aim of most parents was to make their sons engineers.

I could not start as an engineer at twelve, and meanwhile I was in sore need of a pay. I had to find a job of some kind. My teacher at Buchanan's Sunday forenoon meeting, Robert Bolton, found me a situation as a message-boy in Murdoch's printing-works in Buchanan Street, Glasgow.

Bolton lived in Springfield Road, fully a mile from where I lived. I set out from the foot of Westmuir Street at seven o'clock in the morning for Springfield Road to meet him, and we walked together along the London Road to Buchanan Street every morning – a trudge of about three miles.

I worked till six o'clock at night, and then walked home again. All I had to eat was a 'piece' in my pocket. My wage was 3s 6d a week. After a fortnight the Factory Inspector came on the scene, pronounced me to be too young, and Murdoch's were forced to dispense with my valuable services. I was one of the first victims of the social legislation of which I was later to demand more. On that occasion I heartily disapproved of it.

That was my first experience of being unemployed, and there was no dole. To the poor, experiences come early.

I ran about for nearly a fortnight, until I got a job as message-boy with Archibald Scott, grocer, on the west side of Bellgrove. It was a high-class shop, and I carried messages to Dennistoun.

On occasions, I had to take a two-wheel porter's barrow loaded with messages to Springburn, three miles away, and most of it uphill. It was agony. I was small for my age, and so lightly built that I was known among my friends as 'Wee Davie.' What awful struggles I had, straining every nerve and muscle to pull that two-wheel barrow up the steeps of John Knox Street, with the great walls of the prison on one side, the Cathedral and the Necropolis on the other, and in front of me the Royal Infirmary! The solid masonry made me feel 'awfu' wee.'

As I passed these great buildings and went on uphill through Castle Street, Springburn seemed to be miles and miles away. I cannot remember any occasion when anybody gave me a hand up that hill with my barrow, though sometimes I have stopped in the middle of the hill, dead-beat and weeping . . .

I stuck it for six months, because the four shillings a week was of vital importance. Then I heard that Watson's at Parkhead Cross required 'a message-boy with experience.' That was meant for me . . .

I was so glad to have the job that, when the Fair came round, I went to the shows where a man took photographs on tin. I paid sixpence to be taken. I had to cross my legs to hide a large patch in the knee o' ma breeks – an early example of the personal vanity of which I was to hear so much in later years.

My mother was so proud to have my picture that she forgave the extravagance. Real photographs were rather a novelty and quite the fashion. They were called '*cartes de visite*' by the photographers. We simply called them 'photies.'

Each works had a 'photie club,' into which the workers paid sixpence a week until enough was gathered to allow us 'to hae oor photies ta'en.'

I was with Watson's for two years, until I was old enough to be apprenticed as an engineer. I started off at J. and T. Boyd's (Shettleston Iron Works) to serve my time as an engineer. I worked from 6 o'clock in the morning till 5.30 at night, and my wage was five shillings weekly.

At 8.30 we stopped for three-quarters of an hour for breakfast, and every morning I ran full pelt from the works to my home for my breakfast, a distance of about one mile and a half. Then I ran back, taking my dinner in my pocket. My dinner consisted of 'breid and jeely.'

At 5.30 I came home for my supper – porridge and buttermilk, and sometimes bread and butter and a cup of tea. Our principal food was porridge and buttermilk. Only on Saturdays and Sundays did we have a hot meal, which usually consisted of broth, made with half a pound of boiling beef and a marrow-bone and potatoes. We were very fond of broth.[3]

Davie Kirkwood indeed became an engineer, but not all apprenticeships were successfully completed. Robert Barclay, in a small Aberdeenshire town, described being taken on by a tailor when he was only eleven:

A tailor in our district wanted an apprentice, and hearing of a lad some miles away, who wanted to learn the tailoring trade, I became the bearer of a letter to his folks stating that this man would take him as an apprentice. I brought word back that he was engaged to a tailor in another district. The tailor's wife remarked that I might come and learn myself. The suggestion seemed to open a way of escape from having to go to school; and so in a short time, from being a scholar, I was an apprentice tailor. There were no sewing machines in country districts in those days, although some tailors in towns had them; all was hand work. I commenced in August, 1861. I served a short period on trial; then an agreement was made out, by which I had to serve for four years, receiving one shilling per week the first year, two the second, two and sixpence the third, and three and sixpence the fourth; getting my food etc., at home. I got on pretty well; but found all was not smooth sailing here more than at school. I got punished at times for not doing my work properly, once to the effusion of blood. I tried to get home and show my bleeding nose, but was held back, and made to wash my face, and thus obliterate any trace of undue punishment. One day, however, he struck me on the thigh with the board used for pressing clothes on, causing a mark that remained a while. This, and other complaints I was making, led to my leaving his service. By this time I had served a year and a half; and as no convenient place was found where I could serve out my time, I was put again to school.[4]

For girls, apprenticeships and well-paid jobs were out of the question, but by the first half of the twentieth century there were jobs for teenagers (leaving school in this case aged fifteen) in the big new department stores like those on Princes Street in Edinburgh, as this example from the 1940s shows:

I remember my mother making me stay on at school till I was about 15. Her ambition was for me to work in an office but I never wanted to work in an office. I went to Binn's, it was Maule's then, at the West End.

We thought we were frightfully posh yet we got a lot less pay than in a factory. There was a thing which you could call class distinction. There was the 1st Sales (Assistant), the 2nd Sales, the 3rd Sales and, when you started, you would be the 4th Sales. If a woman came in and the 1st Sales wasn't busy she got the sale, and if another woman came in, well the 2nd Sales got that. Sometimes you never got a sale because by the time it came round to the 4th there weren't enough customers in the department.

I remember I was promoted just before I was married, up to 1st Sales, and oh dear! – we had a different canteen. There was one for the bosses, one for the 4th, 3rd and 2nd Sales, and 1st Sales went to another canteen. Mind there was just an urn and it was just that one lot sat on benches and another lot sat on chairs but that was real distinction. I wasn't conscious of class distinction but of being a bit better than a 4th Sales. I think I got 10/- and the supposed encouragement of a 1d. in the £1.00 commission.

I remember the buyer always wore a long black dress, made of crepe, right down to the floor. We all had to wear black dresses – you were lucky if you had two.

The buyer we had was the most terrible woman. You weren't allowed to stop for a second. You had to clean out, or dust tops of cupboards, or fold all the stuff in the glass drawers, whether or not they'd been done the day before, rather than stand about. She was like an eagle ready to pounce and we all had to, "watch out here's the boss". So it wasn't a very nice atmosphere but I liked the work. We got a Saturday half day like all the shops in Princes Street. We worked 9–6 or 9–7 on the other days.

If you were allowed back to work (after marriage) they would have said "What a shame she's got to go and work" so, even if you were hard up, the last thing was to go back to work. It was not the done thing – Oh no! In those days the man was supposed to be the provider. It was ridiculous if you look back – there was no liberation.

The funny thing was when you left they made paper hats

and chains for round your neck and flowers and you all had a
bask in the cloakroom – no drink – sausage rolls and cups of tea
and we'd all giggle and ask personal questions like, "do you
know the facts of life?" and, "do you know what you're in for?"
... When it was my turn I was so mortified I locked myself in
the toilet.[5]

Even for the university graduate the day came when he had to find
his first job. John Boyd Orr, later to be one of the most distinguished
nutritional scientists of the century, did not like schoolteaching at
all at first, but he returned to the fray with more satisfaction the
second time:

As I had won a Queen's scholarship to the teachers' training
college and the university, it was incumbent on me to teach for
a short time to justify taking the scholarship. Immediately after
graduating in 1902 I applied to the Glasgow School Board for
a job and was given one in a school in the slums. The playground
was a small area laid with concrete. The rooms were overcrowded, and the children were ill-clad. Looking back now, I
realise that the majority of them were obviously suffering from
malnutrition and some of them from actual hunger. Some came
to school with no breakfast, and others with only tea and bread
and butter. Going round between the seats one could see the
lice crawling on their heads and on their clothing. We were
supposed to teach them grammar, arithmetic and all the other
subjects in the educational curriculum. I went home the first
night feeling physically sick and very depressed. I had another
look at the school the next day, and came to the conclusion that
there was nothing I could do to relieve the misery of the poor
children, so I sat down and sent in my resignation. I returned
home to work in my father's business where I could make £3 a
week instead of a little less than £2 a week which was the
remuneration of a university graduate schoolteacher at that time.
The work was much more enjoyable than trying to forcibly feed
education down the throats of children who did not want it and
received little or no benefit from it.

After three or four months working with my hands I thought

it was time to go back to teaching for a bit to give some return for the scholarship, and was appointed to the Kyleshill School in Saltcoats about seven miles from where we lived, which meant I was able to stay at home. This was a school in the east end with children from the poorer part of the town. I was given the senior pupils aged from twelve to fourteen years. Nearly all the children came from poor homes and were compelled to start work as soon as they left school at fourteen, or earlier if they could get exemptions. As none of them was going to university or even a secondary school there seemed little point in teaching them formal grammar, higher arithmetic and the other subjects needed for examinations. The more common sense view seemed to me to be to give them as pleasant a time in school as possible and not set them home lessons which could not be done properly since the only table in the whole house was the kitchen table.

Although these children were all from the lower income groups they were by no means inferior in mental ability to the children from better-off families. At one of the local teachers' meetings – which I seldom attended – I heard some disparaging remarks made about the poor school I was in, and wondered what could be done to show that these children were as clever as those in the other schools, including the fee-paying schools. I discovered a way out through an endowment which gave six bursaries to school children in the area. I picked out four of my cleverest boys, told them to send in their names for the bursary examination, and then kept them in after school hours for about half-an-hour for three weeks before the examination teaching them the subjects I should have been giving them if I had adhered to the curriculum. The boys obtained the first, second, fifth and sixth of the six places in the examination. This result gave an increased feeling of self-respect to the senior pupils and to the teachers in the school. It was obvious that the system of primary school education at that time lost the country the services of many potential first-class leaders and scientists from the poorer ranks of society.

As I was very fond of singing, a good deal of the time which should have been spent on academic subjects was devoted to chorus singing of Scottish songs which the children enjoyed. By this time, however, the school inspectors instead of coming once a year for a one-day examination had taken to popping in unexpectedly at any odd time. One day the inspector came in when we were singing and wanted to know what should be taught at that hour according to the curriculum. As a matter of fact I was not sure . . .[6]

Luckily, he got away with it.

CHAPTER VI

FISHING AND FARMING

The coastline of late eighteenth-century Scotland was dotted with little fishing villages. The small open boats used by the fisherman hunted for white fish, using long lines. During the nineteenth century this activity shrank in relative importance as Scottish fishermen's lives were increasingly dominated by the pursuit of herring. Government support helped put the industry on its feet; Eastern Europe – especially Russia – welcomed its catches.

The herring fleets moved around the coast, following the shoals of fish down as far as East Anglia. The work the industry offered drew in people from the Highlands. In this account of 1848 the author records their movement to join east-coast fleets.

The fishermen on this eastern coast go out about the middle of July; previous to which they have been for some weeks employed in preparing their boats, overhauling their tackle, and engaging extra hands, generally Highlanders, who come down to the coast at this season in order to hire themselves to the owners of the boats for the six or eight weeks during which they are out at sea. These men earn during the season from three to six pounds, a perfect godsend to the poor fellows, whose eyes are seldom gladdened by the sight of hard money during the rest of the year. Just before the time when the herring boats go out, the roads are dotted with little groups of Highlanders, each man having a small parcel of necessaries tied up in a handkerchief and carried on a stick over his shoulder. They are sadly footsore and wayworn by the time they have traversed the island from the west coast. Being little accustomed for the most part to walking anywhere but on springy heather and turf, the hard roads try them severely. Most of them are undersized and bad specimens of the Celtic race. Very little English is spoken amongst them, as not one in ten understands a word of anything but Gaelic. When they have occasion to go into a road side shop to purchase anything, or to ask a question, a consultation is first held amongst the party, and then the most learned in Saxon is deputed to act as spokesman. Wearily and heavily the poor fellows labour along the road, and by the time they reach Forres, Nairn, and the other towns near the shore, they are sadly knocked up, their food during the journey having been poor and scanty, consisting generally of potatoes, and perhaps oatmeal, mixed up frequently with cold water, a sorry mess for a Highlander who is taking the unaccustomed exercise of tramping along a hard road. Many of these men know pretty well where, and by whom, they shall be hired, but others have to seek employment where they can. Their faces grow visibly shorter as soon as they are engaged: and they set to work, though possessing little seamanship, to assist in putting into order the nets, floats, stores, &c. In a few days every boat is afloat and ready. Then comes the parting-glass with their shore-staying friends, which, by the bye, is often multiplied until it amounts to a very fair allowance.

As the boats set sail from the small harbours and piers, the wives and families of the fishermen who belong to the place come down to see their relatives off; and many groups of weather-beaten women sit and watch the boats till out of sight, discussing anxiously the chances of a good or bad season, a matter of no light import to them, as their comfort during the rest of the year almost entirely depends upon it.

I have frequently seen some stout boy, strong and fearless, but too young to be allowed to accompany his father, hide amongst the nets, sails &c., in the boats, hoping to get taken out unobserved, till they were too far out at sea to send him back. The little fellows, however, seldom succeeded, and were generally chucked unceremoniously enough out of the boat, either on to the pier whilst the boat was passing alongside of it, or into some of the numerous haddock and other fishing boats which lie at anchor in the harbour.

The herring season, although a time of hard work to the

men, is for the most part a time of rest to the women. Instead of having to tramp, as they shortly hope to do, miles into the country with a weight of fish on their back which would be almost a burthen for a donkey, they have little else to do than to gossip with each other, and set lines about the harbour and shores, excepting in those places where the herrings are cured, and put into casks for foreign consumption, where they are busy enough. The boats which go out from many of our small towns seldom return home again until the season is over; but leave the produce of their fishing at the curing stations every night if possible.

The herring fishermen have not only much hard work, but many dangers to contend with. Whilst far out at sea tending their nets during the night-time, storms of wind suddenly come on; and a scene of hurry and confusion ensues which can scarcely be imagined. Anxious to save their tackle and unwilling to lose any chance, the men in some boats are busily engaged hauling up their nets; other boats are driving past them with everything in confusion and their sails flapping in the wind. Others, manned by more prudent and able hands, who have foreseen the coming storm, are scudding with everything snug for the nearest port, and lucky are the boats which reach it without loss of tackle or life. Frequently by waiting too long, whilst endeavouring to save their nets, the poor herring fishers are placed in the utmost danger, and are driven helplessly out to sea, where they either toss about at the mercy of the winds and waves till the storm somewhat abates, or are swamped and lost, the men probably having been wearied out by their efforts to keep the boat's head straight to avoid shipping the broken waves which surround them. The crews, too, the chief part of whom are generally landsmen, or, at best, men accustomed only to the calm waters of the west-coast lochs, become disheartened and useless at the hour of need, affording little assistance to the "skipper" of the boat, who is probably the principal owner also, and who, if he saves his life, has the prospect before him of heavy loss or ruin. Many a herring boat founders this way at sea, her crew worn out by their exertions. At other times an inshore wind dashes the boats on the iron-bound coasts off which they have been fishing, and the crews perish before the eyes of their wives and families. Instances have occurred of a crew reaching some rock within a short distance of the shore, and within hearing of those assembled on the beach, who, after having vainly attempted to afford them assistance, see the poor fellows gradually washed off one by one as their strength fails them during the rise of the tide. There are but few harbours on the east coast into which the boats can run if caught in a storm and riven away from the safer parts of the coast. If a heavily-laden herring boat is over-taken by rough weather, it is very difficult to get rid of the cargo quickly enough to escape being swamped. In fact the throwing them overboard is a long operation; and sometimes, when they have a lucky haul, they load until the gunwale of the boat is but a few inches above the water. In this case the shipping of a single wave is sufficient to swamp them. A cargo of large fish, such as cod or skate, may be thrown overboard with some degree of quickness – not so a cargo of herrings.[1]

By the 1860s the size of herring catches had grown greatly. Bigger boats of better design offered increased catching capacity, using the more extensive light nets made of cotton instead of the much heavier hemp. When Charles Weld ventured (on his Scottish tour) to the port of Wick he was awed by the sight of the herring industry in action.

An hour more and we are in sight of Noss Head, and close to that of Wick. But the eye turns from these to the sea around, which is paved with hundreds upon hundreds of boats, spreading their red-brown sails, all making for Wick. We are, in fact, in the midst of the great herring fishing fleet of Wick. You would have thought that all the boats belonging to Scotland had been off Peterhead last night, but if you do not see those belonging to Wick you will have but a very imperfect idea of the magnitude of our great Scotch herring fishery.

The sea was literally covered by boats, all similar in size and rig, and differing only by numerals conspicuously painted on the bows beneath a huge W. As we drew near the harbour, the boats were closer packed until, at its entrance, we were obliged to go at quarter speed to guard against frequent collision. At length the steamer reached her moorings, and after more than usual confusion, occasioned by disembarking in boats, we landed.

The bustle was amazing. You had to keep a sharp look-out to avoid being tripped up by ropes, or caught in the wet nets which were being hauled out of the newly arrived boats. Besides these, the narrow quay was encumbered by hundreds of carts in readiness to carry the herrings to the gutting troughs. And the herrings – there had been a great take on the previous night, and in every boat were silvery heaps glistening in the rays of the rising sun. Now, indeed, you are enabled to form some idea of the wealth of the deep, and how inexhaustible is that storehouse.

Look at the fine stalwart fishers, clad from head to heel in oilskin garments, their faces shining like the newly risen sun with health. Who could fear the decay of our naval power when we have such men as these? Remember too that there are thousands of them, for the far Western Isles, Sutherland, and in short, all parts of Scotland, and a portion of the north of England, send out fishers, so great and profitable is this mighty herring harvest.

We are not tired of looking at the stirring scene, now more bustling than ever, for stout girls are carrying the herrings to the gutting troughs as fast as they can run ... Wick, at any time, cannot be a lovely town; but during the herring fishing it is odious. The stationary population of 6,722 souls is increased during the fishing season to upwards of 16,000, and as the houses do not increase in the same proportion, and the sanitary arrangements are not of the highest order of excellence, you may imagine that this great influx of population is not calculated to improve the appearance of Wick.

But as we walk through the fishy streets, there is no sign of an overflowing population; the thoroughfares are nearly peopleless, and, with the exception of children making dirt pies here and there, and old crones airing themselves at open doors, there is no one to be seen.

The explanation is easy; the men are in bed, the women at work among the herrings, as we shall soon see. We pass through more streets, the population of which is sunk in slumber, and emerging on the harbour we are amidst a world of women.

The harbour is full of fishing-boats, as close as they can pack; no room for a punt. You wonder how they ever got in, and equally how they ever get out.

Wick harbour is surrounded on the land side by hundreds of erections, looking like abortive attempts at building wood houses, some twenty feet square, for the walls are only about three feet high. These are the gutting troughs. Round them stood rows of what close inspection led you to conclude were women, though at first sight you might be excused for having some doubts respecting their sex. They all wore strange-shaped canvas garments, so bespattered with blood and the entrails and scales of fish as to cause them to resemble animals of the ichthyological kingdom, recently divested of their skin, undergoing perhaps one of those transitions set forth in Mr. Darwin's speculative book "On the Origin of Species." And if a man may become a monkey, or has been a whale, why should not a Caithness damsel become a herring?

Badinage apart, the women do cast their skins. Work over, they don gay dresses, and, flaunting in colours, you would not know the girls that you meet in the evening to be those whom you saw in the morning coated with blood and viscera.

Sixty-five women, side by side, and all silent! A wonder this, you will think; but if you saw the movement of hands and arms you would admit that to keep these going at the rapid rate which they do, is quite sufficient muscular exercise.

Let us watch the operations. First, the herrings are carried as fast as possible in baskets from the boats to the gutting-troughs until the boats are emptied of their scaly treasures. Then, the women, familiarly called gutters, pounce upon the herrings like a bird of prey, seize their victims, and, with a rapidity of motion which baffles your eye, deprive the fish of their viscera. The operation, which a damsel not quite so repulsive as her companions obligingly performed for me at slow time, is thus effected. The herring is seized in the left hand, and by two dexterous cuts made with a sharp short knife in the neck an opening is effected sufficiently large to enable the viscera and liver to be extracted. These with the gills are thrown into a barrel, the gutted fish being cast among his eviscerated companions. Try your hand, as I did, at this apparently simple process, and ten to one but your first cut will decapitate the herring. If this does not happen, you will mangle the fish so seriously in your attempts to eviscerate it that you will render it entirely unworthy of the honour of being packed with its skilfully gutted companions. And even if you succeed in disembowelling a herring artistically, you will probably spend many minutes in the operation, whereas the Wick gutters – I timed them – gut on an average twenty-six herrings per minute.

At this rapid rate you no longer wonder at the silence that prevails while the bloody work is going on, nor at the incarna-dined condition of the women. How habit deadens feeling! Who would imagine that a delicate looking girl could be tempted by even a high wage to spend long days at this work? Such, however, is the fact; for although the majority of the 2,500 women employed in gutting herrings are certainly not lovely nor delicate limbed, still I observed several pretty and modest-looking girls who would apparently have made better shepherdesses than fish-gutters. But here, as elsewhere, the love of gain overcomes repugnance. The damsel who kindly inducted me into the mysterics of the art of evisceration told me that she had some-times made £8, in a good fishing season, a large and welcome addition to her annual wage as a domestic servant.

The same operation is performed at all the troughs, of which there must be many hundreds, and some idea may be formed of the activity that prevailed at the time of my visit by the following calculation: – The take on the previous night amounted to 18,051 crans. Now as the average number of herrings in each cran is 750, we have the prodigious number of 13,538,250 herrings, all of which had to be eviscerated. But this is not all. As fast as the herrings are gutted they are carried off in baskets by sturdy girls as fast as they can run to the curing-houses, and shot into small troughs. From these they are taken by the packers, also women, whose business it is to pack, or, as it is locally called, rouse, the herrings in barrels, disposing them in layers after they have been well sprinkled with sea-salt, which is generally preferred to that extracted from the earth. Here the work is superintended by an owner, for two reasons – one, in order to see that the herrings are properly salted, and the other that they are sufficiently pressed down; for, as the packers are paid by the barrel, dishonest women might pack the fish loosely and thus apparently fill the barrel before it had received its proper complement of fish.

The herrings undergo successive packings at various intervals of time before the barrels are finally closed. At each packing more salt is added, and at the final packing great care is taken to dispose the herrings in even layers.

The viscera is deposited in barrels and sold to farmers for manuring purposes, at the average price of 1d. per barrel.[2]

Women, carrying creels full of fish, walked many miles inland from the fishing communities. The coming of the railways reduced their trade by enabling catches of fresh fish to be rapidly moved to inland places. Nevertheless the street sellers persisted for some time, walking to remote places where no railway reached, as well as selling their wares in the street. Janet Story, who lived through the Victorian period, witnessed the fishwives at work in Edwardian times.

In consequence probably of the convenient multiplicity and the excellence of the Edinburgh fish shops, the once familiar and picturesque figure of the Newhaven fishwife is becoming less evident in our streets; and this fact is greatly to be regretted. They were a hardworking and industrious class of women, a great assistance to their equally hardworking husbands, and most surely an interest and a pleasure to all who looked on their sonsy faces and fascinating costume, with the wide sleeve showing their strong round arms, and the snowy cap that often surmounted a weather-beaten but still handsome countenance.

A certain number of them preferred carrying their fish about with them and calling at the different houses, sending the cry of "Caller haddies" before them to announce their coming. Fearful and wonderful scenes took place on these occasions, especially if the cook was inexperienced and did not understand how to cope with the lady of the fish baskets. A price was invariably demanded far and away beyond reason, and much above what the fishwoman intended to take; so the haggling was lengthy and excited, and might frequently be heard half way down a street: the cook being at first addressed as "Ma lamb" and "Ma leddy," while later, when a tough antagonist had been encountered, it descended to "Od wumman!" and "Ye limmer!" I never heard anything stronger in the way of remonstrance: I never heard a fishwife swear. They seldom quitted a house without selling their fish: they had a very persuading way with them, and few could resist it.[3]

After the Great War of 1914–18 the fishing industry declined. The loss of the Russian market after the 1917 Bolshevik revolution hurt the herring trade. The expansion of rival fleets and over-fishing and its impact on fish stocks have brought a sad decline to a once great industry. Farming, too, has been through enormous changes since the mid eighteenth century and, like fishing, now employs but a tiny number of people in comparison to the labour force it once occupied.

During the second half of the eighteenth century improved methods of farming spread from the home farms of enlightened lairds to many of the smaller farms. Improved drainage, crop rotation, better feeding of the land, enclosure of fields and tree planting helped to transform the landscape. In Buchan, James Milne and his father attacked the problem of improving unpromising land.

In 1836 my father succeeded to the remainder of a lease that expired in 1841. Before renewing, the then factor for the estate went over the holding. He declared it was in a wretched state, and that he would put a rent on it which would cause it to be "given up or redd up." This rent was fixed at £25 during the first half and £30 for the remainder of the lease. My father agreed to this heavy rent, and a struggle for bare existence began. Economy had to be practised; we had to be content with the most frugal food and clothes. I can remember my father and mother taking but one cup of tea, and that only in the morning, sweetening it with treacle because that was cheaper than sugar. The children never got tea, excepting one cup on sabbath morning, while tobacco was a luxury not to be thought of. When meal got scarce before harvest, we had, Irish-like, to fall back on potatoes. Everything had to give place to rent and manure. Being the only boy, I had to work as soon as I was able – and, indeed, before I was able – and 'tis with sadness I look back on those early years. My education was curtailed and interrupted, partly because I could not be spared, and partly because there was no money to pay school fees. Even when at school in winter, I had to work morning and evening, plying the flail when I should have been at lessons. My father began his improvements by draining the bogs with stone drains. Part of my first work was to fill the stones into a barrow when the ground was too soft to carry carts, or to hand them to my father as he built the drains. During the lease we put in about 4000 yards of these stone drains. The labour and the quantity of stones required – a load to the yard – were immense, but at that time we were glad to get rid of the stones. Some of the neighbouring farmers also carted away our spare stones, a thing which I afterwards regretted when we began to build dykes. We broke up some of the hard land every year, spade-trenching the parts which were too stony to plough. We had also to spade two acres of moss which was too soft to carry horses.

My father applied the first crushed bones in 1838 – just £1 worth that year, gradually increasing year by year. At first he could not afford to bone all the land that fell to be turnip crop, so he sometimes allowed a neighbouring farmer to lay down a part in turnips, on condition that he applied ten bushels of bones per acre. But in general part of the turnip break lay in summer fallow. The year 1846 saw the last of the fallow land on Atherb. After that we were able to lay down all the shift in turnips. We had to apply guano for oats on new land. Though costly, it was a powerful stimulant, and proved a great boon to Aberdeenshire. Like everything else, it just came when required, for without guano many an acre of new land would never had paid the expense of working it. It just set the ball a-rolling, and paved the way for better and more permanent manures. Our new land in damp years grew light crops, but in dry years the oats were so puny that they would scarcely cut with the scythe, and we had to pull up the bands by the roots. We still ploughed with a horse and an ox, and now kept four cows, four stirks, and four calves, selling the stirks about two years old for about nine pounds a-head. About this time we sold three stirks to a dealer who failed. Well can I remember the bitterness of that disappointment, not so much for the money as for having to thresh with the flails for another year. In 1856, however, we were able to put in a threshing mill. This was our first great start, as it allowed more time for other work. The threshing mill was a great factor in the making of Aberdeenshire. Great efforts were made to raise this mill, and the first money that could be spared always went for that purpose. It not only was a great saving of labour, but of grain, as threshing by the flail was often scamped.

By the end of the lease, which expired in 1860, we had all that would break with the plough under cultivation, having during the nineteen years of our lease reclaimed nearly thirty acres.

As soon as we entered on the new lease we began to lime every field in rotation with marked effect. We also began to take out the boulder stones. This was the heaviest and most fatiguing work of all. We had no mechanical appliances except long levers and blocks. They were hard to bore for blasting – four or five feet was all that a man could do per day. Many a time have I set up a box barrow to shelter me from the drifting snow or the sleety shower and drilled a hole. When once we got them loose and free from earth all round, we put on a fire which broke them up. In winter the boulders were dirty, and wore the skin off our hands. Often after a hard day's work among these stones, with tired muscles and aching hands, I have been unable to enjoy refreshing sleep at night, but in a feverish dream repeated the work of the day. During the lease we built 1400 yards of dykes with these stones, entirely at our own cost. We had also to fill up the holes left by the removal of the boulders, which in some cases required five or six loads of earth or clay. We estimated our carting for this purpose at 2000 loads. We also carted 1500 loads of clay to three acres of mossy land, and top-dressed our light land with forty loads of clay per acre every rotation. We blasted off the tops of rocky hillocks, and then carted on clay and mould. We made 1000 yards of a road for farm use, bottomed it with lea gatherings, and finished it with broken rubble granite. Before this there was no road on the farm. We also built new byres for 20 cattle and stables for horses at a total cost of £70, the proprietor paying one half of the price of the walls. The old byres had been partly built of stones and clay, topped with turf, and were about nine feet wide, and so low that the cows polished the couples with their backs.

Our barn was of the same sort, but both it and the dwelling-house had to serve out the lease. When we had more than twenty beasts I had to turn mason and build additional accommodation. Our stock of beasts rose from 16 in the beginning of the lease to 20 in the middle, and some years at the end of the lease we had as many as 26, selling two-year olds at that time at an average of £25 per head. These were the palmy days of farming. Our oat crop also improved from three quarters to five quarters per acre, quality and weight improving in proportion. We now thought we had won the battle, and looked forward to more ease and comfort; farming had become a money-making business.[4]

By the end of the nineteenth century Scots had become predominantly urban dwellers. The male labour force directly engaged in agriculture fell from 30 per cent of the total in 1851 to 14 per cent in 1901. But, a Royal Commission found, a long life of labour still faced even those élite members of the farming community – the ploughmen.

On Sunday it is the general rule for all the ploughmen to attend morning stables. After the stables are cleaned out and the horses groomed, watered, and fed, all but one who is appointed for the day are at liberty either for the whole day or until the evening stable hour. Some masters insist on every ploughman coming to the 8 p.m. stables, others are contented if one of the number takes the whole stable under his charge, and this is done turn about by the men. In summer the horses for at least two and a half months are out at grass all day, and there can hardly be said to be any Sunday work then. But on some farms it is not so.

In summer he is due at the stable at 5 a.m. If his horses have been out at grass all night, his first duty is to catch and bring them in. There is generally an hour's work mowing and bringing in grass for the stables. The stables are to clean out, the horses to groom and feed. He goes home to breakfast about 6.15, returning at 6.45, at once harnesses his horses, ready to leave the stable at 7 sharp. He works till 12 noon, when he unyokes and brings his horses in, waters and feeds them, then goes home for his own dinner. Returns to stables about 20 minutes before 2, harnesses his horses, and leaves the stable for afternoon work at 2 sharp. Works till 6, which is "loosing time." Brings his horses in, takes off harness, gives them a rub over with a brush or wisp, waters them, and gives them a feed of oats. Either goes off to his own tea, returning in half an hour to put his horses out to grass for the night, or quietly waits till his horses have finished their feed, then turns them out, and his day's work is finished. On farms where the horses stand in the stables all the year round the men return at 8 p.m. give them a thorough grooming, do up the stables, and fill the racks with grass, vetches, or hay. The 8 o'clock stabling takes from 30 to 45 minutes.

In winter those who breakfast before going to work appear at stables at 6 a.m. Clean out the stalls, feed the horses, do any odd jobs about the steading, sometimes clean out the byres, and so on till near daylight, then they harness their horses. A few minutes before day breaks they leave the stable door for the field, there they remain till 12 noon. Their object being to have nine hours actual work in the field, they occupy no more time at home than is required to take their dinner, returning at once to the stables and leaving for afternoon work at 1 p.m. They work till the light dies out, the horses are then put in, and a little corn and hay given. If they are cool, a drink of water precedes the corn and hay. The ploughmen then go home for supper, returning at 8 p.m. to groom the horses and do them up for the night. This occupies from half an hour to three-quarters of an hour, and concludes the day's work.

The 8 o'clock hour is seriously objected to in some localities, and has been given up in many parts of Clackmannan and Fife. In Kinross it is still the general custom. During winter and spring there are times when the ploughmen have very easy work.

On wet days when the horses do not go out, most of the

men's time is spent in cleaning the harness or doing simple little jobs about the barn or steading. In harvest they work energetically, and when carrying the corn there are few spare moments.[5]

Women formed an important part of the labour force on the nineteenth-century farm. Their work kept the farmhouse and dairy running smoothly. They were needed in the fields for tasks like weeding, thinning and gathering up harvested crops. The following account comes from a lecture given at Rhynie in 1849.

Female servants form probably one twelve part of our whole population, thus having a large influence, either for good or evil, according to their general character. They are generally strong and healthy; this may be attributed to their youth rather than to proper attentions to food, clothing, etc. In other occupations are found persons of every age, but in this class few continue working as servants after they are 40 years of age, by the time they have reached that period of life they are married, or get into less laborious situations. The ages of this great majority range from 13 to 35 years, and that period may be regarded as a time when a greater share of health is enjoyed than at any other.

Their wages are small. They will average £3–10/- in the year, exclusive of board. With this sum they have to provide clothes and [it] is sufficient for this purpose and something more. Yet many a female servant spends the whole of her wages in dress leaving nothing for other purposes, such as provision for days of sickness, or assisting parents. I would not condemn in female servants necessary attention to decent and respectable clothing, but other fondness of dress and outward display is often evidenced by this class, whereby they often entail future distress upon themselves and those connected with them.

I must here make some allusion to those females engaged in outwork; surely their lot is far from desirable and their work far from effeminate. Many of them are hired at very low wages to pull turnips during the winter. Conceive a female having to work in the open air all day amidst perhaps drifting snow, drizzling sleet, or drenching rain, and this day after day. Is this fit and proper work for a woman? Add to this, those thus engaged are of the poorest class and not able to procure for themselves anything like comfortable clothing. Such a mode of life is sufficient to undermine the strongest female constitution and I have no doubt many are thereby ruined in health for life. What a contrast to our drawing room ladies who will hardly venture out on a frosty day even though loaded with cloaks and furs. Female servants like all their sex are addicted to tight lacing, which must ever have a pernicious effect on the bodily system, but especially in their case where so much exertion and activity is required, it must prevent the proper circulation of the blood and free action of the muscles. We will now look at their intellectual conditions. They are by no means educated. For the most part they are the daughters of working men who have large families depending on them for subsistences. At a very early age they are sent away to service, and afterwards have no opportunities of attending schools, except for a quarter or two during the winter season. Female servants thus are bad readers, worse writers and no arithmeticians. In this country few of that class till lately got any instruction in arithmetics, and the present race of them may be considered as having no knowledge of counting. Their general knowledge must be very limited. There is no reading with them, except when some of the menservants may chance to have a book to read aloud, this may be regarded as a rare occurrence. Their principal mental furniture is comprised of the gossip and tittle-tattle of the neighbourhood, the occurrence of a marriage may be fit subject to them for a week or even a month's talking. Particularly are they pleased while listening to the musical powers of the males called forth in singing ballads and songs which have not always a good tendency.[6]

Through the nineteenth century and into the early twentieth century workers obtained their farm employment at the twice-yearly feeing markets held in major villages and in towns. Joseph Mitchell attended one of these occasions in mid-Victorian times.

At Elgin there was held what is called a "Feeing Market," that is, a fair where all the country servants go to get places. There was an immense assemblage of lads and lasses, and of course the chapmen and packmen did not neglect the opportunity of doing the "Johnny Raws;" and there were stalls of clothes, shoes, trinkets, and sweetmeats, which it was supposed would tempt the rustic beaux and belles.

There was much of kind and friendly greeting among the people. In the crowd we encountered Mr. Peter Brown, the great agriculturist of the district, and while chatting with him a country fellow came up, tapped him on the shoulder, and said, "Are ye Peter Brunn?" "Yes," says Peter, turning round, "and you're d----d familiar." So we left Mr. Brown to discuss his business with the man.

In the passage of the inn there was a group of people hargaining about wages. "Noo, Mr. Collie, just gie the loon (lad) the even siller," cried an elderly country peasant to a jolly farmer-like person. "Deil a bit o' me'll do that, he'll get forty-aught shillings, and a shilling of arles" (a fee of agreement). "No, but I winna tak' that," says a raw lad standing by, about 5ft 8 in. in height, and about eighteen years of age; on his head he had a broad bonnet, and on his feet a pair of shoes well shod with hobnails. He had a hazel stick in his hand, with a large knob naturally bent, and the end of a cutty pipe was seen peeping out of his waistcoat pocket. "Na, but he winna tak' that," said the old man; "come, come, Mr. Collie, just gie him fifty shillings, he's a smairt chiel, and will do your bidding in a' things. I'm his uncle and I maun say he's been weel brocht up." "Weel, then," says Collie, "I'll gie him the forty-nine shillings, and the shilling o' arles will mak' the even siller." "Na, na," says the old man again, "we mauna dispute about a shilling. I ken weel if the loon gives to you, he will be well guided, he'll hae a guid maister at any rate; it is his ain fault if he's no weel aff." Mr. Collie evidently mollified at this little touch of flattery, said "Weel, then, there's the arles to ye, my lad, ye'll get fifty shillings, and ye must be hame on Thursday nicht." This being amicably settled the parties separated. The lad in high exultation no doubt spent the shilling with his sweetheart or an acquaintance at the next public house.

All the domestic and farm servants claim the right of attending these "Feeing Markets," as a holiday, and large crowds assemble in the various towns where they are held. No amusements or simple refreshments are provided for them, nothing but drink, drink. The result is that most of the poor people return home in a half-excited state, which does not improve the morality of the districts.

We lounged about the fair for a while, and amused ourselves watching a few thoughtless lads flirting with a sergeant, who was dressed very gaudily, and about securing them as recruits. How very suddenly the whole tenor of our lives may be changed! These young fellows had come to Elgin to be hired as farm-servants, had got a little excited with drink, and charmed with the gay apparel and military music of the soldiers, at once joined the army. What a change forthwith takes place in the outward appearance of the rustics. In the course of a few weeks' drilling, instead of the round shoulders, the awkward, hobbling gait, the open mouth, and the ungainly appearance, the lads brighten up to be well-dressed, handsome men. Captain Campbell declares that a soldier has a far more pleasant life than a peasant; they are well clothed and fed, and have about sixpence a day to drink or lay by. Some of the Scotch soldiers are very careful, for he has frequently had sums of money to keep for them. One man deposited £21, the savings of his pay.[7]

Low wages and long hours on the land encouraged men and women to leave for work in towns and cities. The growing mechanization of farming in the twentieth century meant that far fewer workers were needed anyway. Alexandra Stewart saw these changes from her home in Perthshire. She also saw the need for women's labour that the Great War brought.

I can remember when, in the late '40s, the first motor tractors came to the glen farms. They ended an old partnership between farmers and horses – the big, docile Clydesdales that had served and sweated for so long. The first day the men at Balnahanaid – the farm in the glen where I was at the time – treated the tractor like a new toy, and had a few spills and trachles with it.

It seemed like progress. It made things easier. Yet somehow it also led straight downhill. One by one, and finally in quick succession, deaths or retirement put paid to farming as the old men had no successors. The big, mechanised farms to the south and east, in Strathearn and Strathmore, look more like factories than like the couthy steadings we used to know, and it sometimes seems as if the beasts are treated as little more than units of production; the wretched dairy cattle of the Lowlands, with their painfully distended udders that must impede them as they amble along, would hardly manage a 28-mile journey over the hills, and the milk pumped out of them by machine is put into tankers and driven off to the cities, or to swell the surpluses of the European Community.

It baffles me to understand how milk carried long distances in crates during hot summer weather is healthier than milk supplied by a good clean housewife milking her own cows in spotlessly clean surroundings and feeding her family with pure, undiluted food. Where would you get purer butter, cream and cheese? For all the talk of brucellosis, I cannot recall that any family in Glenlyon ever came to harm from drinking milk from cows reared in that healthy place. Most folk were very particular about milking, which was always done by the woman of the house, and most took pride in keeping the dairy well scrubbed and scalded.

The principal ambition of a Highlander in the old days was to live a pastoral life and obtain land to which he and his family had some rights. Deprived of this he was lowered and broken of spirit. To become a mere labourer in his own country at a pittance and be forced to beg for daily hire and daily bread in sight of his own native mountains was a continual insult. That is why some of the bravest and best were the first to emigrate in the early days of depopulation. There is even a tendency in incoming proprietors of the present day to think of the natives as an inferior race and almost subject them to a caste system. All too often those who swallowed their pride to keep their homes ended losing both in 1914. Most of the young men of the glens and villages were conscripted to the army or munitions. Young women went for nurses or into the ancillary services, or

joined the land army if they were too young to be drafted. I
opted to be a land girl. I knew I could milk a cow and toss the
hay on our little croft, but I had never worked a horse or built
a corn stack (a special task), nor yet shawed a row of turnips. I
gradually managed to do the jobs fairly well: milking, feeding
the calves by pail (a hard job with the lively animals all wanting
more than their share), seeing to the pigs – but corn stacks had
me stumped.

The farmer, who had no other help, was a hard taskmaster.
One day I was assigned to building the stack, which has to be
done differently from hay – soft, pliable stuff that can be pushed
into shape. Building the stack had to allow for the shape of the
individual sheaves and the stiff, unbending straw. The top end
where the grain is different from the end that was nearest the
ground, where the cut is – like a shoe, say, with its heel and toe.
The sheaves had to be laid to take account of this, just as you
pack a pair of shoes facing opposite ways. The farmer seemed
to assume that I knew this already, or should work it out for
myself.

I thought I was doing fine myself until I was near the top.
The boss was to complete the job. You need to have got this
sort of work wrong to realise the deeper meaning of what comes
before a fall. I was just a young lassie, I was already tired and I
had no experience and so no "feel" for the stack getting off
balance. All of a sudden – whoosh!, the stack and I collapsed
and I was buried under a mountain of scratchy, itchy sheaves.

I had to listen to a roar of anger that was neither complimen-
tary nor parliamentary, I was jerked to my feet without ceremony
and put to rebuilding the stack with me forking the sheaves up
to the boss on the stack. The pain of that is that you are forking
the sheaves furthest towards the end of the job, when the stack
is highest. At the end of the day I was so tired that I fell asleep
in the chair over my supper. The farmer wanted to wake me
up to clear the table but his wife, a more kindly soul, let me
sleep on.

During the war I found myself moving all over the place
where there was work to be done. I couldn't last the pace too
long at the farm, and when my father discovered how I was

being treated he took me away. I worked in Edinburgh and Dundee helping round the house, and I was a while with a relative in Stirling where one of the things we did was laundering soldiers' uniforms, and you had to iron down the seam carefully to kill off the parasites' eggs. With so many away at the war, there were two effects: there was always work to do and social life was meagre. We used to spend our evenings knitting socks for the poor lads in the trenches. Our only treat was an occasional night at the pictures.[8]

The massive modern farm buildings, the huge fields, and the frequent roar of motorized machinery all add up to a modern environment the Victorian farmworker would not readily recognize. Whether he would look back to the age of the horse with nostalgia and regret is, however, quite another matter.

CHAPTER VII

FACTORY AND MINE

It would be wrong to imagine that the Industrial Revolution herded the workforce into the factories. The first cotton mills were built in Scotland around 1780, and there were 112 in operation by 1812. Flax mills, jute mills and woollen mills followed in due course, and there were a few large iron works (like Carron, founded in 1759) even before the application of the hot-blast process to smelting in 1828. But the factories could not at first command every process, even in textiles: they could card the fibre and spin the yarn, but weaving, until about 1830, was still mainly done at home or in small workshops by an army of handloom weavers, and their numbers did not begin to fall until the 1840s. Similarly, hosts of women 'tambourers' or embroiderers finished off the fabrics in rural cottages; they were often the wives of farm labourers, and agricultural employment increased rather than declined in most Lowland counties of Scotland until the middle of the century. It was, in fact, rather difficult to recruit and hold factory workers. Women and especially young children were reckoned to be more amenable to discipline than adult men, and were preferred where possible because it was important to train the workforce to the constant rhythms of the machines. It did not matter if a handloom weaver left his work-bench for a cup of tea or a chat with his neighbour, but if a cotton spinner did the same except at a pre-arranged break period chaos would result on the shop floor.

All this created new problems for management. One employer, whose name became a byword for philanthropy and consideration towards his workforce, was Robert Owen of New Lanark. In 1816 he was examined by a Parliamentary Commission on the conditions in his factory:

26 April, 1816, Sir Robert Peel, Bart., in the Chair: examination of Mr Robert Owen.

What is your situation in life? – I am principal proprietor and sole acting partner of the establishment of New Lanark, in Scotland.

How many persons, young and old, are immediately supported by the New Lanark manufactory and establishment? – About 2,300.

To how many out of that number do you give employment? – This number varies occasionally, but upon the average about sixteen or seventeen hundred.

The remainder of the 2,300 are the women and children? – Children too young, and persons too old, of the same families; some of the wives are employed.

At what age do you take children into your mills? – At ten and upwards.

What are the regular hours of labour per day, exclusive of meal times? – Ten hours and three quarters.

What time do you allow for meals? – Three quarters of an hour for dinner, and half an hour for breakfast.

Then your full time of work per day is twelve hours, out of which time you allow the mills to cease work for an hour and a quarter? – Yes.

Why do you not employ children at an earlier age? – Because I consider it would be injurious to the children, and not beneficial to the proprietors.

What reason have you to suppose it is injurious to the children to be employed in regular manufactories at an earlier age? – The evidence of very strong facts.

What are these facts? – Seventeen years ago, a number of individuals, with myself, purchased the New Lanark establishment from the late Mr Dale, of Glasgow. At that period I find that there were 500 children, who had been taken from poor-houses, chiefly in Edinburgh, and those children were generally from the age of five and six, to seven and eight; they were so taken because Mr Dale could not, I learned afterwards, obtain them at a more advanced period of life; if he did not take them at those ages he could not obtain them at all. The hours of work at that time were thirteen, inclusive of meal times, and an hour and a half was allowed for meals. It [was] very soon discovered that although those children were very well fed, well clothed, well lodged, and very great care taken of them when out of the mills, their growth and their minds were materially injured by being employed at those ages within the cotton mills for eleven hours and a half per day. It is true that those children, in consequence of being so well fed and clothed and lodged, looked fresh, and to a superficial observer, healthy in the countenances; yet their limbs were generally deformed, their growth was stunted, and although one of the best school-masters upon the old plan was engaged to instruct those children regularly every night, in general they made but a very slow progress, even in learning the common alphabet . . .

In consequence, then, of your conviction that children are injured by being employed the usual daily hours in manufactories, when under ten years of age, you have for some time refused to receive children into your works till they are ten years of age? – Yes.

Do you think the age of ten the best period for the admission of children into full and constant employment for ten or eleven hours per day, within woollen, cotton or other mills or manufactories? – I do not.

What other period would you recommend for their admission to full work? – Twelve years.

How, then, would you employ them from ten to the age of twelve? – For the two years preceding, to be partially instructed; to be instructed one half the day, and the other half to be initiated into the manufactories by parties employing two sets of children in the day, on the same principle that two sets of children were employed when proprietors thought it their interest to work day and night.

Do you think ten hours and three quarters a day the proper time for children to be employed in manufactories? – I do not.

What time do you recommend? – About ten hours of actual employment, or at the most, ten hours and a half.

Do you give instructions to any part of your population? –

Yes, to the children from three years old, upwards; and to every other part of the population that chuse to receive it.[1]

Not everyone, however, was persuaded of either the benevolence or sense of Owen's methods. William Cobbett, a radical English journalist with a countryman's sceptical dislike of the factories and the new political economy that justified them, visited New Lanark to see the factory school which Owen had established. It was part of Owen's belief that singing and dancing was an essential part of a healthy education. Cobbett thought it was scandalous.

Here I saw boys in one place, and girls in another place, under masters appointed for the purpose, carrying on what is called "education". There was one boy pointing with a stick to something stuck up upon the wall, and then all the rest of the boys began bawling out what it was. In one large room they were all *singing out something* at the word of command . . . and the fellow who leads the lazy life in the teaching of whom, ought to be sent to raking the kennel, or filling a dung-cart. In another great apartment of this house, there were eighteen boys and eighteen girls, the boys dressed in Highland dresses, without shoes on, naked from three inches above the knee, down to the foot, a tartan plaid close round the body, in their shirt sleeves, their shirt collars open, each having a girl by the arm, duly proportioned in point of size, the girls without caps, and without shoes and stockings: and there were these eighteen couples, marching, arm in arm, in regular files, with a lock-step, slow march, to the sound of a fiddle, which a fellow, big enough to carry a quarter of wheat or to dig ten rods of ground in a day, was playing in the corner of the room with an immense music book lying open before him. There was another man who was commanding officer of the marching couples, who, after having given us a march in quick step as well as slow step, were disposed of in dancing order, a business that they seemed to perform with great regularity and elegance; and it is quite impossible to see the half-naked lads of twelve or thirteen, putting their arms round the waists of the thinly-clad girls of the same age, without clearly perceiving the manifest tendency of this mode of education to prevent "*premature marriages*" and to "*check population.*"

It is difficult to determine, whether, when people are huddled together in this unnatural state, this sort of soldiership discipline may or may not be necessary to effect the purposes of schooling; but I should think it a very strange thing, if a man, calculated to produce effect by his learning, could ever come to perfection from a beginning like this. It is altogether a thing that I ABHOR.[2]

Most commentators, however, failed to follow Owen's ideas because they regarded them as too liberal to be widely applicable. Managers were left to puzzle out for themselves how to mould and control a workforce. William Brown in Dundee, running a flax mill around 1820, made this memo for himself:

A master or Manager of a Mill should be chaste, temperate, modest and devout, scrupulously just in his ministrations and severely exact in the discipline of his hands; upon which he should know his glory and his success in a great measure depend. Hands in a Mill should always be kept busy. The more closely they are held at their work, the more comfortable they are. If allowed to leave their places they are continually sighing after something they have no business with and rendering themselves uneasy. It is mistaken humanity to indulge them in ease, idleness or play. When in fault they should be reprimanded first calmly then seriously then sharply. Great care should be taken to point out their faults and explain their duty to them. Young ones or beginners especially should have their business frequently pointed out and explained. There is scarcely anyone so backward or corrupt that may not be improved by unremitting attention and patient and persevering efforts on the part of the overseer.

The giving of orders and directions to servants is a thing that has to be practised in a Mill perhaps several hundred times a day and ought to be well understood; yet notwithstanding of its importance most people pay no attention to the manner of it. In giving orders no apology should be made however hard the order but great care should be taken not to demand anything that is ill-timed or unreasonable. If orders are given in a sensible, reasonable sort of way, the servant will likely do his utmost to fulfil them; but if given in a rude, ill-humoured way he will probably do but bare justice. Masters reap great benefit from having the art of making their servants interested in their work, exerting on all occasions their own ingenuity, being responsible in character for what they perform, enjoying their own merit and not being depressed and offended by sulky looks or harsh expressions. Masters who are properly up to the management of their hands are always welcome among them and their presence is agreeable; but those who rule by wrong methods are disliked and their absence is always earnestly wished for.[3]

We have seen in an earlier section how terrible could be the experience of a child starting work in a badly run mill (see pp. 69–72). A further account of James Myles' experience shows how far management could fall short of William Brown's ideals – though notice how in the end he found a fair employer.

On the approach of winter I began to feel severely the terrible infliction of long hours. As the mill went on at half-past five a.m., I had, as I have already stated, to get out of bed at five, and as trade was very dull at the time, to be behind the hours was not only to lose *double* wages for the lost time, but to run the risk of being instantly discharged. At that time mill-masters did not employ men for rousing their hands in the mornings, and each individual had to grope away as he best could. I wish I knew the benevolent person who first conceived and carried into execution the plan of warning them each morning. I certainly would have woven an humble chaplet of literary flowers to have adorned his memory. The plan at once removed a load of anxiety and pain off the minds of the young, as the terror of sleeping in kept them in a nightly state of unhappiness. I know the effect it had on myself, and to use a common expression, it like-wise kept my mother on "heckle pins." We had no clock in the house, and my mother used to rise at all hours of the night, and sit until she heard the Cowgate clock strike an hour.

Often has she sat from a little past three until five, when she would waken me and return to her bed. I have frequently risen myself, put on my clothes, gone out, and discovered afterwards that it was only about three in the morning; but rather than return to my bed, and run the risk of lying too long, I have gone to a stair in the vicinity of the mill, laid myself down on it, and fallen fast asleep, and on the arrival of the fireman I would creep alongside the boiler to catch a little heat to my cold overworked body. The stair still stands. It is the only outside one opposite the Quarry Lands in the New Roads. A few days ago I visited it, and the sight of it kindled a fire of contending emotions in my breast. I thought on the time when necessity, that iron-hearted slave-driver, backed by the voracious demands of competition, ground the health and strength of children in mills; and I could not help contrasting it with our own time, under the dominion of the Ten Hours' Bill. The contrast was in every way gratifying, as the hours are not only diminished, but corporeal punishment is prohibited, and a more healthy system of usage generally in practice. The recollections I have of sleeping on stairs, and the many severe beatings I got, steal over my mind like something cold and even criminal, and I involuntarily shudder as if I had done an evil deed . . .

It was during this winter that I got the first unmerciful beating from a mill overseer. I was attending a spinning frame. It got too full in the shifting, and I was unable to keep up the ends. The foreman challenged me. I told him I was doing the best I could. He flew into a furious passion, dragged me into the turning shop, cut a strap off a lathe, and lashed me cruelly. He then seized me by the ears and hung me for a few moments over a window three storeys from the ground. In reading of such a ferocious action as this, methinks I hear the reader exclaim, Surely that is not true; but I beg solemnly to state that it is true to the very letter, and there is one mill foreman in Dundee who can corroborate all I have said. I know such inexorable tyranny is not and cannot be practised nowadays, but when I was a boy it was, I regret to say, too common in such places. On the evening of this unlucky day, when I returned home, my eyes were red, and my head sore with weeping, and a second time I gave vent to my pent up feeling under the wings of my mother's sympathy . . .

When I detailed the usage I had got from my foreman, her indignation rose so high that she burst into tears, and vowed vengeance on his head. On the following day she called on Mr H---, the proprietor, and made her complaint. She was told that he never interfered in such matters, and she left without getting any satisfaction. Determined to wreak her wrath on the unfeeling perpetrator of the assault, she proceeded straightway to the mill, and met the foreman at the top of a stair which led down to a malt barn. Made strong by passion, without a moment's warning, she seized him by the neck, and hurled him to the bottom of the stair as if he had been a child. He had scarcely time to think, far less to rise, when she bounded out at the door and vanished from his sight. A few of the workers who witnessed this scene enjoyed it highly, for overbearing masters and foremen receive no sympathy from their workers when an accident happens or the talons of adversity seize on them . . . The event I have detailed made me more miserable than ever. I knew that my overseer would seize on the first petty fault I might commit, and make it a pretext for dismissing me from my employment . . . According to my anticipations a fault was soon picked out, and pretext discovered for paying me off. One day, at breakfast time, I had been amusing myself sailing little bits of wood with masts and paper sails in the mill pond. My cravat, unknown to me, got all wet in the ends while I was bending. On returning to my work it got warped round a shaft that propelled my rose, or elevator. In a moment it was whirled round the shaft, and my head came violently in contact with it; but my cravat providently nipt in two, or I would have been instantly suffocated. My neck was a little ruffled, and my head sore, and I entered a small room off the flat where yarn was kept, and lay down until I should recover from the stun and fright I had received. It was impossible for mill boys then to sit down to rest themselves without falling asleep and I was of course no exception. In a few minutes I was asleep, and dreaming of falling over precipices, and being worried by wild beasts, which was necessarily caused by the fright I had got. While in this state, a roguish boy of the name of Fleming poured oil on my neck, and painted my face all over with ink and grease. He then went and told the foreman I was lying in the yarn-room sleeping, and for this petty fault – petty when it is considered what happened previous to it – I was instantly discharged. As the spring was approaching, and trade improving, moreover, as I had had some experience as a mill-boy, I was not afraid of getting work. I had heard much of the kindness and generosity of Messrs ---- as employers, and I applied at their establishment and was successful. The reports I had heard of these gentlemen were fully verified by my experience, and, years after I had left their employment, I was pleased, on reading the evidence which was taken before the Committee of the House of Commons on the Factory Question in 1833, to find it stated, by a witness of extensive experience and knowledge, that Messrs ---- were favourable to a reduction in the hours of labour, and were considered the most kind-hearted employers in Dundee.[4]

Bad though the reputation of factory work might be in the working class, the great workshops were themselves a source of awe and pride to the Victorians. In the second phase of the Industrial Revolution, after 1830, the blast furnaces of West Central Scotland dominated both the landscape and the economy, as recounted in this description of 1869.

Though Coatbridge is a most interesting seat of industry, it is anything but beautiful. Dense clouds of smoke roll over it incessantly, and impart to all the buildings a peculiarly dingy aspect. A coat of black dust overlies everything, and in a few hours the visitor finds his complexion considerably deteriorated by the flakes of soot which fill the air, and settle on his face. To appreciate Coatbridge, it must be visited at night, when it presents a most extraordinary and – when seen for the first time – startling spectacle. From the steeple of the parish church, which stands on a considerable eminence, the flames of no fewer than fifty blast furnaces may be seen. In the daytime these flames are pale and unimpressive; but when night comes on, they appear to burn more fiercely, and gradually there is developed in the sky a lurid glow similar to that which hangs over a city when a great conflagration is in progress. For half-a-mile round each group of furnaces, the country is as well illumined as during full moon, and the good folks of Coatbridge have their streets lighted without tax or trouble. There is something grand in even a distant view of the furnaces; but the effect is much enhanced when they are approached to within a hundred yards or so. The flames then have a positively fascinating effect. No production of the pyrotechnist can match their wild gyrations. Their form is ever changing, and the variety of their movements is endless. Now they shoot far upward, and breaking short off, expire among the smoke; again spreading outward, they curl over the lips of the furnace, and dart through the doorways, as if determined to annihilate the bounds within which they are confined; then they sink low into the crater, and come forth with renewed strength in the shape of great tongues of fire, which sway backward and forward, as if seeking with a fierce eagerness something to devour.

The most extensive ironmasters in Scotland are Messrs Baird and Co., who own forty-two blast furnaces, employ nine thousand men and boys, and produce about three hundred thousand tons of pig-iron per annum, or one-fourth of the entire quantity made north of the Tweed. Twenty-six of their furnaces are situated in various parts of Ayrshire, and the remaining sixteen are concentrated at Gartsherrie, in the neighbourhood of Coatbridge. Gartsherrie Ironworks are the largest in Scotland, and it is stated there is only one establishment in Britain which has a greater number of furnaces. The quantity of pig-iron made is one hundred thousand tons per annum, and the number of men and boys connected with the works is three thousand two hundred. More than a thousand tons of coal are consumed every twenty-four hours; and, as showing how well chosen is the site of the works, it may be mentioned that nineteen-twentieths of the coal required is obtained within a distance of half-a-mile from the furnaces. One coal-pit is situated close to the furnaces, and has been in operation since the works were established, forty years ago. The coal from this pit is conveyed to the furnaces by means of a self-acting incline. Most of the ironstone was at one

time obtained from pits in the neighbourhood, but now it has
to be brought from a distance of from two to twenty miles; and
a complete system of railways connects the pits with the works.
The total length of the railways is about fifty miles, and the
traffic is carried on by means of six locomotives and an immense
number of trucks. The establishment is also connected with the
great railway systems of the country, and possesses additional
facilities for transport in a branch of the Monklands Canal,
which has been carried through the centre of the works. For the
canal traffic, there is a fleet of eighteen barges, of about sixty tons
each; and eight of these are screw steamers. A great proportion of
the manufactured iron is sent out by the canal.

As the Gartsherrie Ironworks have a wide-spread reputation
for producing iron of a superior quality, and are among the best
organised manufactories in the country, a description of them
may be interesting.

The furnaces, sixteen in number, stand in two rows, one on
each side of the canal, and about forty yards distant from it. A
constant supply of coal and ironstone can be reckoned upon,
and therefore only a small stock is kept at the works. The mineral
trains are worked with unfailing regularity, and their cargoes are
deposited conveniently for immediate use. There is thus no
superfluous shovelling about of the materials, nor is any expense
incurred by piling them into heaps. The proportions of ironstone, coal, and limestone laid down are exactly what are required
in the process of smelting. Manual labour has, by a variety of
ingenious appliances, been reduced to a minimum, and the
amount of waste is infinitesimal. Everything is done according
to a well-defined system, and nothing connected with the works
is considered to be too insignificant to merit attention. No heaps
of rubbish are allowed to accumulate, no scraps of iron or cinder
lie about, and every nook and cranny about the vast place is as
tidily kept as it can possibly be. The workmen are liberally
treated, but they must do their work carefully and well. Negli-
gence and irregularity are unfailingly punished, while merit is
as certainly rewarded. All the men employed about the furnaces,
even the firemen and engineers of the blast engines, are paid
according to the quantity and quality of iron produced. This

arrangement is found to work admirably, as each man knows that, by attending to his work, he is not only putting money into the pockets of his fellow-labourers, but also improving his own earnings.[5]

Behind heavy industry lay the need to mine coal to fuel the blast furnaces and the steam engines, and miners developed their own powerful cultures born of the work experience. In the early days of the Industrial Revolution, women in Scotland (though not in England) were employed to carry coal from the hewing face to the pit bottom, and then up spiral stairs to the surface. The following account was published by Robert Bald, mining engineer at Alloa, in 1812:

> In those collieries where this mode is in practice, the collier leaves his house for the pits about eleven o'clock at night, (attended by his sons, if he has any sufficiently old), when the rest of mankind are retiring to rest. Their first work is to prepare coals, by hewing them down from the wall. In about three hours after, his wife (attended by her daughters, if she has any sufficiently grown) sets out for the pit, having previously wrapped her infant child in a blanket, and left it to the care of an old woman, who, for a small gratuity, keeps three or four children at a time, and who, in their mothers' absence, feeds them with ale or whisky mixed with water. The children who are a little more advanced are left to the care of a neighbour; and under such treatment, it is surprising that they ever grow up or thrive.
>
> The mother, having thus disposed of her younger children, descends the pit with her older daughters, when each, having a basket of a suitable form, lays it down, and into it the large coals are rolled; and such is the weight carried, that it frequently takes two men to lift the burden upon their backs: the girls are loaded according to their strength. The mother sets out first, carrying a lighted candle in her teeth; the girls follow, and in this manner they proceed to the pit bottom, and with weary steps and slow, ascend the stairs, halting occasionally to draw breath, till they arrive at the hill or pit-top, where the coals are laid down for

sale; and in this manner they go for eight or ten hours almost without resting. It is no uncommon thing to see them, when ascending the pit, weeping most bitterly from the excessive severity of the labour; but the instant they have laid down their burden on the hill, they resume their cheerfulness, and return down the pit singing.

The execution of work performed by a stout woman in that way is beyond conception. For instance, we have seen a woman, during the space of time above mentioned, take on a load of at least 170 pounds avoirdupois, travel with this 150 yards up the slope of the coal below ground, ascend a pit by stairs 117 feet, and travel up on the hill 20 yards more to where the coals are laid down. All this she will perform no less than twenty-four times as a day's work ... The weight of coals thus brought to the pit to by a woman in a day amount to 4,080 pounds or above 36 hundredweight English, and there have been frequent instances of two tons being carried. The wages paid for this work, are eightpence per day! – a circumstance as surprising almost as the work performed ...

From this view of the work performed by bearers in Scotland, some faint idea may be formed of the slavery and severity of the toil particularly when it is considered that they are entered to this work when seven years of age, and frequently continue till they are upwards of fifty, or even sixty years old.

The collier, with his wife and children, having performed their daily task, return home, where no comfort awaits them; their clothes are frequently soaked with water and covered with mud; their shoes so very bad as scarcely to deserve the name. In this situation they are exposed to all the rigours of winter, the cold frequently freezing their clothes.

On getting home, all is cheerless and devoid of comfort; the fire is generally out, the culinary utensils dirty and unprepared, and the mother naturally seeks first after her infant child, which she nurses even before her pit clothes are thrown off ...[6]

Such work by women underground was abolished by Act of Parliament in 1842. At the start of the present century their place had been taken by pitponies and boys who took the coal loaded into small wagons or 'hutches', underground, as recounted by an American student, Kellog Durland, who took a job for a time as a miner in the Fife coalfield to see what is was like:

> "Light your lamp. This way – mind the hutches." He led and I stumbled after.
>
> Even here, twelve hundred feet down, there was the same deafening, clattering roar as above. Races of six, eight, nine and ten hutches came rattling out of the black passages drawn by fast-going ponies, guided by a single rope which took the place of reins. Wee boy drivers, not so high as the undersized ponies some of them, grotesque in their patched muddy clothes, cried in piercingly shrill voices at the animals, deep-chested men shouted back and forth as they rolled the coal-weighted hutches off the rails on to the smooth sheet plates and then on to the cages, or jerked the empty ones back to the rails.
>
> "Follow this man," and without a word my new guide, a grizzled old miner, turned abruptly to the right down a dark passage – a "level" – where the last echoes of the noisy pit bottom were quickly lost and only the weird babbling swish of an unseen stream and the sucking of the mucky ooze beneath our feet was audible.[7]

As late as the 1950s the miner's life remained dirty, dramatic and dangerous, and gave rise to a fierce sense of comradeship from shared toil and peril. Charles Brister recounted a shift below ground in another Fife mine that ended in an industrial accident:

> The two men filled their water bottles and drew their lamps. Then, after submitting to a search, they waited with a crowd of others for the "cage."
>
> Before their eyes the vibrating steel cable rushed heavenwards and the cage, with its slatted iron gates, emerged from the depths. The safety lock shot home, a bell rang, the gate clanged. And a mass of black, sweat-soaked flesh pushed and shoved its collective way through the waiting nightshift.
>
> Words were flung and hurried questions caught.
>
> "Has it been rainin' –?"

"What won the three o'clock –?" and from a young but cynical voice, "Ooh, yu lucky people!"

A bell rang vibrantly, the banksman waved, and they surged forward into the steel box dangling on the end of its slender thread. Behind them, others continued to push and soon they were packed like sardines. They heard the "snack" of the safety lock being withdrawn. Again a bell rang and the cage dropped swiftly into the damp, dripping darkness.

Somewhere in the crush a humorist said, "Even numbers breath in, odd numbers breath out."

The whirl of flying metal against the guides became a tormented, howling shriek which died slowly to a rattling dirge and stopped. The cage hung motionless, then it suddenly dropped and stomachs reached crazily to throats. "What does that bastard think this is," demanded a plaintive voice, "a muckin' yo yo?" Then somehow it was all over and they were walking up the firm, concrete pavement of the brightly-lit pit bottom.

At the outer end of the Sea Level the two propdrawers switched on their lamps and, accompanied by the two cuttermen, settled down to the long, stumbling, slipping, clutching, twisting, splashing, crouching journey. Five thousand weary yards later they reached their own Section, where the deputy awaited them.

"Yure coalcutter's picked an' ready tae go," he said, and waved the two cuttermen up the heading. Then he turned to the propdrawers, "Ah'm told it's pretty bad up at the top end o' the run, Tom," he said to the old man. "So watch what yure doin'. But fer Christ's sake get me oot. Ah'm told that this new Manager's a bastard, so try no tae lose any props or there'll be hell tae pay."

"There'll be none lost if we can help it," Tom said steadily.

"An' neither o' us'll be lost either," snarled Benny with fire in his eyes. "We're no chuckin' oor lives awa fer the sake o' a ten bob prop. Ah'll gie yu that, richt now. Yu mebbe aint discovered it, but them muckin' days is over."

The deputy said bad-temperedly, "That's yure job unt it? That's the job yure paid fer, yure the steeldrawer o' this section."

Benny opened his mouth for a devastating reply but Tom

silenced him with a look. He turned to the fat deputy with a glance of arid disdain in his eyes. "We ken what oor job is," he said in his dour, hard voice, "an it's a job you'll never be able tae do as long as yu've a hole in your ass."

The deputy looked confused as Tom turned away and, followed by Benny, scrambled slowly up the narrow heading.

The deputy said sourly, "That's a miserable ole bastard, that. 'Ve yu ever heard him laugh?" Then he sat down and opened his snack-box. "He'd hurt hissel' if he laughed," he said, before anyone could reply.

The shotfirer said suggestively, "His only son got killed wi' the Argyles in Korea."

"That's muck all tae do wi' it" the deputy snarled. "Korea wis only a few years back. That old bastard's been like that as long Ah've kent him, an' that's twenty years if it's a day."

It was three in the morning and near the end of the shift when Tom and Benny reached the "bad bit." Slowly they had worked their weary way up along the hundred yard face, drawing props from the waste and throwing them over to the face to be used again the next day. As the last prop came out of each "drift" the roof collapsed in a crashing roar of rock and rubble, making them leap frenziedly for the comparative safety of the face. In the centre track, the long snake-like, steel conveyors wound away between lines of standing props.

The next day the face would advance and the conveyors would be shifted into what was now the face track. Where they now crouched watchfully on the conveyors would have become the waste. And the props that sheltered them now would to-morrow night also have to be drawn. An endless cycle, ever to be repeated, until the seam was worked out or reached the "boundary" or struck a "fault."

Down the face they could hear the rumbling clatter as the low, steel-clad monster crawled deliberately along the face in the care of the two cuttermen, its whirling picks tearing into the hard, glistening, diamond-bright glitter of the wall of coal. Snarling, growling, spitting and cracking as though in an insane rage.

They crouched together in the darkness and soberly surveyed

the "bad bit." Several of the props had been forced more than a foot down into the pavement under the relentless pressure, and in the bulging roof were ominous, dripping cracks.

Benny popped a sweet into his mouth. "This is where the muckin' fun begins," he grunted. He dragged off his black singlet and wrung it out in wiry hands, the sweat forming a pool on the pavement. He slipped the cold wet garment on again and it began to steam the moment it came in contact with his heaving body.

Tom rubbed a corrugated palm over the sweat-matted hair on his old naked chest. There was a sound nearby and the second cutterman stopped beside them. He turned on his knees and began to haul the heavy power cable, coiling it between his own body and the coalface.

Tom and Benny started gingerly, cautiously to the withdrawing of the props. Frequently they paused to listen and stare around them. Twice Tom tapped the roof with the shaft of his pick and listened attentively to the resulting, all-revealing sound. Finally there was but one set left. Two steel props supporting a huge wooden bar, nine feet long, a foot wide and six inches thick.

Willie, the cutterman, threw down the last coil of cable with a sigh of relief, wiped the dribbling sweat from his eyes and looked about him. "Christ," he began, "this is a braw bit, Ah don't thi—"

Tom's suddenly-lifted hand silenced him. The wooden bar cracked as though it were matchwood. Then there was a tomb-like silence. Benny took the end of the short chain, crawled carefully into the menacing waste and fixed it gently around a prop. Once it was secure he hurriedly rejoined Tom and, getting as far away as the length of the chain permitted, they prepared to haul.

The cutterman, suddenly realising their intentions, got hurriedly to his knees. "Just a meenit," he cried, "yure no goin' tae draw that set, are yu?"

"Aye," Tom told him doggedly, "aye, it has tae come oot."

Willie crawled rapidly down the face.

"Let me oota here," he shouted, "yu bastards can bury

yusel's if yu like, but yure no goin' tae happ me up. Ah've a wife an' weans at hame." They heard him shouting to his neighbour to stop the machine, that the steeldrawers were going to "shut the bloody, muckin' place."

Tom and Benny strained to their work. The prop moved slightly. As it shifted, so the bar and the roof it supported sagged even lower. In his black face Tom's white, protruding eyeballs stared unwinkingly at the prop, with the bar and the threatening roof looming above it all.

Benny sucked frenziedly at a sweet. "Christ," he said. "Ah could do wi' a smoke." Then, miraculously, the prop was clear, the roof sagged down and the bar cracked again, protestingly, but somehow it held.

Benny sighed with relief. "Ah do believe we're goin' tae get awa wi' it after a'," he said softly.

They waited apprehensively for several minutes, ears and eyes straining, then Tom inched forward over the conveyors and reached for the prop, which in falling had jammed on the waste side. As he strained at the stubborn steel Benny, with one eye on his neighbour's safety, began to pull in the slack chain.

A thin trickle of flour-like whiteness drifted down from the roof. Benny roared a warning and flung himself away. Tom hurled his heavy body backwards as there was a thunderous, crashing rumble above them and an avalanche of rock smashed down on the steel conveyors, buckling and twisting them.

The remaining prop lurched crazily. The bar, under its shattering load of stone, drove into Tom's back, pinning him like a fly to the pavement. There were a few lesser rumbles and then a deep, deep silence.

Benny flung himself on the mound of rock, tearing wildly with his bare hands and screaming madly to where the two cuttermen were waiting below him in the darkness.

It took half an hour to dig Tom out and not only was he alive but he claimed to be unhurt. "Ah'm richt enough," he said brusquely, struggling to his knees.

"Are yu sure?" Benny was not convinced.

"Sh'm right enough Ah tell yu, just that ma back's a wee bit sair."

They helped him from the cramped space out to the comparative roominess of the "top road" and as they emerged from the face the deputy appeared on the scene.

"What's up?" he demanded.

"Yu an' yure muckin' props," snarled Benny, "an' yure muckin' bad bits, pity it wisnae that muckin' Manager that got this. But nah—," Benny was almost in tears. "The bastard'll be lyin' snorin' on his wife's shirt tail the noo."[8]

It is no wonder that, between the 1830s and the 1980s, so many of the bitterest industrial disputes between union and management involved the traditional factories and the mines.

CHAPTER VIII

RELIGION

Attendance at church was part of the very pith of Scottish life. The great majority of the population in the mid eighteenth century were Presbyterians of the Church of Scotland, though by the end of the century some 300 congregations of Seceders (Presbyterians who had fallen out with the established church) had formed, mainly in the central Lowlands. There was also a declining Episcopalian church tainted by its links with Jacobitism and in the process of being reduced, in Sir Walter Scott's words, to the 'shadow of a shade'. A few thousand Catholics hung on in remote parts of the Highlands and Islands, though hardly any were in the Clyde area – Alexander Webster in his population *Survey* of 1755 could find only five 'papists' in the whole of Lanarkshire, Renfrewshire and Ayrshire.

Church life around 1800 still engaged the attentions and affections of most of the people in the countryside, where a service was a social affair as well as a religious one. It also involved dogs as well as people, as this passage about a Border parish makes very clear:

Talking of the dogs suggests another great improvement made on the church. There were no doors on the seats, and nothing but a narrow deal in each as a footboard, and no separation below between them. The planking on the passages was very deficient, a great deal of the earthen floor was thus exposed; and it can easily be imagined that when the shepherds from Ettrick, as well as from Yarrow, came to church, each man as regularly accompanied by his dog as encased in his plaid – no matter what the weather or the season – frequent rows ensued. On the slightest growl from one, all pricked up their ears. If a couple of them fell out and showed fight, it was the signal for a general *mêlée*. The rest that were prowling about, or half asleep at their masters' feet, rushed from their lairs, found a way through below the pews, and among the feet of the occupants, and raised literally such a *dust* as fairly enveloped them. Then the strife waxed fierce and furious, the noise became deafening, the voice of the minister was literally drowned, and he was fain to pause, whether in preaching or in prayer. Two or three shepherds had to leave their places and use their *nibbies* unmercifully before the rout was quelled, and the service of the sanctuary could be resumed.

These scenes were more unseemly than a solitary cur, with some rude ear for music, joining in the psalmody, and were of old standing in Yarrow. Old Mr Scott of Eldinhope used to relate how Dr Cramond bade the old beadle, Sandy Rae, put out the noisy delinquents, and got for answer, "I dinna like to meddle wi' the folk's dougs, sir;" somewhat more polite than another rejoinder, "I'm no gaun tae get mysel' bitten; they may pit them oot that brought them in." The appearance of a strange dog any day in church was the signal for the whole fraternity holding a conclave; and if not satisfied with its appearance, giving it no peace during the service, unless it could find an open door to beat a retreat. So much, indeed, were the curs recognised as a regular portion of the congregation, that the closing arrangements were made with reference to them. The going round of the elders with the ladles put them all on the *qui vive*, and, for peace's sake, the congregation sat till the blessing was pronounced. Their rising was attended by a perfect storm of barking, a general canine jubilee.[1]

The social side of the church was especially visible on Communion Sunday, when the population would gather from miles around for both spiritual and material refreshment.

None could preside over the services with more grace and gravity than the minister of Yarrow, whether in the palmy days of youth or when in the enjoyment of a green old age. His commanding appearance and benevolent expression and dignified bearing at all times won the respect of his people; and when on a sacramental occasion he walked out in his court-dress and cocked-hat and powdered hair, there was something more striking and venerable still in the eyes of his rural flock. When he entered the pulpit he came fresh from his study and his closet, his memory charged with the careful meditations of the week, and his feet shod with the preparation of the Gospel of peace. In the crowd that thronged every pew, some standing in the passage, and others seated on the graveyard without, he found a most eager and sympathetic audience; and it was out of the abundance of the heart the mouth spoke – it went from the heart to the heart. Thoughts that breathe and words that burn fell from his lips. More especially when he came to the consecration prayer and Communion address, his lips seemed touched as with a live coal from off the altar . . .

The Sabbath service was a protracted one. It began at 10.30, and with an hour and a quarter of interval, did not close till about 7 p m ; so that those who came from the extremities of the parish – Corsecleugh, Dryhope-hope, Redfordgreen, and Ashiestiel – had to start at an early and return at a late hour. There were seven full Communion tables. Refreshments of bread and cheese and milk were provided in the kitchen of the manse for all comers of the people generally; a bowl put in the "minister's well" for those who liked a cooling draught of spring water; bread and ale in the barn, furnished by some of the publicans of the parish (David Brunton, Yarrowford, was the first I have heard of; then John Scott, Ettrick-bridge, of the sign "Entertainment for man and horse;" then George Turnbull of the Gordon Arms, and John Leigh, his successor); and refreshments in the dining-room and parlour of the manse for the farmers and their families. The ministers and elders dined at the manse during the interval. A sumptuous "Monday's dinner," to which some of the principal parishioners were invited, completed the service of carnal things.'

In the Highlands the kirk similarly encompassed the community with its weekly ritual, though there was no sense yet that Highlanders were particularly serious about their religion. Elizabeth Grant, daughter of the laird of Rothiemurchus, recalled half a century later the kirk where she went as a little girl around 1812:

The stir consequent on our entrance was soon hushed, and the minister gave out the psalm; he put a very small dirty volume up to one eye, for he was near-sighted, and read as many lines of the old version of the rhythmical paraphrase (we may call it) of the Psalms of David as he thought fit, drawling them out in a sort of sing-song. He stooped over the pulpit to hand his little book to the precentor, who then rose and calling out aloud the tune – "St. George's tune," "Auld Aberdeen," "Hondred an' fifteen," etc. – began himself a recitative of the first line on the key-note, then taken up and repeated by the congregation; line by line he continued in the same fashion, thus doubling the length of the *exercise*, for really to some it was no play – serious severe screaming quite beyond the natural pitch of the voice, a wandering search after the air by many who never caught it, a flourish of difficult execution and plenty of the *tremolo* lately come into fashion. The dogs seized this occasion to bark (for they always came to the kirk with the family), and the babies to cry.

When the minister could bear the din no longer he popped up again, again leaned over, touched the precentor's head, and instantly all sound ceased. The long prayer began, everybody stood up while the minister asked for us such blessings as he thought best: with closed *eyes* it should have been, that being part of the "rubric"; our oddity of a parson closed but one, the one with which he had squinted at the psalm-book, some affection of the other eyelid rendering it unmanageable. The prayer over, the sermon began; that was my time for making observations, "Charity" and "Solomon's Lilies" soon requiring no further attention.

Few save our own people sat around; old grey-haired rough-visaged men that had known my grandfather and great-grandfather, black, red, and fair hair, belonging to such as were in the prime of life, younger men, lads, boys – all in the tartan. The plaid as a wrap, the plaid as a drapery, with kilt to match on some, blue trews on others, blue jackets on all. The women were plaided too, an outside shawl was seen on one, though the wives wore a large handkerchief under the plaid, and looked picturesquely matronly in their very high white caps. A bonnet was not to be seen, no Highland girl ever covered her head; the girls wore their hair neatly braided in front, plaited up in Grecian fashion behind, and bound by the snood, a bit of velvet or ribbon placed rather low on the forehead and tied beneath the plait at the back. The wives were all in homespun, home-dyed linsey-woolsey gowns, covered to the chin by the modest kerchief worn outside the gown. The girls who could afford it had a Sabbath day's gown of like manufacture and very ornamented with a string of beads, often amber; some had to be content with the best blue flannel petticoat and a clean white jacket, their ordinary and most becoming dress, and few of these had either shoes or stockings; but they all wore the plaid, and they folded it round them very gracefully.

They had a custom in the spring of washing their beautiful hair with a decoction of the young buds of the birch-trees. I do not know if it improved or hurt the hair, but it agreeably scented the kirk, which at other times was wont to be overpowered by the combined odours of snuff and peat reek, for the men snuffed immensely during the delivery of the English sermon; they fed their noses with quills fastened by strings to the lids of their mulls, spooning up the snuff in quantities and without waste. The old women snuffed too, and groaned a great deal, to express their mental sufferings, their grief for all the backslidings supposed to be thundered at from the pulpit; lapses from faith was their grand self-accusation, lapses from virtue were, alas! little commented on; temperance and chastity were not in the Highland code of morality . . .

There was no very deep religious feeling in the Highlands up to this time. The clergy were reverenced in their capacity of pastors without this respect extending to their persons unless fully-merited by propriety of conduct. The established form of faith was determinately adhered to, but the *kittle questions*, which had so vexed the Puritanic south, had not yet troubled the minds of their northern neighbours. Our mountains were full of fairy legends, old clan tales, forebodings, prophecies, and other superstitions, quite as much believed in as the Bible. The Shorter Catechism and the fairy stories were mixed-up together to form the innermost faith of the Highlander, a much gayer and less metaphysical character than his Saxon-tainted countryman.[3]

As the nineteenth century proceeded the kirk was to alter its character in many respects. The arrival of tens of thousands of Irish immigrants, especially in the middle decades, produced a revived and numerous Catholic Church, especially in the industrial west. In 1878 the Catholic hierarchy was re-established in Scotland for the first time since the Reformation. The Episcopalians, too, staged a recovery, particularly among the upper classes and in Edinburgh. The Church of Scotland itself became more puritan and evangelical in tone, and in 1843 split in half over the question of patronage and the church's relations with the state. The Disruption created two churches, the Church of Scotland continuing, or Auld Kirk, led by the former Moderate party, and the Free Church, led by Thomas Chalmers, Dr Welsh, and their colleagues in the Evangelical party. The schism was not finally healed until the reunion of 1929. To many contemporaries like Henry Cockburn, the Disruption was a dramatic example of men putting principles before self-interest, since for the ministers leaving the Church of Scotland meant leaving the security of their livings and manses and depending for their future on the voluntary support of generous laymen:

8th June 1843. The crash is over.

The event that has taken place was announced so far back as November, when the Convocation proclaimed that their adhering to the Church would depend entirely on the success of the last appeal they meant to waste upon Government and Parliament. These appeals had failed, and all subsequent occurrences flowed towards the announced result. On the two Sundays preceding the Assembly hundreds of congregations all over the country had been saddened by farewell sermons from pastors to whom they were attached. The general belief that there would be an extraordinary move, combined with the uncertainty as to its exact time and form and amount, had crowded Edinburgh with clergymen, and had produced an anxiety far beyond what usually preceded the annual Assemblies of the Church . . .

Dr. Welsh, Professor of Church History in the University

of Edinburgh, having been Moderator last year, began the proceedings by preaching a sermon before his Grace the Commissioner in the High Church, in which what was going to happen was announced and defended. The Commissioner then proceeded to St. Andrew's Church, where the Assembly was to be held. The streets, especially those near the place of meeting, were filled, not so much with the boys who usually gaze at the annual show, as by grave and well-dressed grown people of the middle rank. According to custom, Welsh took the chair of the Assembly. Their very first act ought to have been to constitute the Assembly of this year by electing a new Moderator. But before this was done, Welsh rose and announced that he and others who had been returned as members held this not to be a free Assembly – that, therefore, they declined to acknowledge it as a Court of the Church – that they meant to leave the very place, and, as a consequence of this, to abandon the Establishment. In explanation of the grounds of this step he then read a full and clear protest. It was read as impressively as a weak voice would allow, and was listened to in silence by as large an audience as the church could contain. Whether from joy at the prospect of getting rid of their troublesome brethren anyhow – which they professed, or from being alarmed – which to a great degree was the truth, the Moderate party, though they might have objected to any paper being read even from the chair at that time, attempted no interruption, which they now regret. The protest resolved into this, that the civil court had subverted what had ever been understood to be the Church, that its new principles were enforced by ruinous penalties, and that in this situation they were constrained to abandon an Establishment which, as recently explained, they felt repugnant to their vows and to the consciences.

As soon as it was read, Dr. Welsh handed the paper to the clerk, quitted the chair, and walked away. Instantly, what appeared to be the whole left side of the house rose to follow. Some applause broke from the spectators, but it checked itself in a moment. 193 member moved off, of whom about 123 were ministers, and about 70 elders. Among these were many upon whose figures the public eye had been long accustomed to rest in reverence. They all withdrew slowly and regularly amidst perfect silence, till that side of the house was left nearly empty. They were joined outside by a large body of adherents, among whom were about 300 clergymen. As soon as Welsh, who wore his Moderator's dress, appeared on the street, and people saw that principle had really triumphed over interest, he and his followers were received with the loudest acclamations. They walked in procession down Hanover Street to Canonmills, where they had secured an excellent hall, through an unbroken mass of cheering people, and beneath innumerable handkerchiefs waving from the windows. But amidst this exultation there was much sadness and many a tear, many a grave face and fearful thought; for no one could doubt that it was with sore hearts that these ministers left the Church, and no thinking man could look on the unexampled scene and behold that the temple was rent, without pain and sad forebodings. No spectacle since the Revolution reminded one so forcibly of the Covenanters.[4]

Whatever church the believer belonged to, the Sabbath in Victorian Scotland retained and even intensified its hold as a day given over to silence and worship. In a well-to-do and pious Episcopalian home in Edinburgh in the 1880s, family prayers were the custom, but the sharp eyes of a little girl saw a great many other things between her fingers:

One awoke on Sunday morning to a city of silence. No sound in the streets of trams or carts, and no cries of coalmen. The rare rattle of a cab and the clip-clop of the horse's feet on the stones have an ungodly ring. For to drive in a cab on Sunday, except in the case of "needcessity", as Ann would say, was to break the Sabbath, and to break the Sabbath was to imperil the soul, *and* to pay double fare into the bargain, and I really don't know which we in Scotland considered the worse penalty of the two.

No sweet chimes usher in the morn as in lighter-minded lands. Early church-goers, Catholic or "English Church", must walk in quietness. Not till the forenoon is well advanced, when every steeple and tower will set harsh bells a-clanging, must there be any disturbance of the Presbyterian Peace.

The signs of Sunday are all about me as I run downstairs, dressed in my Sunday frock. The shine and polish of yesterday, but no bustle of today. I hear Forbes in the kitchen grinding the coffee-beans in the little coffee-mill. The beans make a scrunchy sound and the smell is delicious.

The round table in the dining-room is laid for breakfast and the big brass kettle is beginning to sing on its gas ring attached by rubber piping to one of the jets of the chandelier. My father has cleared a space for the enormous fat family Bible and found his place. The first bell is rung, for prayers. The second bell will mean breakfast. On week-days there is a third bell, for porridge, between prayers and breakfast proper. Very confusing for the stranger within our gates.

Forbes and Christina come in and sit near the door in their clean prints and aprons, their hands folded primly in their laps, their fine thin Scottish faces models of Sabbath solemnity. Ann slips unobtrusively into a corner and shakes her head at Louis and me as a warning to behave properly. If Aunt Louisa is there, she sits in the velvet armchair, her mouth drawn down, her face grim with disapproval of my father's method of reading the psalms and prayers, which is scholarly but breezy. When we say the Lord's Prayer she does her protesting best to slow down the pace, and caps my father's cheerful "A-men" with an evangelically emphatic "*Ay*-men", and I feel quite sure that "*Ay*-men" is more religious than "A-men".

No emotional memory of family prayers stirs in me. But one picture remains of a happening brought about by our custom of the three bells.

A morning in summer when Madame Davy was our guest. She was a Catholic, so did not come in to prayers, and being French she was not expected to like Scottish porridge. So she had been bidden to wait until the third bell had sounded before joining us in the dining-room. But this morning she must have forgotten which bell meant which. My father had finished the psalm and shut the Bible with his characteristic gesture of decision, not to say with a bang, at which signal we all with one accord turned our backs on him and knelt down. I counted the buttons on the leather padding of the chairs while I let the words of the General Confession creep in my ears. Suddenly I heard the door open, and turned my head to see Madame Davy standing there irresolute, startled by this unusual and peculiar back-view of the household.

Now I knew all about Roman Catholics from Aunt Louisa, and conceived of them as a people plunged in the darkness of superstition. What would Madame Davy do? Would she turn and flee as from mortal sin, or would she stay and risk damnation? I watched, fascinated. And then I saw her close the door softly and kneel down, in her black gown and her wondrous snow-white coiffure, and with bent head and meek devotion join in our Protestant prayers. My childish mind, imbued with prejudice, took a leap forward, and I saw a new vision of understanding and tolerance.

"A-men," says my father; "*Ay*-men," comes Aunt Louisa's stern correction. And up we all spring. My father makes the coffee in the "Napier" machine, to my mind, the cleverest and prettiest of all coffee-making devices. Forbes brings in the hot muffins, English muffins, a new bakery venture of "Makie's" perhaps, and a new luxury on our Sunday breakfast-table. Christina scorns them even while she serves them. She knows well that all the muffins in England cannot compare with her scones, especially her triumph of triumphs, the "scoople" scone. This is not so much a scone as a World's Wonder. Flattened to a wafer-like thinness, buttered with lavishness, tenderly rolled, it is devoured lusciously, the butter oozing out at each end, and vanishes like a succulent dream.

When I was a child there was no talk of making Sunday a happy day for children – children had just to try to be happy though Sunday. Aunt Louisa said all good children loved Sunday better than all the other days of the week. I knew that. All my story-books were full of such children, like Marianne in *Anna Ross, the Orphan of Waterloo*, who was converted by Anna and almost immediately died, words of piety on her lips and forgiving all her relations. I realised that Marianne was a pattern, but I didn't want to be as good as all that. I think our half-conscious feeling about Sunday was that it was the waste of a perfectly good day which, under happier auspices and more skilful plan-

ning, might have been another Saturday. But we knew there was
no getting past that first chapter in Genesis, so we accepted
things as they were, thankful for alleviations, like coffee for
breakfast, and that at least it wasn't another Monday. But it was
certainly a day of bans and restrictions. The toy cupboard must
not be opened, my dolls must lie abed. It was accounted sin to
be seen with a needle in your hand. There must be no music,
except what is called "sacred"; no singing unless hymns; and as
for whistling, if one of the boys so far forgot himself, or the day,
as to let forth one solitary trill, down in the lower regions
Christina heard, and rushed, a thin little creature all fire and
fury, up the kitchen stairs, and breathless with horror, "Laddie!"
she gasps out, "d'ye no' ken it's the Sawbath? An' a' the folks is
stannin' in the street lookin' up at the windeys!"

   To affront the neighbours – that, for Christina, is sin
unpardonable.[5]

Religion, however, had a different emphasis in different places and
classes. In Glasgow, despite much talk about 'the godless multitude'
and the 'unchurched masses', the bulk of churchgoers as late as the
1880s were still working class – which is not the same as saying that
most of the working class still went to church, for that they plainly
did not do. Popular religion, though, had its entertaining sides, as
recalled at the end of the century by Tom Johnston, who was later
to become Secretary of State for Scotland in the Second World
War. (The Band of Hope was the children's temperance society.)

Religious revivals swept us periodically. There was, of course,
the annual Orange turn-out on 12th July, when Swanky Semple
would put on his pit buits "to fight for an unchained bible," and
a band would march through the town playing "Kick the Pope"
and "Boyne Water," while the local priest strove manfully to
shepherd his fighting men into bye-ways.
   But the real emotional frenzies with their penitent forms and
testimonies and hot gospelings were exciting while they lasted.
Once a woman called Maggie McPhee was converted and an
announcement made that she would, at a succeeding séance,
give her emotional experiences. Maggie, whose cross, borne with

more or less fortitude during her wedded life, had been a rather shiftless husband, drew a crowded attendance for her testimony; and it was a sheer if unexpected delight to the more irresponsible elements in her audience when she began clasping her hands in prayer and looking skywards in the most approved petitionary fashion, and in a shrill voice crying: "Oh Lord, but it's hard tae be a Christian and merrit tae Sanny McPhee!". . . .

One great institution of our childhood was the Band of Hope. It met on Friday evenings and provided an occasion for the appearance of old gentlemen with magic lanterns showing entrancing pictures of mice being poisoned in beer, and of dipsomaniacs, wife and child beaters, being ultimately buried in paupers' graves, or hanged for murder committed while under the influence of the demon Rum. Once or twice there arrived an old fellow with a board upon which were stuck a dozen candles, and after a discourse upon "Let your light so shine," one candle at the end of the board was lit, and from it the light was dexterously passed to the other candles. The process was simple enough but was rather spoiled when two bad boys, of whom I was one, surreptitiously wet the wicks so that they refused to light. The other bad boy was one George Whitelaw who later became an eminent press cartoonist in London.

Of the Sunday School I have no great memories but that we maintained, or at any rate were supposed to maintain, a coloured brother at an African Mission School. The coloured brother went by some such name as Tababeer, and it was a sore point to many that this dusky child of Africa should be steeped in the luxury of our pennies while Cheuch Jean, at her little shop in the West High Street, should have splendid sticky balls for sale, and we go without.[6]

For Tom Johnston the Orange marches were scarcely more than incidental to his early memories, but for Harry McShane, on the other side in the 1900s, the Catholic-Protestant divide dominated his early life.

My father was a catholic and my mother a protestant. They met and married while they were working in a fish-hook factory in

Pupils in the infant department of Harris Academy, Dundee, in the 1900s.

The rooftop playground of Frederick Street School, Aberdeen, 1907. This school was built to serve part of the city's poorest and most densely populated district.

Housewives in Aberdeen's Fisher Village of Fitty in the 1930s.

The Caldrum Street (Dundee) Steamie in 1958, shortly before launderettes replaced such establishments.

46, Saltmarket, Glasgow, in the 1860s: the worst slums of the city centre.

Near the Gallowgate, Glasgow, around 1930: unemployment and the pawnshop.

Lipton's, St Andrews, around 1930: the modern grocer and his prices.

Life in a Glasgow single-end, early twentieth century.

A Glasgow council estate of the post-war years: decanting congestion to the rim.

A 'Titan' tractor at work in the Aberdeenshire countryside, 1923.

A country smithy in Fife, 1937: still the age of the horse.

Flora McAulay of Bundalloch, Loch Long, Ross-shire, 1929.

Kingston, Glasgow. My father's family were Irish catholics; both his parents came from County Tyrone. My mother's name was Janet Sanson and her family were Scots, obviously of French descent, and originally from Edinburgh. After their marriage my parents lived in a two-roomed house, the top flat of a tenement in Govan Street, Glasgow. I was born there, the eldest of the family, on 7 May 1891.

Mixed marriages were denounced bitterly in those days, by both catholics and protestants. In Glasgow the catholic was looked upon with only a degree less hatred than in Belfast at the present. When I was a few months old my parents separated, and my father took me to live with his family. The differences were over status as well as religion. My father and his father were builders' labourers. My mother's father, Tom Sanson, was a blacksmith and a member of the Church of Scotland. He was fired by John Knox and was very anti-catholic.

It wasn't long before my father and mother got back together – my sister was only a year younger than me – and they never separated again. There were another ten children that came after me, eight boys and two girls. But I didn't go back home with my father: I stayed with my grandparents and I never saw much of my mother, though my father came regularly to the house and I went out with him a lot.[7]

As he grew up his political education began with hearing the sectarian debates that drew large crowds on Glasgow Green:

Every Sunday, at Glasgow Green, people would gather to hear open-air lectures and debates. Three or four hundred people would listen to a well-known lecturer, and there would be speakers and their audiences all the way along the Green up to Nelson's Monument. Shortly after my father stopped me reading 'bloods' he took me to hear the lecturers and the debates, though I don't think he was very keen on any particular school of thought.

A large number of the debates were between catholic and protestant speakers, and they lectured on their doctrines in a way that they don't do now. Two of the greatest disputes were about papal infallibility and transubstantiation. Were the popes infallible? Was the Pope the real successor to Peter, and did Christ refer to the Catholic Church when he said: 'On this rock I'll build my Church'? Was the bread and wine the true body and blood of Christ – during the Last Supper when he passed bread and wine and said 'This is my body, this is my blood' – was that a literal statement? Of course the protestants were refuting all this and arguing for their doctrines: predestination, and whether baptism by immersion was eligible.

The thing that made Glasgow Green different from Hyde Park and other open-air speakers' places was that the speakers could challenge one another to debates. Near the Green, across from Jail Square where the mortuary is now, was the Bird Market, a wooden market where they sold birds and goldfish all week but on Sundays they put down seats and had a platform . . . You had to pay twopence, but you heard a real debate. Both speakers brought their authorities and had piles of books on the table; each of them was given fifteen minutes, then ten minutes, then five.

The popular time for speakers to challenge each other was on Sunday afternoon at two o'clock; all the lecturers would be speaking and suddenly there would be a challenge from one to another. A debate between James Cotterell, an English catholic lecturer, and Harry Alfred Long, a protestant minister, attracted a tremendous crowd. Long would debate with anybody, atheist or catholic: he debated with G. W. Foote, a freethinker and one of the leaders of the Secular Society. Long would say: 'You say we come from monkeys. Speak for yourself.' . . .

Sometimes debates were held on some aspects of Irish history. There was one outstanding lecturer on this subject, a man called James Ward. He was a big hefty fellow, a navvy; I never heard anyone with such a grasp of Irish history. There was also a man called Weir, a very bitter Orangeman who was obsessed by King Billy crossing the Boyne but who could really debate. When he and Weir debated each other they were really informative and worth listening to. Of course the one political question most often raised at Glasgow Green was Irish Home Rule, because it was so closely bound up with religion.[8]

The twentieth century saw, ultimately, a wide decline in old-style religious observance and disputation, partly because the old certainties were challenged by science and biblical criticism, partly because other leisure activities developed that competed with church-going, and partly because it no longer appeared to Protestants to be either so fashionable or so essential to salvation to attend the services. The nutritional scientist, John Boyd Orr, who had himself lost his faith, reflected after the Second World War on the changes since his youth. He did not consider them all for the best:

Today we have labour-saving devices, electricity and other modern conveniences, but it is doubtful if people are happier than they were in the 1880s. At that time there was no fear of war. There were frequent skirmishes to maintain law and order in the Empire, but there had been no great war in which Britain was engaged since the Crimean War. With the advance of science everything was thought to be on the up-and-up. God was in His Heaven and Queen Victoria was on the throne, Britain maintained the Pax Britannica and there was no thought of wars or conscription.

In the 1880s almost everybody attended church regularly, and most believed in the authenticity of the Scriptures and thought of the Christian religion as the only true religion which would ultimately be accepted by all mankind. But changes were beginning to take place, and with some of these I became involved. The theory of evolution which suggested that man had been specially created about four thousand years before the appearance of Christ began to be replaced by Darwin's new idea that man was related to and had evolved from a lower species nearly a million years ago. The people began to be divided between those who had at least a partial acceptance of the new ideas and the fundamentalists who still believed in the verbal inspiration of the Bible. The Churches with the wider outlook began to amalgamate, but the Fundamentalists held out for the old Calvinistic Presbyterian religion. At the time of the amalgamation of the Churches my father, who was a Fundamentalist, vigorously supported the minority, and as feeling ran high he came in for a great deal of criticism. I, who had discarded the old beliefs after leaving home and never attended church, rallied along with my brothers in his support in the exciting battle. As the majority were in favour of the Union of the Churches and the newer and freer outlook, there was little propaganda for the minority. I had just completed my arts course at Glasgow University and I wrote a book, *The History of the Scottish Church Crisis*, in favour of the orthodox group. Such was the interest in the controversy that the book was sold out within a few weeks.

Today, instead of about 99 per cent of the people attending church regularly, there are only about 10 per cent. Whereas, on the Sabbath Day, all the blinds of the shops used to be pulled down in case people going to church should have their thoughts distracted by worldly affairs, now the shops are almost as well lit on a Sunday as they are during the week. The old reverence for the Sabbath Day still exists in the Highlands of Scotland . . .[9]

We have not yet by any means become a country of atheists – most people believe in some kind of a God – but the old centrality of the kirk has left Scottish life. Catholics are the most regular at church services, and Free Presbyterians in the Hebrides the strictest sabbatarians. But dogs have given up church attendance in every denomination.

CHAPTER IX

SEX AND COURTSHIP

There is nothing more difficult for historians to explore than the personal and sexual lives of a past age. The Victorian period has a reputation for prudery: it would be truer to say that it was an age of marked differences between the classes in their sexual behaviour. There were many brothels. William Tait in 1842 estimated that there were 200 in Edinburgh alone, employing at least 800 girls working full time and another 1200 who drifted into the business when other employment was hard to get. Most of the customers were middle class, but some working-class groups were also involved – the military, and Irish navvies with full pockets on pay-day and a long way from home, were often mentioned.

Isabella Bird was a famous Victorian lady explorer, better known for her books on the Rocky Mountains and Japan than for investigating the squalor of her adopted city. Here she explores the seamy side of tenement life in Edinburgh High Street with the same spirit of observation and record that she brought to her travels in distant continents.

> . . . on opening a door we entered a room 12 feet square, with direct light, but with rotten partitions, like all the rest, and so pervious to sound that we heard every word of a narrative of our visit which the "decent widder" before mentioned was giving to an incomer. This room was miserable. Ashes, the accumulation of days, heaped the floor around the fire. There was no other furniture than a bedstead with a straw mattress upon it, a table, and a stool; but it was the occupants, rather than the apparent poverty, who claimed our attention. A girl about eighteen, very poorly dressed, was sitting on the stool; two others, older and very much undressed, were sitting on the

floor, and the three were eating, in most swinish fashion, out of a large black pot containing fish. I have shared a similar meal, in a similar primitive fashion, in an Indian wigwam in the Hudson's Bay Territory, but there the women who worshipped the Great Spirit were modest in their dress and manner, and looked *human*, which these "Christian" young women did not. An infant of about a month old, perfect in its beauty, and smiling in its sleep, "as though heaven lay about it", was on the bed, not dressed, but partly covered with a rug . . . "Where are you from?" one of my philanthropic companions asked of the girl of eighteen, the mother. "Dundee; mother and I came here five weeks ago. I was a mill-worker." "Will the father of your child marry you?" "No, sir." "Have you got work here?" "No, sir; I can't get any." "What are you going to do, then?" "I suppose I must do as the others." She gave this answer without shame, and without effrontery. An upbringing in a Dundee "pend" had not acquainted her with shame as an attendant upon sin. Alas for the hundreds of girl-children growing up among the debasing circumstances of the crowded "lands" of our wynds and closes, without even the instincts of virtue!

The next room, though miserable in itself, was clean and well finished, with pictures hanging upon the partitions. A mother and daughter, both widows, but earning a good living by needlework, were the occupants. They complained bitterly of the gross viciousness of the stair, and of the "awful riot" kept up all night by those newcomers. They told us that the wretched old hag who had come from Dundee had five female lodgers, with only two gowns among them all, and that they were of the poorest and most degraded class. These respectable widows, both elderly women, had lived in that room for seven years, and in the main had had quiet neighbours. They now found themselves in this close proximity to a den of vice, unable to exclude the sounds which came through the partition, and too terrified at night by the drinking and uproar to be able to sleep. The term had lately passed, so they were compelled to bear it.[1]

Many middle-class men appear to have obtained their first sexual experience in such places, but middle-class women were expected to observe absolute chastity before marriage and complete faithfulness afterwards. The double standard did not begin to fall into disrepute until well into the twentieth century.

For the working class, however, there was more sexual freedom and, in a sense, equality. The courtship customs of the rural population were much discussed after 1855, when the publication of the Registrar General for Scotland's annual reports revealed a rate of illegitimacy of almost ten per cent of total births nationally, rising to more than fifteen per cent in Lowland country areas like the north-east and south-west. Dr Strachan, a doctor from Dollar, produced evidence that most working-class girls were pregnant when they got married, and in 1870 in a surprisingly frank article tried to explain to the middle-class readers of the *Scotsman* how the other half loved:

> In courtship – Here it is especially difficult to make the two classes understand the immense difference that exists between them. Working men will not believe that it is possible to court a wife without stolen interviews, with the lady sitting on the gentleman's knee, or enfolded in his arms for hours in the dark; and they are totally incapable of conceiving that a kind look or a gentle pressure of the hand will yield delight a thousand times more exquisite than the coarser freedoms in which they themselves indulge. Consequently, they do not believe that their manner of courtship is confined entirely to themselves. And, on the other hand, even the middle class can scarcely credit the manner of courtship that is almost universal among those who are very little beneath them in station.
>
> Among the working classes, those who are attached to each other never meet in public or in the social circle. If they did, from an excessive desire to 'behave themselves before folk', they would conduct themselves towards each other as entire strangers . . .
>
> The ordinary custom is for the lover to visit his sweetheart after bed-time, when, at a preconcerted signal, the fair one steals out of the house [or] more frequently the lover is secretly admitted into the house . . .
>
> The back of a haystack, or in the barn, or the coal-house,

although not so poetical as among the rigs o' barley, is the more frequent scene of courtship. But the most frequent of all, especially in the case of servant maids, is the girl's bed-room. But, wherever the place, the meeting is by stealth, in the middle of the night, in darkness, lasts for two or three hours, and is repeated weekly.

This is the uniform mode of "courting" amongst the working class in Scotland. It is not confined to engaged lovers, but even acquaintances, who may or may not become lovers, go a-courting. A girl prides herself on the number of such lovers she may have, and young men do not think it wrong to visit different girls after this fashion. It must be remembered that no one in the working class, not even the most particular of parents, thinks there is anything wrong in such courtship. The upper classes would be astonished if they knew how long such visits were continued without a fall from virtue. In many cases they are so continued for years. In some, even under such temptations, no fall from virtue ever takes place. But for too many the following quotation is applicable: ". . . they learn, when it is too late – what women can never learn too early, or impress too strongly on their minds – that a lover's encroachments, to be repelled successfully, must be repelled and negatived at the very outset."

When a fall from virtue does take place, in the great majority of cases, blame cannot be ascribed to one party more than the other; both have fallen victims to the powerful temptations to which they have exposed themselves by ignorantly and thought-lessly following old-established customs in which they have been trained to see nothing wrong.

But there are cases – the upper classes would be astonished if they knew how many – where at least one of the parties deserves no sympathy but utter detestation. Many young men, and this is especially true of agricultural labourers, are in the habit of going a "courting" merely as a bit of fun, and with the deliberate intention of seducing the poor girl if they can. They know well the shame and misery to which she must be subjected; but calculating on their own chances of escaping all conse-quences, they do not hesitate to gratify their passions at her expense; and it is very common for such persons to boast of their successes to each other. The apathy and indifference with which such deliberate seducers are treated among their own class is a sad manifestation of the low tone of feeling which I have been endeavouring to describe ... if there were a spark of manly spirit in the father, the brothers, the cousins, the friends of the girls, the cowardly scoundrels would not escape being kicked and cudgelled wherever they dared to show their faces.[2]

In our own century there has emerged a greater uniformity of culture in sexual matters, as a result of changes in education and an exposure to the common media of film, radio, television and popular press. Nevertheless, for a long time differences between the classes persisted. Middle-class children still often found it difficult to discover the facts of life or to meet the opposite sex. David and Lionel Daiches were the children of a famous rabbi in Edinburgh, and in the interwar period the family used to take its holidays in the East Neuk of Fife. They found the local chip shop was a place where the youth of Crail met:

These were the years of my adolescence, and the young men and women hanging around Mrs Aird's stood for a world of sexual adventure whose very thought was absolutely incompatible with the atmosphere of our family life. As far as Lionel and I were able to discover, sex did not exist in the Daiches family. Neither of our parents ever addressed to us a single word about it, at any time. My father's notion, I think, was that one kept oneself pure by hard work and idealistic ambitions until one had completed one's professional training, and then a suitable bride was brought to one's attention, with whom one fell in love and in marriage to whom one's sex interests were first awakened. I found my own adolescence disturbing and embarrassing, and I thought the imaginations to which it gave rise were both unique and guilty. I suppose it is comic or even pathetic that a small confectioner's-cum-fish and chip shop in a little seaside town should have represented to me, and I think to Lionel as well, a world of forbidden desire. For years afterwards the smell of fish and chips had a more erotic tang to me than perfumes named

'Ecstasy' or 'Desire', though by the time I was really grown up my taste had become more conventional in this respect.[3]

Very different from this was the experience of another Jewish boy, Ralph Glasser, who grew up in the Gorbals when they were among the most deprived inner-city areas in Europe. He worked in a clothier's sweat shop, where he met Annie. Elsewhere in his book he describes the immediate but squalid and casual sex of the closes and the ash-pits, the sexual exploitation of women and the anxieties of men: but this first love was for real.

The commonest injury at the sewing machines was a needle through a finger tip. The trade joke was that you were not a proper machinist till that had happened to you. But it was far from a joke when it did. In the immediate agony the victim instinctively pulled her impaled finger away and the needle broke, leaving part of itself embedded under the nail. Blood-poisoning, and sometimes amputation, could follow.

One day Annie's hair caught in the sewing foot of her machine. Some was actually drawn down to the shuttle and sewn into the seam she was working on, and her head was pulled down and banged hard against the fast moving vertical piston of the sewing head. No great injury was done, but she sustained a nasty bruising on the forehead and some blood was shed. Her cry was heard, as might the high-pitched mew of a kitten, through the general clamour and roar. Her bank of machines was the nearest to where I stood at the pressers' table and I got to her first, seized a pair of shears and cut her hair free, and then ran and got the first aid box from the boss's office and dabbed iodine on the cuts on her forehead. She wept a little but set her lips together and tried to push me away so that she could turn back to her work. Fearfully she glanced round at the other machine hands pushing pieces of garments along the wooden trough towards her work place and then at the passer who was getting worried because of the blockage of work beginning to grow at this point. For when an accident happened, unless it was a serious one, as when Jack Nimms dropped a press iron and burnt and tore the flesh all down his leg and broke the shin bone and some bones in his foot, never to walk properly again, the pace of work did not slacken. So now the machinists to Annie's right continued to push their completed pieces along the trough to her, and the two on her left were sitting waiting for work, losing working time, and money. Until she did *her* seaming up on these pieces, they could not do their part on them. If the hold up lasted much longer we would all be losing money. Even as I put a bandage round her forehead she reached under the sewing machine to remove the shuttle and began to clear it of shreds of her hair preparatory to re-threading.

Her voice shaky with the pain she said: 'Ye'd be'er le' me go! Thanks all the same. Ah've got tae ge' on wi' ma pieces now!'

'Can ye that?' I asked, for she was white as chalk.

'Ah'll have tae!' She gave me a quick taut smile and bent her head to re-thread the needle.

And so we drew close.

Annie had fiery red hair, greenish eyes, dimpled, laughing features, creamy skin, and a lovely, taut, sinuous figure. She did not walk so much as strut, swinging her body on flexed muscles in a way that shocked some of the older folk.

'There's that Annie Dalrymple flaunting herself! The brazen girl!' I did not think the word brazen fitted her. With me she was innocent. She had, however, a hungry awareness, an impatience for experience, that might have been misunderstood. Or perhaps it was I who misunderstood?

She seemed to look far into me, eyes wide in wonder, face aglow; and her body sweat, a hot vapour sweeping up from the depths of her, overwhelmed me like a potent drug. That first experience of mingling chemistry was like a magical discovery long imagined, and claimed at last.

We sought to know everything about one another at one breath, one glance. Miraculously that did seem to happen as we walked the pavements at night hand in hand, or stood on the Suspension Bridge over the Clyde, feeling it vibrate with passing footsteps, and watched the lights along the river bank reflected in the dark oily waters; or sat in silence in the front seat of the upper deck of a tram and let our dream worlds flow together.

We played the game of telepathic sympathy, comparing what we had each thought at a certain hour when we had been apart and taking delight in finding that we had been closely in tune.

Sometimes we bought a tuppenny bag of chips to eat together as we walked, and after a time would be amazed to find that we had forgotten to eat them, and that the greasy chips were stone cold.

One day, some weeks after we had first gone out together, we wandered in silence to some long grass in the Park, and lay down and looked up at the sky, and after a while timidly turned to each other. Innocents, we learnt from each other intuitively, slowly. After a few months we went for the first of many hiking weekends to the Socialist Camp at Carbeth, a few miles north of Glasgow.

Before we set off she whispered shyly: 'Will ye put somethin' on yersel' when – when we're taegither?'

'Aye, ah've bought some.'

Our sublime unity continued for about a year.[4]

Finally, in any age there is sexuality at another level, of the frustrated but hopeful person in a crowd. Edwin Muir's portrait of the Edinburgh streets in the 1930s, with their pedestrian life not yet driven away by traffic fumes and with fewer amusements like television to keep the people indoors, evokes this intensity. Notice how one of the attractions of pubs, then, as opposed to now, was that women were generally kept out of them.

In Princes Street you are seen, whoever you may be, and this knowledge, partly alarming and partly exhilarating like a plunge into cold water, forces the pedestrian to assemble his powers and be as intent as his neighbours. The concentrated force of observation sent out by the people he passes is sometimes so strong that he has the feeling of breaking, as he passes, through a series of invisible obstacles, of snapping a succession of threads laden with some retarding current. In London he can walk the most crowded streets for hours without feeling that he is either visible or existent: a disconcerting, almost frightening experience for a Scotsman until he gets used to it. But the crowd in a

London street is mainly composed of people who are going somewhere, while the crowd in Princes Street is simply there; and even if you are going somewhere you cannot ignore it; it acquisitively stretches out and claims you. For it is there not only to observe, but also to be observed, and if you omit one of these duties you strike at its *amour-propre*, and perhaps at its existence. If a continuous relay of absent-minded philosophers could be let loose in Princes Street, the very foundations of its life would be shaken, and it would either rise and massacre these innocent revolutionaries or else die of disappointment.

This apparently unmotivated intentness of Scottish street crowds is filled with unsatisfied desire. It is as if the eye were trying to undertake the functions of all the other senses, and the accumulated frustration and hope of a people were thrown into a painfully concentrated look. In such unnatural circumstances the eye acquires an almost prehensile power; it flings out invisible tentacles which draw its victims to it and into it, so that it can devour, digest and excrete them with lightning rapidity. This process resembles a sort of reciprocal and incorporeal massacre, in which eater and eaten remain unchanged. It is finally a little exhausting for such a diet does not allay hunger; after the thousandth meal the eye remains as starved as after the first: it may in the course of time assume a brazen, defiant, even a pleading expression, but it is always unsatiated.

This yearning again is drenched in unsatisfied sex. Nowhere that I have been is one so bathed and steeped and rolled about in floating sexual desire as in certain streets of Glasgow and Edinburgh. This desire fills the main thoroughfare and overflows into all the adjacent pockets and backwaters: the tea-rooms, restaurants and cinema lounges. The only refuges from it are the pubs, which convention forbids women to enter, but which, nevertheless, are always well attended. There, like sailors after a difficult and nerve-whipping voyage, the men put into harbour and wrap themselves in the safe cloak of alcohol, which Luther thought such a secure defence against the flesh. But those whom Princes Street leaves still unsatisfied resort to the tea-rooms and lounges, where they languidly steep themselves until they are quite saturated. Among the tea-rooms in Princes Street there are places more strange than a dream. Passing through a corridor one enters an enormous room filled with dull and glassy light, and as silent as if it were miles under-sea. Nereids float in the submarine glimmer, bearing trays in their hands; and over glassy tables the drowned sway like seaweeds, the sluggish motion of the tide turning their heads now this way, now that, with an effect of hypnotic ogling. When one gets used to the light one sees that these amphibious sea-plant-like forms are respectable members of the Edinburgh bourgeoisie, that their clothes are quite dry, and that the sea change they have suffered is temporary, having been paid for. They are well-dressed people, and they are drinking tea and eating scones.[5]

CHAPTER X

DRINKING

Like many northern peoples (the Swedes, the Finns, even the American Indians), the Scots have a reputation for being free to the point of abandon in their drinking habits. In Victorian times it was very normal for the poverty of the working class to be attributed to their misuse of alcohol rather than to their low wages: however unfair, the accusation let the middle classes off the hook of responsibility. Certainly very large quantities of drink, especially of whisky, were consumed. In the 1830s it was measured as two-and-a-half gallons of legally distilled spirit a year per head as a population, and quantities of illicit whisky were drunk as well. It was still about a gallon a head as late as the 1910s, when the Chancellor's taxes and the start of modern licensing laws during the First World War began to bring consumption under control. Today, except in the Highlands, beer has largely replaced whisky as the regular tipple, but Scotland continues to be cursed by an abnormally high incidence of alcohol-related illness.

There is no doubt that all classes imbibed freely, and had done so even in the eighteenth century. Henry Cockburn remembered as a child in the 1790s encountering his father's friends in the legal and political élite of Edinburgh relaxing in an inn in the Moorfoots.

The old ale-house at Heriot was the first inn I ever entered. My father, who, I think, was then convener of the county of Edinburgh, went out to attend some meeting of road trustees, and he took a parcel of us with him. He rode; and we had a chaise to ourselves – happiness enough for boys. But more was in store for us; for he remained at the mansion-house of Middleton with his friend Mr Hepburn, and we went on, about four miles farther, to Heriot House, where we breakfasted and passed the day, fishing, bathing, and rioting. It was the first inn of most of the party. What delight! A house to ourselves, on a moor; a burn; nobody to interfere with us; the power of ringing the bell as we chose; the ordering of our own dinner; blowing the peat fire; laughing as often and as loud as we liked. What a day! We rang the hand-bell for the pure pleasure of ringing, and enjoyed our independence by always going out and in by the window. This dear little inn does not now exist, but its place is marked by a square of ash trees. It was a bright, beautiful August day.

We returned to the inn of Middleton, on our way home, about seven in the evening; and there we saw another scene. People sometimes say that there is no probability in Scott's making the party in Waverley retire from the Castle to the Howf; but these people were not with me at the inn at Middleton, about forty years ago. The Duke of Buccleuch was living at Dalkeith; Henry Dundas at Melville; Robert Dundas, the Lord Advocate, at Arniston; Hepburn of Clerkington at Middleton; and several of the rest of the aristocracy of Midlothian within a few miles; all with their families, and luxurious houses; yet had they, to the number of twelve or sixteen, congregated in this wretched ale-house for a day of freedom and jollity. We found them roaring and singing, and laughing, in a low-roofed room scarcely large enough to hold them, with wooden chairs and a sanded floor. When their own lacqueys, who were carrying on high life in the kitchen, did not choose to attend, the masters were served by two women. There was plenty of wine, particularly claret, in rapid circulation on the table; but my eye was chiefly attracted by a huge bowl of hot whisky punch, the steam of which was almost dropping from the roof, while the odour was enough to perfume the whole parish. We were called in and made to partake, and were very kindly used, particularly by my uncle, Harry Dundas. How they did joke and laugh! with songs, and toasts, and disputation, and no want of practical fun. I don't remember anything they said, and probably did not understand it. But the noise, and the heat, and the uproarious mirth – I think I hear and feel them yet. My father was in the chair; and he having gone out for a little, one of us boys was voted into his place, and the boy's health was drank, with all the honours, as "the young convener. Hurra! hurra! may he be a better man than his father! hurra! hurra!" I need not mention that they were all in a state of elevation; though there was nothing like absolute intoxication, so far as I could judge."[1]

Different pubs had different appearances: in the nineteenth-century inner city the contrast between the glitter and show of a public house and the shabby character of its clientele was the subject of much comment from temperance reformers, and Alexander Brown, describing Glasgow in 1858, added a further description of public drunkenness which became all too familiar in the streets of the city after closing time.

The public house next to the house of God, by far the most important institution in the city, if we may judge from the encouragement it receives, is now reaping a "delightful harvest!" In almost every street, almost every shop seems a public house, just as if the authorities had licensed them all out of a gigantic pepper-box, sending them all broadcast over the city, in accordance with the popular adage, "the more the merrier." One can scarcely realise the enormous number of these houses, with their flaring gas lights in frosted globes, and brightly gilded spirit casks, lettered by the number of gallons, under the cognomen of "Old Tom" or "Young Tom," as the case may be, with the occasional mirror at the extreme end of the shop, reflecting at once in fine perspective the waters of a granite fountain fronting the door, and the entrance of poor broken-down victims, who stand in pitiful burlesque in their dirty rags, amid all this pomp and mocking grandeur! We have often thought, as we have seen these mirrors, that they must be the appropriate gifts of some benevolent institution, or Total Abstinence Society, desirous of realising the sentiment of the poet,

> Oh wud some power the giftie gie us
> To see oursel's as ithers see us.

*

But this institution – the public house – is really deserving serious attention; and we wonder, that while it continues among us, "time honoured" and "hallowed," no effort is made to put it on a perfect equality with the church. Had every public house a spire, no one can have any idea how far it would go to give ornament to the city. It would then realise to the stranger its ancient character, spoken of by local historians, as being "the most beautiful city of the world," and, at the same time, pay a graceful tribute to *modern* opinion of its present character, such as that given by Mr. Kohl, the German traveller, who calls it at once "the most religious and the most drunken city in Europe or the world . . ."

[After closing time] if the moving masses are now a little thinned, very certain it is, that a few of them do not walk precisely in the same straight line as they were wont an hour ago. Here, one poor fellow from the left wing approaches us somewhat obliquely. He now falls out of the ranks – his head a little drooping. At length he commits it to the care of a shop-shutter, which he affectionately embraces. Some way on, another "half-seas-over" is met, who retires into the privacy of a back street, and, after sundry violent hiccupings, he blames "the air" for the consequences.[2]

Scenes like these led to accusations from outsiders that Glasgow was 'miles worse': the aspersion was indignantly denied by James Devon, the medical officer at Glasgow Prison, in 1913.

In Glasgow we are accustomed periodically to learn from the testimony of English visitors that we are the most drunken city in the kingdom; and tourists write to the newspapers and tell their experiences and impressions of sights seen in our streets, quoting statistics of the arrests for drunkenness. This alternates with panegyrics of the city as the most progressive in the world – "the model municipality." We are neither so bad nor so good as we are sometimes said to be. That the streets of Glasgow – or rather some of them – are at times disgraced by the drunkenness of some who use them, is quite true; but the fact that some travellers at some times see more drunk people in a given area than may be seen in any English city does not justify the inference that the inhabitants of Glasgow are more drunken than those of other cities. In no English city is there so large a population on so small an area. If there are more drunk in a given space there are also more sober people; but only the drunks are observed. In Glasgow, moreover, the ordinary drink is whisky, which rapidly makes a man reel. It excites more markedly than the beer consumed so generally in England, which makes a man not so much drunk as sodden. If it were worth the retort, one might point out that even if it be true that in Scotland you may see more people drunk, in England you see fewer people sober.[3]

It was also a recurrent theme that different people took their drink in different ways. Sir Archibald Geikie's journeys on the First Geological Survey of Scotland carried him the length and breadth of the country in the Victorian period. In this reflection on Scottish drinking habits, he concluded that Highlanders drank steadily but held their drink, while Lowlanders aimed to get drunk in order to obliterate the miseries of industrial life. (The 'lowdamer' mentioned was laudanum, an unconcentrated form of opium in solution.)

The question is often asked why so much whisky should be consumed in Scotland. One explanation assigns as the reason the moist, chilly climate of the country, and this cause may perhaps be allowed to have some considerable share in producing the national habit. No small proportion of the spirit, especially in the Highlands, is drunk by men who are certainly not at all drunkards, and who can toss off their glass without being any the worse of it, if, indeed, they are not, as they themselves maintain, a good deal the better. But it must be confessed that, especially among the working classes in the Lowlands, tipsiness is a state of pleasure to be looked forward to with avidity, to be gained as rapidly and maintained as long as possible. To many wretched beings it offers a transient escape from the miseries of life, and brings the only moments of comparative happiness which they ever enjoy. They live a double life – one part in the gloom and hardship of the workaday world, and the other in the dreamland into which whisky introduces them. The blacksmith expressed this view of life who, when remonstrated with by his clergyman for drunkenness, asked if his reverend monitor had himself ever been overcome with drink, and, on receiving a negative reply, remarked: 'Ah, sir, if ye was ance richt drunk, ye wadna want ever to be sober again.'

The desire of getting quickly intoxicated is perhaps best illustrated among the miners in the great coal-fields. Thus an Ayrshire collier was heard discoursing to his comrades about a novel way he had found out of getting more rapidly drunk: 'Jist ye putt in thretty draps o' lowdamer into your glass and ye're fine an' fou' in ten minutes.' In the same county a publican advertised the potent quality of the liquor he sold by placing in his window a paper with this announcement: 'Drunk for three bawbees, and mortal for threepence.'

The quality of the whisky is often bad, since much of what is sold is raw-grain spirit, sometimes adulterated with water and then strengthened with some cheap liquid that will give it pungency. There was some truth in the reply of the Highlander to the minister who was warning him against excess, and assuring him that whisky was a very bad thing: 'Deed an' it is, sir, specially baad whusky.' The mere addition of water would do no harm, rather the reverse; but it would be detected at once by the experienced toper. 'This is no' a godly place at all, at all,' said a discontented labourer in the Perthshire Highlands. 'They dinna preach the gospel here – and they wahtter the whusky.'

Strangers are often astonished at the extent of the draughts of undiluted whisky which Highlanders can swallow, without any apparent ill effects. Burt tells us that in his time, that is in the third decade of the eighteenth century, Highland gentlemen could take 'even three or four quarts at a sitting, and that in general the people that can pay the purchase, drink it without moderation.' In the year 1860, in a walk from Kinlochewe through the mountains to Ullapool, I took with me as a guide an old shepherd who had lived there all his life. The distance, as I wished to go, amounted to thirty miles, mostly of rough, trackless ground, and among the refreshments for the journey a bottle of whisky was included. Not being used to the liquor, I hardly tasted it all day, but when we reached the ferry opposite Ullapool, Simon pitched the empty bottle into the loch. He had practically drunk the whole of its contents, and was as cool and collected as when we started in the morning.

All over the Highlands 'a glass' serves as ready-money payment for any small service rendered, such as when a driver has brought a guest to a farm or country-house from some distance, when a workman has completed his repairs and has some miles to walk back to his home, or when a messenger has come from a neighbour and waits to take back your answer. A piper who has marched round behind the chairs of a dinner party at a great Highland laird's, blowing his pipes till it seems as if the windows should be broken, ends his performance by halting at the side of the lady of the house, to whom is brought and from whom he receives a full glass of the native beverage.[4]

Edwin Muir, in 1932, similarly found cultural differences in drinking habits: he observed that the working class got drunk noisily and in public, the middle class quietly and in private.

Scottish streets are given an atmosphere of their own simply by the number of drunk people that one encounters in them. Whether the Scottish people drink more than other peoples it would be impossible to say; but they give the impression of doing so, because of the abundant signs of public drunkenness that one finds in such towns as Edinburgh and Glasgow and even in small country towns on a Saturday night. During a fortnight's stay in Edinburgh I did not get through a single evening without seeing at least one example of outrageous or helpless drunkenness, and I had spent two years in London without coming across more than four or five. I think the explanation is that Scottish people drink spasmodically and intensely, for the sake of a momentary but complete release, whereas the English like to bathe and paddle about bucolically in a mild puddle of beer. One might put down this difference to a difference of national temperament or of national religion or to a hundred other things; there is no doubt, in any case, that the drinking habits of the Scots, like their dances, are far wilder than those of the English. The question is not a very important or interesting one. Much more interesting is the difference which class distinction produces in drunkenness in a Scottish town. There are as many drunk men and women in Princes Street on a Saturday night as in Leith Walk. But there are far fewer signs of them, and this is mainly due to social causes. Even when a man is in other ways incapable, he tries to conform to his particular code of manners, and so drunkenness in Princes Street is quiet and genteel: shown in a trifling unsteadiness of gait or a surprising affability of aspect by which the middle-class Edinburgh man manages to suggest that he is somehow uphold-ing something or other which distinguishes him from the work-ing classes. He is helped in this purpose by certain benevolent external circumstances, however, such as that the whisky sold in Princes Street is better than the whisky one buys in Leith Walk, and that it is always easy to get a taxi in Princes Street after ten o'clock. By means of these discreet ambulances the unconscious and semi-conscious are inconspicuously removed. In Leith Walk they lie about the pavement until their friends or the police laboriously lead them away. Thus appearances are kept up, appearances upon which a whole host of the most important things depend.[5]

Finally, there was Hugh MacDiarmid's spirited defence of a Glasgow pub of 1952, 'frowsy and fusty enough to suit my taste'; he de-nounced what he saw as an Anglicizing tendency to make drinking cosy and attractive to women as well as men.

I have never been able, despite repeated efforts, to understand the periodicity of those complaints against the Scottish pub which have been made during the past half century. Made, I suspect, when not by women or clergymen, either by English visitors or by Scots who, as Sir Walter Scott said, 'unScotched make damned bad Englishmen'. They are usually accompanied by envious comparisons with the amenities of English inns, which we are told are far more sociable and cater to family parties in a way Scottish pubs do not. For, in the latter, at their most typical, the rule is 'men only' and 'no sitting' – you stand at the counter with your toes in that narrow sawdust-filled trough which serves as a comprehensive combined ash-tray, litter-bin, and cuspidor. So it was when I first began to drink nearly fifty years ago; so it still is for the most part. Certainly nowadays, in addition to the common bars and to the jug (or family) departments to which women, mostly of a shawled, slatternly, and extremely subfusc order, still repair with all the ancient furtiveness, there are bright chromium-filled saloon bars, cocktail bars, and other modern accessories in the more pretentious places. And even in most of the ordinary bars there is now a fair sprinkling of women not only of the 'lower orders' or elderly at that, but gay young things, merry widows, and courtesans. Men (if you can call them that) even take their wives and daughters along with them to these meretricious, deScotticised resorts.

Now, I am not a misogynist by any means. I simply believe there is a time and a place for everything – yes, literally, *every-thing*. And like a high proportion of my country's regular and purposive drinkers I greatly prefer a complete absence of music and very little illumination. I am therefore a strong supporter of the lower – or lowest – type of 'dive' where drinking is the principal purpose and no one wants to be distracted from that absorbing business by music, women, glaring lights, chromium fittings, too many mirrors unless sufficiently fly-spotted and mildewed, or least of all, any fiddling trivialities of *l'art nouveau*. If there are still plenty of pubs in Glasgow which conform to these requirements and remain frowsy and fusty enough to suit my taste and that of my boon companions, in another respect the old order has changed sadly and I fear irreversibly. Our Scottish climate – not to speak of the soot-laden, catarrh-producing atmosphere of Glasgow in particular – makes us traditionally great spirit-drinkers. That has changed. Most of us cannot afford – or at any rate cannot get – much whisky or, for the matter of that, any other spirit. There are, of course, desperate characters who drink methylated spirits. I have known – and still know – resolute souls partial to a mixture of boot-black and 'meth,' and I remember when I was in the Merchant Service during the recent War a few hardy characters who went to the trouble of stealing old compasses off the boats at Greenock (where we had the largest small-boat pool in Europe) in order to extract from them the few drops of spirit (well mixed with crude-oil and verdigris) they contained. But in Glasgow pubs today at least ninety percent of the drinking is of beer – and mere 'swipes' at that; 'beer' that never saw a hop. I can remember the time when it was the other way about. What beer was consumed was used simply as a 'chaser' to the whisky in precisely the same way as a 'boilermaker' in New York. For of course you get drunk quicker on whisky plus water than on neat whisky, and whisky and soda is an English monstrosity no true Scot can countenance at all.

There are other sorry changes in even the lowest-down pubs which in general hold to the grim old tradition of the true Scottish 'boozer'. The question of hours, for example. In London one can still drink legally twenty-three hours out of twenty-four [this in 1935]. That is because London is a congeries of different boroughs which have different 'permitted hours' so that by switching from one borough at closing time it is easy to find another where 'they' will still be open for an hour or two longer. In Glasgow, moreover, unlike London, there are few facilities for drinking outside the permitted hours. For most people, that is. It will hardly be thought that I am pleading for decreased consumption, but I believe that the same amount of strong drink taken in a leisurely way over a fair number of hours is less harmful than the rush to squeeze in the desired number of drinks in the short time the law allows. Our national poet, Robert Burns, was right when he said: 'Freedom and whisky gang thegither.' What he meant is precisely what my own motto means: 'They do not love liberty who fear licence.' I speak for that large body of my compatriots who uphold this great principle and regard respectability and affectations of any kind as our deadliest enemy. There are, of course, clubs and hotels, but *hoi polloi* have nothing to do with either of these.[6]

The modern trend in pubs is, of course, completely in the opposite direction, especially since the move in the 1960s to liberalize drinking hours, to serve food, to allow children into certain rooms, and positively to encourage the women to join the men in the bar. What MacDiarmid would have said about bar lunches for all the family, posterity can only guess.

CHAPTER XI

CELEBRATION

The popular image of Scotland is not of a country given much to celebration, except perhaps on Hogmanay with plenty of drink circulating. The legacy of seventeenth-century Calvinism was certainly to render Sunday very strictly kept, to frown on excesses in weddings and funerals, and to discourage the 'superstitious' celebration of Christmas, Easter and those other Christian festivals that were observed by Catholics, Anglicans and Lutherans in other European countries. Nevertheless, the cheerlessness of life is easily exaggerated, as people will soon find one thing to celebrate if another is banned, and in any case it defied church power to be strict about everything. In traditional rural societies, there was a cycle of special days and special events that punctuated the year, as exemplified in the following description of Orkney first published in 1920 when its author was eighty-two. The 'old style' referred to in the opening line predated the adjustment to the Gregorian Calendar which deleted twelve days in 1752, and it is clear that Christmas Day, 'Yule Day', had always been celebrated in Orkney in one form or another.

Though the time was changed in the year 1752, Orcadians held to the old style, which was twelve days later. Even within forty years back, one old residenter in Finistown stuck tenaciously to old Yule Day and old New Year's Day.

Preparations for these feast days were made by baking scones, brewing ale, and by taking in an extra quantity of peats on Yule Even, the peaty neuk being filled up to the rafters with a supply sufficient to last over New Year's Day. On Yule Day no work was done, the day being spent in visiting and treating. If open weather, one or two of the old men made a pilgrimage in the

early morning to the top of the hill, to see if any trace of frost
could be found, for a green Yule augured ill for the health of
the community. A dance for the young people was held in the
evening, all returning to their homes for supper, for that was
the event of the day. The other meals of the day consisted of
the usual cheese and bread accompanied with ale, but there was
always "flesh" for supper.

The advent of New Year's Day was heralded by the young
people going from house to house singing the New Year's Song,
and this was kept up until a late date. First-footing, still in
fashion, was accompanied wih nettle-burning. The meaning or
origin of the latter custom the writer never heard, but it was a
very common practice. Young folk were on the outlook for
some time previous, and great secrecy was kept regarding the
whereabouts of a good fresh bunch of nettles. Of course he was
the victor who could strike the foremost blow, but it was not
allowable to touch the face, only the hands and feet. Some wily
ones, rising early on New Year's morning, secreted the nettles
underneath the blankets, whereupon the sleeper, on giving a
morning stretch, received a severe burn on his feet coming in
contact with the noxious weed. Otherwise the day was passed in
much the same style as Christmas Day, only with the addition
of ba'-playing for the men and boys, and for others the tamer
amusement of weighing, all and sundry repairing to the barn of
the licensed malster or the miller, to learn how many pounds
avoirdupois they had gained or lost since last New Year's
Day . . .

Other feasts and holidays held by the people in old times
have now passed into oblivion. Aphelly Day came in the end of
January, and was observed, like New Year's Day, by feasting and
ba'-playing.

The quarter days were Candlemas, Beltane, Lammas and
Hallowmas. The airt of the wind on the quarter days betokened
the direction of the prevailing winds during that quarter. The
weather of Candlemas and Beltane days received particular
attention, and even yet one hears it referred to in a jocular
manner:

> If the lavroo' sings afore Candlemas Day,
> Sheu'll greet aifter.
> If Candlemas Day is fair an' clear
> Hid'll be twa winters that year.

On Candlemas "flesh-maet" and rich brose or soup were substituted for the usual vegetarian diet. Beltane was observed chiefly as a term day, but the airt of wind and the weather on that day were regarded as predictive of the quality of the growing crop.

> If the wind is sooth,
> There'll be bread for every mooth;
> If the wind is east,
> There'll be hunger for man an' baste;
> If the wind is west,
> The crop'll be lang an' slushy;
> If the wind is nort',
> The crop'll be short an' trig.

John's Mass was celebrated in June by the lighting of large bonfires in the different districts. In Firth the three most important bonfires were: one above Moan, one in Kingsdale, and another above the shore near the boundary between Firth and Rendall. The superstitious element was strongly evidence in the rites performed round the John's Mass bonfire. Herd-boys and lasses too availed themselves of every opportunity to pull large quantities of heather, which were piled up in readiness for the day. When evening came the fire was lit by a live coal from a neighbouring house. A bone was always thrown into the fire whenever one could be readily got. The farmers who wished a bountiful crop the ensuing harvest had large heathery torches made, lit them at the John's Mass fire, and never allowed them to get extinguished till the whole circumference of the fields had been traversed. This ceremony was gone through with the utmost gravity, after a solemn procession had circled round the blazing pile for some time. The two fires in the north side of Firth could be easily seen by those taking part in each, and probably two miles apart. At a certain previously arranged hour, a party from each fire set out with several heather torches, one of which was lit at each fire and carried along hurriedly till both parties met. This successfully accomplished meant that the farming interests of the two communities would meet with prosperity. As the dusky hour of midnight drew near, merriment waxed fierce and furious. After dancing till the early dawn set in, the young people wound up by jumping through the flames in a manner resembling the orgies of our Pagan ancestors, and by wildly pursuing each other home with blazing firebands.

Hallowe'en, that night when witches and warlocks paced abroad, and special opportunity was given to those who wished "to pierce the shades of dim futurity," was celebrated in Orkney by many of the observances described by Burns in his "Hallowe'en." Kail-runts, pulled at random in the dark, symbolised the stature and build of one's future spouse, while the buds on the stalk intimated the number of one's progeny. In casting glasses, a glass was filled with water, and upon the white of an egg being poured into it, any one gifted with a fertile imagination could portray all the details of one's future.

Then the process which the national bard calls "winnan three wechts o' naething" was very popular among young people. This was done by going out into the dark barn, leaving both doors open, and performing a sham process of winnowing, having nought on the sieve but a pair of scizzors or a knife. An apparition having the appearance of one's life partner was expected to pass the barn door. Another custom was to throw a ball of worsted down into the kiln, retaining the end of the worsted in the hand, and standing in the kiln-door, to unwind the ball, meanwhile repeating: "Wha hauds i' me clew's end?" In confirmation of the verity of these practices, it was told that a young woman winding her clew at the kiln door was replied to by the voice of the herd-boy. Incensed at not hearing the manly tones expected, she struck out in the dark. In after years, when cropping her husband's hair, she remarked on the "norrows" (bumps) on his head. His explanation was: "Du's thoo no mind the whack thoo gaed me i' the kiln-door on Hallowe'en?"[1]

In the early nineteenth-century town there was a strong tradition of horse-play, too. To the historian, one of the most interesting annual celebrations in the burghs was the King's Birthday, riotously celebrated in Edinburgh until 1810. At these celebrations, described here by Robert Chambers in 1825, the line could be crossed between good fun and a political demonstration. In 1792 the occasion was used to demonstrate support for the ideals of the French Revolution, to burn images of Henry Dundas, local MP and Home Secretary, and to break the windows of the Lord Provost's house. Even under less tense circumstances, what was officially intended to be a mark of loyalty and respect to His Majesty easily slid into a ritual mocking of authority and the taunting of the Town Guard (or *Rattens*). The cruelty to animals was, unfortunately, an acceptable part of street life in the pre-Victorian world: cats are being maltreated here, but it was also common to celebrate Halloween with cockfighting in the parish schools, the bodies of the losers being presented to the teacher.

From the time of the Restoration, when the Magistrates celebrated the "glorious twenty-ninth of May" upon a public stage at the Cross, down to the year 1810, when the last illness of our late excellent Sovereign threw a damp over the spirits of the nation at large, Edinburgh was remarkable for her festive observance of the *King's Birth-Day*. This was one of the great holidays of Edinburgh, though one which was usually attended with fully as much licence and outrage as loyalty and happiness.

By the boys, in particular, the fourth of June used to be looked forward to with the most anxious anticipations of delight. Six months before that day, they had begun to save as many of their *Saturday's halfpence* as could possibly be spared from present necessities; and for a good many weeks, nothing was thought of but the day, and nothing was done but making preparations for it. White-washing and partly-painting *stair-fits*, was one of the principal preparations. A club of boys, belonging perhaps to the same street, or close, or *land*, would pitch upon a particular *stair-fit*, or, if that was not to be had, a piece of ordinary dead wall, as much out of the way as possible; and this became, for the time, the object of all their attentions, and their ordinary place of meeting. Here, upon the great day, they were to muster all their arms and ammunition, kindle a fire, and amuse themselves from morning to night, with crackers, serpents, squibs, and certain Lilliputian pieces of ordnance, mounted upon the ends of sticks, and set off with matches or *pee-oys*.

For a fortnight immediately before the day, great troops of boys used to go out of town, to the Braid and Pentland Hills, and bring home whins for *busking* the lamp-posts, which were at that period of the year stripped of their lamps – as well as boughs for the adornment of the *bower-like* stations which they had adapted for their peculiar amusement. Of course, they were not more regular in these forages, than the Magistrates were with edicts, forbidding and threatening to punish the same.

One of the most important preliminaries of the Birth-Day, was the decoration with flowers of the statue of King Charles in the Parliament Square. This was always done by young men who had been brought up in Heriot's Hospital – otherwise "*Auld Herioters*," – who were selected for this purpose, on account of the experience they had had in dressing the statue of George Heriot, with flowers, on *his* birth-day, which was always held on the first Monday of June. The flowers for the statue of Charles and his horse were prepared, on the eve of the birthday, in the large vestry of the Old Church – now the Old Church itself – and, according to report, the Herioters were allowed L.10 for their trouble by the Magistrates.

The morning of the Birth-Day was ushered in by firing of the aforesaid pieces of ordnance, to the great annoyance of many a Lawn-Market and Luckenbooths merchant, accustomed, time out of mind, to be awaked four hours later by the incipient squall of the saut-wives and fish-wives at eight o'clock. As for the boys, sleep of course had not visited a single juvenile eye-lid during the whole night; and it was the same thing whether they lay in bed, or were up and out of doors at work. Great part of the morning was spent in kindling the *bane-fires*, preparing the ammunition, and adorning the public wells with evergreens. The wells thus honoured were the Bow-Head, Lawn-Market, Cross, and Fountain-Wells; and, besides branches of trees, there was always an oil-painting hung at the top, or a straw-stuffed figure set up against the bottom. Both around the fires and the wells were great groups of boys, who busied themselves in annoying the passengers with cries of "*Mind the Bane-fire!*" or "*Mind------*" the person, whoever he might be, that was represented by the painting or the *effigy*. A halfpenny was a valuable acquisition, and of course added to the general stock of the company, to be expended in the purchase of gun-powder. These elegant exhibitions were the wonder and admiration of many a knot of country-people, some of whom had come from a great distance, to witness the *fun* and the *ferlies* of the King's Birth-Day.

About seventy years ago, it was customary to fix figures of the Sun, the Moon, and the Globe, upon the top of the Cross-Well; and these being pierced with small holes, and communicating by a pipe with the cistern, water was made to play from their faces in a very beautiful manner. This continued from twelve to four, and was sanctioned by the Magistrates. It was to this well that the ancient pillory of the city was fixed.

Towards the afternoon, the *bane-fires* were in a great measure deserted; for by that time the boys had usually collected a good sum, and began to bend their thoughts upon the great business of the evening. A new object of attention now sprung up – namely, the meeting of the Magistrates and their friends in the Parliament House, in order to drink the King's health. In the Great Hall, formerly the meeting-place of the Scottish Parliament, tables covered with wines and confectioneries were prepared at the expense of the city; and to this entertainment there were usually invited about two hundred persons, including the most respectable citizens of Edinburgh, besides the noblemen, gentlemen, and the chief military and naval officers who happened to be in the city or its vicinity. About five o'clock, the attention of the mob became concentrated in the Parliament Close. The company then began to assemble in the House; and those arch-enemies of the mob, yclept the *Town Rattens*, drew themselves up at the east entry of the Square, in order to protect the City's guests as they alighted from their carriages, and to fire a volley at every toast that was drunk within the House. The gentlemen who came to honour the Magistrates had often to

Cutting barley in Fife, 15 August 1953.

Peat cutters at West Loch Tarbert, Harris, 1937.

Calum McPhee on Mingulay, 1905: it took fifteen thousand peats to keep a crofter's family in fuel for a year.

Inside a Glencoe bothy, 1953.

Members of an Aberdeenshire cycling club of the 1880s stand confidently by their 'ordinaries'.

The labour force who cared for the gardens of Udny Castle, Aberdeenshire in the 1900s.

purchase the good-will of the mob, by throwing money amongst them; otherwise they were sure to be maltreated before getting into the House. Dead cats, cod-heads, and every species of disgusting garbage, were thrown at them, and sometimes un-popular persons were absolutely seized and carried to the box which covered a fire-pipe in the centre of the Square, and there *burghered*, as it was called – that is, had their bottoms brought hard down upon the ridge of the box three several times, with severity proportioned to the caprice of the inflictors, or determined by the degree of resistance made by the suffered.

While the Town-guard stood in the Square, the mob were seldom remiss in pelting them with the same horrible missiles. Resistance or revenge in such a case would have been vain; and the veterans found it their only resource to throw all the articles of annoyance, as they reached them, into the lobby of the House; thus diminishing, and perhaps altogether exhausting the ammunition of their persecutors.

The healths being drunk, the *Rats* were ordered to leave the Square, and march down the street to their guard-house. Most of these veterans had no doubt participated in the distresses and hazards of many a march and countermarch; but we question if they were ever engaged in any so harassing and dangerous as this. In fact, the retreat of the ten thousand Greeks, or that of the British troops in the late Peninsular War, was scarcely so beset with peril and horror, as this retreat of the *Rats* from the Parliament Square to the Town-guard-house – a distance of only one hundred yards! The uproar was now at its height, and the mob, not content with a distant *fire* of missiles, might be said to charge bayonets, and attack their foes hand to hand. The ranks of the Guard were of course entirely broken, and every individual soldier had to dispute every inch he proceeded, with a thousand determined annoyers. The temper of the good old veterans was put to dreadful trial by this organized system of molestation; but it is remarkable, that a "dam her shoul!" or some such exclamation, was in general the only expression of their wrath. Upon one occasion, however, about the period of the French Revolution, when the mob assumed a much fiercer and more malicious character than formerly or since, John

Dhu, a high-spirited soldierly man, was so exasperated by the persecution of an individual, that he turned about at the Cross, and hewed him down with one stroke of his Lochaber-axe . . .

After the Town-guard was fairly housed, the mob was obliged to seek other objects, whereupon to vent their ignoble rage; and, accordingly, the High Street, from the Luckenbooths to the Netherbow, becoming now the field of action, every well-dressed or orderly-looking person, who happened to intrude upon the hallowed district, was sure to be assailed . . .

It was customary with the blackguards who headed the mob, to commit *forcible abduction, sans remords* upon all the cats which they could find, either at the doors or the fire-sides of their disconsolate owners. These hapless innocents were sometimes killed outright, immediately on being caught, before commencing the sport; but, in general, were just tossed about till they expired. A full-sized dead cat was sometimes so far improved by the process of jactation, as to be three feet long, and fit for being tied round the neck of a gentleman, like a cravat. Pieces of furniture, such as chairs and tables, were also occasionally seized in the Cowgate, and thrown about the streets in the same manner. Country-people were seldom permitted to escape abuse, when observed upon the street. Our informant once saw three unsophisticated rustics, dressed in their best sky-blue coats, standing at the head of the Old Assembly Close, amongst the women and children who usually took such stations in order to *see the fun*. The poor men were laughing heartily at the mischief they witnessed, – their cachinnations being no more heard amidst the uproar, than their persons were seen amongst the crowd. But suddenly, for some reason or other, the noise of the mob, sinking down to a low note, like the sea subsiding round a stake, left the voices of the honest country folks quite prominent above the circumjacent *hum*; and of course had the effect of directing the attention of all towards the close-head where they stood. The eyes of the mob instantly caught their happy faces, and, in the course of the next moment, an hundred hands were raised with the purpose of throwing crackers, serpents, dead cats, &c., at their heads. Seeing themselves thus made objects of attack, they turned in horror and dismay, and fled down the close. Having the start of their pursuers, they had almost effected their escape, when a stout fellow, more impetuous than the rest, rushing headlong through the *close-mouth*, hurled after them a bruised and battered calf's-head, which had been a well-known and familiar missile throughout the High Street during the whole afternoon, and which, striking the last of the fugitives full in the back, went to pieces where it alighted, darkening with blood and brains the shade of the coat, and laying the luckless rustic prostrate on the ground.

After the mob succeeded in chasing every proper object of mischief from the street, they usually fell to and attacked each other, in a promiscuous *mêlée*, till, worn out by fatigue, and fully satisfied with *fun*, they separated perhaps about ten o'clock, after having kept undisputed possession of the town for at least ten hours.

It is needless to say, that, since the organization of the present system of Police, the celebration of the King's Birth-Day has ceased to be distinguished by any of the above outrages.[2]

As Chambers suggested, the transition to orderly celebration came about quite quickly, but as it did, the population lost interest in marking royal birthdays at all.

In many parts of the Lowlands, celebration by the early Victorian period had indeed become distinctly measured and sober. Here is a page from a handloom weaver's diary from Fenwick, Ayrshire, covering a cold December 1844 and early January 1845. Notice that Christmas day does not even merit a mention – but the author was a Seceder, a strict old-fashioned Calvinist.

The first day's curling this season took place on December 7th. The Fenwick Curling Club, and the Kilmarnock Town End Club played on Crawfordland Loch on the 24th. The Fenwick curlers obtained victory by 19 shots. Another game took place between the Fenwick and Stewarton clubs on the 26th. Fenwick players beat their opponents by 56 shots.

December 26th: A congregational soirée was held in the Secession Meeting House in behoof of the library connected with the congregation, the Rev. Mr Orr in the chair. The speakers were the Rev. Mr Graham from Duke Street, Glasgow, the Rev. Mr Low of Barrhead, the Rev. Mr Robertson of Irvine, and the Rev. Mr Carswell of Eaglesham. The Fenwick vocal club also gave their services. The brilliant display of naptha lamps with which the building was lighted had a fine effect. The lower part of the church was nearly full, tickets eightpence. The money drawn amounted to £13.7.4 and the expenses £7.6.4.

Time is ever pressing onward – 1844 has now passed away – yes! 1844 with all its cares, sorrows, conflicts, crimes; its joys, pleasures, hopes and happiness has gone, gone never to return. We now turn to another year.

January 1st: A most beautiful day, the frost moderate – fine sunshine cheers the face of nature. Bright day, be thou the harbinger of as bright a year! Very little drinking took place this New Year's Day. Men are now given more to reflection than to noisy revelry.

Numbers resorted in the afternoon to Crawfordland Loch, and amused themselves on the strong and transparent ice. It was a beautiful sight to see: The clear frozen loch bounded by woodlands, the blue heaven above, while round the edge of the horizon the clouds glowed like burnished gold. The sun, just seen above the trees, throws his long, slanting beams on the ice and woods at the upper end of the loch, where numbers of the Fenwick lasses sport in its light (true to their nature, for woman ever seeks the sunshine rather than the shade of human life); while enamoured swains hover near the bright band, that they may bask and live in the influence of their smiles, which also show to the curious spectator that though frost reigns all around, at least in their hearts thaw is to be found. Thus passed away New Year's Day![3]

In Victorian Inverness, however, there was a great deal of obviously traditional Christmas gaiety: the description is of a middle-class home, but the spirit of the season engulfed the whole community.

Christmas was then, more than now, a time for hearty, social gatherings. On Christmas and New Year's Day people always went in the afternoons to see their friends and wish them happiness, and though there were no Christmas cards and no decorating of churches, it was the custom at that season to make little gifts for all one's friends, relations, and servants which cost little money, but a great deal of labour, and were, on the latter account, highly valued.

For four or five days before Christmas, boys, who were called "Bulliegeizers" – whatever that may mean – went round every night at seven or eight o'clock singing loudly at the street doors, and of course expecting pennies. The arrival of these boys outside was always a source of delight to the children within, for it reminded them that Christmas was close at hand.

On Christmas Eve a great packing of baskets with tea and sugar, currant loaves, and pieces of meat, for favourite retainers and pensioners, went on in many households, at which the children were not only permitted to assist, but were allowed to accompany a servant with the baskets to the houses of the various recipients, in order that they might acquire a *personal* interest in those whom their parents befriended.

On Christmas morning in most households the servants were sent for to the dining-room to drink the health of their master and mistress, and receive a piece of shortbread, and some little gifts worked for them by the children's own hands; and during breakfast a message often came from the kitchen that some of the pet beggars of the family – such as Walter Sim and "Water Lexy" – had "called to wish every one a merry Christmas," which, of course, was the signal for some eager child to run down stairs with a shilling for each of the grateful visitors.

Thus, in many homes in Inverness in those days, Christmas was a day of more satisfying happiness for the children than it is at present, when they are surfeited with Christmas cards and costly gifts. In those days toys and books were much more expensive than they are now, and children did not get so many of them: therefore they dearly prized the few they did get. They were not loaded on their birthdays with jewellery and all manner of splendid presents from all their relations and acquaintances, but were quite satisfied with a sixpenny or shilling book from their parents, and no remembrance from any one else, except perhaps, a pen-wiper or pin-cushion from some kind aunt. A shilling book with one of Miss Edgeworth's or Mrs. Hofland's tales – carefully written in excellent English – was more highly prized than a five shilling book is by any child now, and even a penny book (with the history of "Cinderella" or "Beauty and the Beast," "The Yellow Dwarf" or "The Invisible Prince"), or a penny toy such as a tin kettle or saucepan, could bestow a degree of happiness which children in the same rank of life could not possibly realise at the present day.[4]

Two celebrations in the year, Hallowe'en and Hogmanay, were perhaps quintessentially Scottish, and have even now escaped the commercialization that has overtaken Christmas and Easter. Halloween, mischief night when the spirits fly, was essentially a children's celebration by the late nineteenth and earlier twentieth centuries, and Molly Weir explains how its gaiety and energy crept even into the poor tenements of Glasgow.

When I was a wee girl in Glasgow, Hallowe'en was celebrated by all of us with keenest enjoyment. The weather always seemed clear and frosty, the skies filled with stars, and there was the exhilaration of dressing up in strange garments, with the added tension and nervousness of a performance about to begin. I usually wore Grannie's old hat, when it had got beyond the stage when a bunch of cherries or a spray of flowers could rejuvenate it, and I sat it on top of my head at a rakish angle, over my blackened face. A long skirt of my mother's, and Grannie's tartan shawl completed the disguise, but I wasn't able to round off the effect with my mother's high-heeled shoes because I couldn't even hobble in them, so my long-legged boots and black woollen stockings just had to be worn, even though they were completely out of character. This was a terrible disappointment, for I longed to prance about in elegant high heels, but for running out and in closes and up and down dozens of stairs sure footing was vital, and boots it had to be.

There was much giggling and mutual admiration when we all met after tea, and set out on the rounds of all the neighbours' houses. Sometimes, greatly daring, we went beyond our own district, and we shivered with excitement and a little dread at the thought of knocking at such strange doors. We were very critical of the brasses, and surprised to find that in some posh closes the name-plates weren't a patch on the glittering gold polish our own mothers managed. We each carried a little bag, home-made from an old petticoat or blouse, with a draw-string top, to hold the expected apples and nuts and sweets we hoped we would collect, and we prepared our acts as we raced along from close to close. We never expected to be handed our Hallowe'en gifts just for knocking on a door and chanting, 'Please gi'e us wur Hallowe'en!' We knew we were expected to do a turn to entertain our benefactors.

We would be invited into the house, and the family would sit round in lively anticipation as we went into our performances. I usually sang the latest popular song, and I particularly liked one requiring the use of my hostess's flue-brush, which I stuck over my shoulder and used as a bayonet. Very dashing I thought this, and so did my audience! There were recitations and ballads, and we generally finished with all of us doing a Highland Fling. We received our applause with flushed and happy faces, and we opened our draw-string bags to receive the apples, and the nuts, with maybe a piece of puff candy or some home-made tablet. Tablet was a great treat and so tempting that it was devoured on the spot, and seldom rested in the bag for a second. A turnip lantern lit our way and we went bobbing through the darkness like glow-worms. The preparation of those magic lanterns was a great ploy. We hollowed out swede turnips skilfully, made two slits for the eyes and a perpendicular line for the nose. A curved slit made a smiling mouth. A little hollow in the bottom held our candle, and the complete effect was golden and delightful. I may say everybody in our district ate mashed swedes for days afterwards, using up the discarded inside of our lanterns.

A party was a great excitement at Hallowe'en, and everyone went in fancy dress. Home-made, of course, for these were unsophisticated as well as hard-up days, and only 'toffs' would have known about hiring clothes. Angels and fairies, their wings fashioned from cardboard boxes coaxed from the Co-operative, and covered with coloured crinkled paper, were ten a penny, for the girls. The boys favoured pirates and cowboys, which were easily fashioned from old hats, and their father's leather belts, and toy guns. All this helped to break down the shyness we would have felt in ordinary clothes, although Hallowe'en fun was so different from any other form of merriment there was never a minute of sitting still wondering what you were expected to do. After the tea, with its salmon sandwiches if we were lucky, or corn mutton if money was tight, followed by the jellies, the games started. The big zinc bath was pulled from under the bed and filled with cold water, then rosy-cheeked apples were tumbled in in a colourful shower. A chair was placed with its back to the bath, the apples and water given a vigorous stir to send them bobbing as wildly as possible and make a difficult target, and we would each kneel, one at a time, on the chair, head sticking out over the top edge just as though we were about to be guillotined. A fork was held between clenched teeth, and we'd gaze at the bobbing fruit below us, waiting for the moment when the biggest and reddest apple was exactly placed for our aim, then *plonk*, down went the fork, usually to slither off between the bouncing apples. There would be howls of glee from the onlookers, and gulping disappointment from the unlucky contestant as he or she climbed down from the chair to go to the end of the queue again. Not till everybody had speared an apple would the next game start, and, of course, it became harder and harder to succeed as the numbers of apples grew fewer and fewer with each win, and the final apple had the whole room shouting opposite advice. 'Drap yer fork noo. *Noo*, Wullie. Ach missed it', 'Gi'e the watter a steer, it's easier when it's movin'', or 'Don't steer it noo, gi'e 'im a chance seein' there's only wan'. And from the faint-hearted, or those who wanted to go on to another game, 'Ach just gi'e 'im it, and let's get on wi' the party.'

There was a lovely game, unpopular with parents but beloved by us children, where a huge home-baked soda scone was covered in treacle and suspended on a string from the centre gas bracket, or hung from a string stretched across the room. It was sent spinning by the leader, and then, with hands clasped behind our backs, we would leap into the air and try to snatch a bite. What a glorious mess we were in at the end of this caper, hair, eyes, cheeks and neck covered in treacle. Mothers and aunties and uncles urged us instantly towards the kitchen sink, 'Go and dight yer faces noo, we don't want treacle a' ower the hoose,' and what a splashing there was under the cold tap, and a battle for the solitary towel as we removed the mess.

And, of course, we loved the trinkets which were buried in a mound of creamy mashed potatoes. Even the poorest family could afford tatties, so everybody could enjoy this traditional bit of fun. The quantities of potatoes we consumed in search of our favourite ring or threepenny piece must have saved many an anxious hostess from worrying how she was going to fill us up.[5]

Hogmanay, of course, with its strong connotations of neighbourliness and drinking, was much more for adults. The best side of it is described by Abe Moffat, miners' leader, writing in 1965 about a Fife boyhood between the wars. He has unexpected things to say about the place of music in his life, as well.

But if anyone wants to see miners and their families enjoying themselves, despite hard times (and that goes for today), then they should visit a mining village in Scotland for Hogmanay. It won't matter if you are the biggest stranger in the world, you will be made welcome. In Lumphinnans, I have seen fifty people in our own house, and Helen would make a special dumpling and cook potted meat so that nobody was hungry during the night. When the bells rang at 12 p.m., the bottles would get drawn, sometimes before 12, and then the singing and dancing would go on until eight and nine o'clock in the morning. And although I am now sixty-seven years of age, I, my wife and family still carry on this tradition, as it is still done in every mining village.

We had no radio or television in my childhood, and we had to make our own music and entertainment. It so happened that when I was at school, my father decided to buy me a violin, and my teacher was his younger brother, Maxwell, who is still alive at eighty-nine years of age. I do not know why I was selected – possibly because I was called after him, and it certainly was impossible to supply musical instruments to all the members of the family. However, it brought enjoyment to all of us when I used to sit and play, not only at New Year, but on many other occasions when they would all dance together.

The violin came in handy in later years when I took part in a Miners' Strike Band to raise money for the strikers. I also played in a dance band for Saturday-night dancing for the miners and their sweethearts.

Then I had an experience during the First World War in France. We had no musical instruments, and I happened to say I could play a tune on the violin. There was an Irish lad in our battalion, and he got down to the job of making a violin. The only tools he possessed were a jack-knife, a poker and a chocolate box. He made the bow out of a piece of tree, and it may be difficult to believe, but I played that violin on the streets in France while British soldiers danced with the French mademoiselles.

Even at my last British Miners' Conference at Rothesay, I gave some of my English and Welsh colleagues a shock, when we were all in a hotel having a sing-song, when I took up courage and played the violin belonging to the proprietor. The eyes stared in their heads, as they obviously thought I could only concern myself with pits or politics.

Every New Year Helen would do the cooking and the singing, as she always had and still has a good singing voice, and I would play the violin. However, in later years, I have been able to sit back and take part in the fun and dancing, as my son, Abe, is able to play the piano-accordion, and so relieve me of this responsibility.

Although out of practice, I still appreciate my violin, and can still play the beautiful melodies of "Bonnie Mary of Argyle" and "Rowan Tree", which were always my favourite tunes, and several Scotch reels and strathspeys. I appreciate that it was a big sacrifice on the part of my father and mother to spend £5 to purchase a violin for one of their family. That was a great deal of money then. It was a good violin 100 years old when my father bought it, which means it is well over 160 years old now.

One time we had Sorimus, the well-known Russian violinist, and his wife living with us in Lumphinnans, when they were doing a series of concerts in Fife, and he played this violin in the house and he said it had a grand tone. So for many reasons, no money in the world could buy this violin that belongs to the Moffat family.

However, I did try to repay my parents for giving me a violin, so I found a job as paper-boy in my native village. I had a complete monopoly, as there was no other paper-boy in the place. I received 3s.6d. per week, which I handed over to my mother. On Friday mornings, I got leave of absence from the school until 11 a.m., and I had to wheel a large barrow to supply all the papers. Of course, in addition to my weekly wage, I got a lot of tips, and all my school mates, both boys and girls, were always waiting on me coming into school, as my pockets were full of chocolates and sweets.[6]

Finally, the Scots have always been extremely enthusiastic in celebrating weddings. Of many descriptions which could be given, we have chosen this account of an Aberdeenshire wedding in a farming family at around the time of the First World War. As was so often the case in Scotland, the wedding took place at the home of the bride, not in church.

It took place at Dungair. Preparations went on for days. Miss Betsy, the sewing woman, worked in the dining-room for a whole month making dresses ... My grandmother baked for hours on end, until the sweat stood out in little moons all over her nose and dropped into the shortbread, to give that delicacy its exquisite lightness, as she said. Boxes of fruit arrived, and cases of bottles that the Old Man took into his charge. Then the wedding cake in a tea box that had the dry fragrance of the perfumed East. Then the greybeard, a five gallon jar of whisky which the Old Man cached beneath his bed and watched over as if it had been his one ewe lamb. On the morning of The Day everything was ready.

The company assembled in the dining-room at three o'clock. As if indeed to celebrate the end of an epoch, Dungair had invited all his old friends, some of whom were like himself, farmers of the third and fourth generations in those parts. He sat in his easy chair in the corner between the window and the fire with the greybeard between his feet and a tray of glasses and a jug of cold water from the pump on a small table at his side. As the old men came in with their wives, they walked over to shake his hand and he, without rising, gave them a stiff dram from the greybeard while the maid helped their ladies to a glass of wine. They then sat down in a wide circle around him. The younger guests, friends of Sally and Peter, disposed themselves in odd corners and laughed among themselves while Peter stood in the middle of the room and was congratulated after the coarse fashion of the countryside by all who came in. The minister arrived last of all and, after taking a little wine, turned to Dungair and said they might begin.

Sally came in with her mother, wearing a plain tweed skirt and a white blouse on which she had pinned a black cat that Tom the second horseman had given her at the games. The company stood up, the minister took his position on the hearthrug with Sally and Peter before him, the Old Man made sure that the greybeard was safe between his knees, and the service began. We sang the Hundredth Psalm, led by Uncle Scott, whose rolling bass was like the elemental let loose in that crowded room. Then the minister prayed and began to read the ancient and somewhat pagan service. When he asked who gave the woman to be married, the Old Man replied from his chair with a wave of his staff, Sally and Peter swore to love and cherish each other for the good of their souls and the comfort of their bodies, the minister blessed them, and so they were married. It was usual for the company to have to endure a long discourse on the more refined joys and the less obvious responsibilities of marriage, but it was cut mighty short on this occasion, which was just as well, for the Old Man was quite capable of putting a sudden end to the address if it had lasted one minute after the five. So the minister talked briefly if not to the point, the papers were signed, the benediction pronounced, and the healths of the man and wife were drunk in noble bumpers.

The interval of half an hour until the feast was ready was spent in amiable discourse. The younger guests walked in the garden, Dungair and the old men went for a round of the steading, the women looked at Sally's clothes, and my grandmother drew order out of the imminent chaos in the kitchen.

We sat down thirty in the dim gold drawing-room around a board spread with my grandmother's patterned linen and decorated with the last flowers from her beloved garden. The Old Man sat at the top of the table with Mrs. Lambert and Mrs. Brown, two of his oldest friends, on his right and left, and the rest of his neighbours beside him. My grandmother sat at the foot near the door where she could keep in touch with the kitchen. Sally and Peter were on either side of her and the rest of the young people were at her end, for her sympathies were always with the young against the cantankerous interference of the old.

How can I describe that feast? I have no words to set down the ripe humanity around that table, the wrinkled whiskered faces of the men, the faded primness or the rosy pink exuberance of the women, the dark and exquisite flush of beauty on the young bride's face, the slow Scottish wit, the roars of laughter, the steam of food, the clink and clatter of the dishes, the thin light of evening deepened in the gold of whisky or kindling a dim radiance in the wine – these and the suns of long gone summers that lingered in the faded gilding of the room. I can only say that it was such and such and hope to evoke from your own past the warmth and laughter of humanity.

To me it was very heaven. I had never seen, never imagined there could be such a wealth of lovely food. First, soup with sherry; then a turkey trimmed with bacon and three hens wreathed in sausages; then a giant roast with sauce; then cold meats in abundance; then sweets, dessert and chocolates; and birse tea last of all. Good drink accompanied them – port and sherry wine for women and boys and whisky from the greybeard for the men. So the Old Man feasted his friends at his daughter's wedding and, when the cloth was drawn, hardly a one of us was sober though none of us was drunk.

The dark had fallen. Lamps were lit. The night was growing cold. Sally dressed herself for the road and prepared to take her leave. That was soon over. A few women wept, but they were guests who had drunk too well. The Old Man gave Peter a final dram. My grandmother kissed Sally and said good-bye. They ran out of the hall, out of the house, into a car and drove away.

The Old Man listened till the car ran out of hearing, then he returned to the greybeard.

'Weel, that's that,' he said. 'Lat's mak a night o't.'

We did and the fun began immediately. Some of the young men, Sally's rejected sweethearts, had brought fireworks to give her a grand send-off. Very pretty they were too as they rocketed into the frosty sky, but one, imperfectly exploded, fell on a rick of old hay in the Home Field which immediately went up in a blaze. Everybody got tremendously excited except the Old Man. When he saw that the wind was blowing away from the steading and that the fire would not endanger the stack-yard, he made himself comfortable at the drawing-room window where he could enjoy the spectacle with the aid of the greybeard and his friends. This was too much for one of the old gentlemen who protested:

'Dungair, man, ye're fiddlin' whan Rome's burnin'. That's what ye are.'

'Drink up, Stripe, drink up,' the Old Man replied. 'The stuff's weel insured.'[7]

CHAPTER XII

LEISURE

The last two hundred years have seen a revolution in both the amount of time free from work enjoyed by ordinary people and the occupations available to fill that time. The expansion of leisure activities was a consequence of a growth in wealth and a shrinkage in working hours, developments of especial significance from mid Victorian times onwards. It was only in the later nineteenth century that organized sport became widely popular as a form of entertainment. A vigorous burst of construction provided Scotland with galleries and museums, theatres and parks. Alongside the expansion of organized leisure there also developed a street culture which encompassed both children's games and the gossip of adults. In the 1950s this culture began to shrink, partly as a result of the growth in traffic and partly in response to the growing attractions of more comfortable, warm and spacious homes filled with increasing quantities of entertainment-providing machinery.

The sports that flourished in late eighteenth-century Scotland had yet to be organized, codified, and disciplined by national bodies. Huge chaotic games of football were enjoyed. Men boxed without gloves – one bare fist fight in 1825 lasted for forty-four rounds. Enterainments included some that were later to be abolished as bloodthirsty, including cock-fighting. In 1830 Pryse Lockhard Gordon looked back on his schooldays in north-east Scotland.

50 years ago cockfighting was a sport permitted at the schools in Scotland at Shrovetide. On the day fixed at our school for the great warfare the room was fitted out by the removal of the benches as the arena and every boy brought with him a few cocks. They were generally dunghill, but one fellow had got a better breed and generally became the victor. The owner of the

best cock is crowned king of the day and is crowned with the tail feathers of the enemy's birds. I was ambitious of this honour and having seen some English cocks at the little seaport of Portsoy I got a few chickens and at the next campaign I was ready with a brace of such game cocks as had never before been seen in the parish. They were shaved and trimmed. When they were produced, disfigured from lack of plumage, there was a general laugh at my expense. The former victor, Peterkin, thought himself sure of victory and produced a bird that looked twice the size of my half-naked stranger. By my triumph was immediate. In half a dozen fights my 'black crested red' laid his enemy prostrate to crow no more. A similar fate awaited all Peterkin's brood except a brace of them which were consigned for cowardice to the master's larder.[1]

Organized and elaborate entertainments were beyond the pockets of ordinary people. But for the rich a range of lavish events were offered in the major cities. Henry Cockburn looked back on the end of the eighteenth century: he observed the last traces of strictly regulated social occasions, and bewailed the arrival of evening dinner.

In my youth the whole fashionable dancing, as indeed the fashionable everything, clung to George Square; where (in Buccleuch Place, close by the southern-eastern corner of the square) most beautiful rooms were erected, which, for several years, threw the New Town piece of presumption entirely into the shade. And here were the last remains of the ball-room discipline of the preceding age. Martinet dowagers and venerable beaux acted as masters and mistresses of ceremonies, and made all the preliminary arrangements. No couple could dance unless each party was provided with a ticket prescribing the precise place in the precise dance. If there was no ticket, the gentleman, or the lady, was dealt with as an intruder, and turned out of the dance.

If the ticket had marked upon it – say for a country dance – the figures 3.5; this meant that the holder was to place himself in the third dance, and fifth from the top; and if he was anywhere else, he was set right, or excluded. And the partner's ticket must correspond. Woe on the poor girl who with ticket 2.7, was found opposite a youth marked 5.9! It was flirting without a licence, and looked very ill, and would probably be reported by the ticket director of that dance to the mother. Of course parties, or parents, who wished to secure dancing for themselves or those they had charge of, provided themselves with correct and corresponding vouchers before the ball day arrived. This could only be accomplished through a director; and the election of a pope sometimes required less jobbing. When parties chose to take their chance, they might do so; but still, though only obtained in the room, the written permission was necessary; and such a thing as a compact to dance, by a couple, without official authoritiy, would have been an outrage that could scarcely be contemplated. Tea was sipped in side-rooms; and he was a careless beau who did not present his partner with an orange at the end of each dance; and the oranges and the tea, like everything else, were under exact and positive regulations.

The prevailing dinner hour was about three o'clock. Two o'clock was quite common, if there was no company. Hence it was no great deviation from their usual custom for a family to dine on Sundays "between sermons" – that is between one and two.

The hour, in time, but not without groans and predictions, became four, at which it stuck for several years. Then it got to five which, however, was thought positively revolutionary; and four was long and gallantly adhered to by the haters of change as "the good old hour". At last even they were obliged to give in. But they only yielded inch by inch, and made a desperate stand at half-past four. Even five, however, triumphed, and continued the average polite hour from (I think) about 1806 or 1807 till about 1820. Six has at last prevailed, and half an hour later is not unusual. As yet this is the farthest stretch of London imitation, except in country houses devoted to grouse or deer, where the species called sportsmen, disdaining all mankind except themselves, glory in not dining till sensible people have gone to bed. Thus, within my memory, the hour has ranged from two to half-past six o'clock; and a stand has been regularly made at the end of every half-hour against each encroachment and always on the same grounds – dislike of change and jealousy of finery.

The procession from the drawing-room to the dining-room was formerly arranged on a different principle from what it is now. There was no such alarming proceeding as that of each gentleman approaching a lady, and the two hooking together. This would have excited as much horror as the waltz at first did, which never showed itself without denunciations of continental manners by correct gentlemen and worthy mothers and aunts. All the ladies first went off by themselves, in a regular row, according to the ordinary rules of precedence. Then the gentlemen moved off in a single file; so that when they reached the dinning-room, the ladies were all there, lingering about the backs of the chairs till they could see what their fate was to be. Then began the selection of partners, the leaders of the male line having the advantage of priority: and of course the magnates had an affinity for each other.[2]

Residential seaside holidays were, in the nineteenth century, lengthy occasions enjoyed by the well-to-do but not normally available to ordinary people. Janet Story stayed in St Andrews.

Tuesday, 15th August, 1854. We went out for a walk on the delightful links; not always a safe proceeding, however, on account of the risk from golf balls; only a very small portion of the turfy expanse being available for ordinary pedestrians. The 'fore! fore!' of the advancing parties is not always as distinct as it should be. The sky became extremely threatening when we were on the links, and we returned home just as some huge drops of rain began to fall; a very severe thunderstorm followed, quite the most beautiful I ever saw, and I have seen many. To the horror of the two old ladies I sat at the drawing-room window and watched the progress of the magnificent storm. Very bright sheet lightning and continuous dazzling forked flashes played in the lurid sky, and were thrown into relief by a background of hills in the distance, now-a-days quite invisible from Hope Street, as new and very obstructive houses have ruined that once beautiful view.

A most lovely evening succeeded this wild war of the elements. We went out later for a turn on the Scores, my aunt's very favourite strolling place, which in those days I regarded as 'dull as ditchwater', because very few people ever walked there, and the links or South Street were very much gayer and more to my taste. Now-a-days I dearly love the Scores; and have often, while promenading soberly up and down their breezy front, recalled the depressed feelings with which I lounged beside my old aunt, and wondered what on earth she saw to attract her to such a dull exercising ground.

One day I had a curious adventure on the links, a very fierce fight with a large bumble bee. I was slowly walking along one of the most attractive of the flat parts of the sward, when a heavy thump on my parasol startled me, and on lowering it to see what had caused it, a large bee made straight for me, and was only prevented from stinging me by a smart rebuff from my parasol. It returned to the charge, however. I prodded again. The bee, evidently very angry, retired to a short distance, only to gather up his forces and bear strongly upon me; while I, now getting rather frightened, ran a little way off, and then turned round just in time to administer a smart rebuff to my adversary. I retreated, it pursued: the day was hot, and I was getting very blown and exhausted, and should presently have been at the mercy of the bee, when fortunately for me a party of golfers came round a low hill, and seeing from my unusual antics that a game of another kind was in progress, they advanced to my assistance, and my trouble with the bee was a thing of the past.[3]

The game of golf attracted new adherents in the Victorian age and new courses were established to cater for them. The growing army of wealthy golfers provided a source of revenue for men who chose to take up caddying. This mid-nineteenth-century account describes one of their number.

One of the strangest peculiarities of this eccentric old caddie was the way in which he wore his clothes. He may be said to have literally carried his wardrobe with him wherever he went. All the clothes he got he put on his back, one suit above another.

To admit of his wearing three or four coats at once, he had to cut out the sleeves to let them on. True to the uniform which invariably distinguished golfers in those days, an old red coat was always worn outside of them all. He also wore three or four vests, an old worn fur one being outermost. It was the same with his trousers – three or four pairs on, and the worst outermost; and three bonnets, sewed one within the other!

When Willie first came from the Highlands, he had been in the habit of going about the country selling tracts; and happening to come to Edinburgh, and passing through Bruntsfield Links, he stood to look at the golfers.

It being a busy golfing day, the golfers could not all get caddies, and one of them asked Willie to carry his clubs; which he did, and got a shilling for his hour's work. With an eye to the main chance, Willie forthwith took to the Royal and Ancient Game; and in order to be near the Links, took up his quarters at Bruntsfield, renting a garret from Mr. John Brand, gardener, lessee of the lands and mansion-houses of Level Lodge and Valleyfield. Willie was very honest, paying his rent regularly, and for his bread and milk as he got it. He lived entirely on baps and milk, never having a warm diet, or a fire in his garret, even in the coldest winter. He was always happy and cheerful. I was a favourite of his, as, when I saw the caddie boys annoying him, I used to say that I would tell the gentlemen of their conduct, which had the effect of stopping them. They knew that the gentlemen would not employ them if it was known that they annoyed Willie.

Possessed of an inborn love of sport, Willie used to go to the village fairs round about Edinburgh with a view to picking up a few pence. His apparatus for enticing the youth of a sporting turn was exceedingly simple, consisting of three turned pieces of wood about a foot long, with turned base about one and a half or two inches in diameter, something like what you see in milliners' windows to put their caps and bonnets on. Cutting three holes in the earth the size of the base of his sticks, in the form of a triangle, he put a penny on the top of each stick. He had a wand about three feet long. The player stood about ten feet off; and paying a penny for his shot, tried to skim the pennies off the top, which was very seldom done; the wand either going too high and missing, or too low and knocking away the sticks, when the pennies dropped into the holes – either result being equally in Willie's favour. I will never forget Willie's face and his happy chuckle as he used to cry out, 'All in the hole!' Many people were attracted around Willie by his odd appearance, and tried their skill at his pennies for the sake of giving him a few coppers. These village fairs were a great treat to us boys. They were called Carters' Plays, and were looked forward to by all the lads and lasses for miles round about, as the great event of the year, there being a grand equestrian procession, when both men and horses were laden with ribbons and flowers. The lasses vied with each other who would turn out their sweethearts with the grandest display of ribbons and flowers. It was a great pleasure to visit the villages on these occasions, and to see so many happy people.

Gunn was in the habit of going to his Highland home every autumn, selling his tracts by the way, and was generally away about six weeks. The last time he bade me good-bye (which was about the year 1820), he told me that he had as much money saved as would pay his funeral expenses, as he had a horror of a pauper's burial. From this journey poor Willie never returned. All the inquiry the golfers made, they could never learn his fate.[4]

The pleasures of golf were beyond the purses of the bulk of the working class. They had neither the time nor the money for the sport. William Haddow grew up amid a late nineteenth-century family that could not afford expensive toys nor contemplate seaside holidays. His grandfather, the head of the household, was a skilled craftsman whose wages at least enabled him to provide his family with the entertainment of a regular newspaper.

My maternal grandfather was a dour, stern, calvinistic Scotsman, a man of few words, just and honest in all his dealings, but feared by his family.

He was a joiner by trade and had been with the same East-end firm all his life. Working hours in those days were from six o'clock in the morning till six o'clock at night. He was never late and never idle and consequently was highly respected and valued by his employers.

On his way home from work he would buy the *Evening Citizen*, the only evening paper then published in Glasgow which upheld Liberalism. After supper, the paper was unfolded and the old man began the reading of the four pages; woe betide if any noise or talking was indulged in by the family until the task was completed. By nine o'clock preparations were made for bed. An exception was made on Friday evenings, possibly because of the shorter working day on Saturday, but principally because the *Weekly Mail* (sometimes called The Cairter's Bible) was published on that day. This was the great family paper of the Eighteen-sixties/seventies and it had a large circulation. It specialised in all the lurid exciting events of the week and ran a serial story with plenty of heart-throb in it. One story entitled Wee Curly created a sensation and must have been read by tens of thousands of working-class folks in the country. After tea on the Friday night we would gather round my grandmother (she was a great reader), and listen with bated breath while she read of Wee Curly's latest adventures and when "To be continued" was reached, we wondered and discussed with great excitement what Curly was likely to do next week. To the modern child such a simple scene as this may seem foolish but in those far off days family life was very different from what it is to-day.

In the winter we had to make and devise our own amusements. Cinema, Gramophone and Wireless were unknown. An occasional concert in the Church Hall, and perhaps an annual visit to the Circus or the Pantomine were keenly anticipated pleasures and were talked about for many a long day afterwards.

In the summer evenings we had street games and every game had its own reason. There was Marbles for the boys, played in various ways, such as "Moshie", Ringey, Three-holey, Plunkers, etc., and a considerable amount of barter took place with the different kinds of "bools" – two "commies" equalled one "glassie" and six "glassies" equalled one "plunker" – a large marble which caused great destruction among the "commies" in the "ringey" game.

Smugglers or "Smuggerlieres," was played by both sexes.

Jumping ropes and hop-scotch (or Peever) were the great games with the lassies. "Cat and Bat" was another favourite game. "Kick the Can" was a noisy game and went on until the policeman appeared. But the most famous of all was the game called "Rounders." A bat (generally home made) and a ball (the harder the better) were used. Four places called "Dens" were marked out. "Sides" were chosen and the game went on fast and furious until both sides were exhausted or until, as often happened, a window was broken, and then there was a hurried scamper for home.

St. Patrick's Day was another great event. Bands of boys from the Catholic Schools and from the near-by Board (Protestant) Schools met in battle array after lessons were over and many a broken head and torn clothes testified to the fight. The fights had little to do with either St. Patrick or with religion; it was simply considered to be a question of use and wont with which to celebrate that day.[5]

David Daiches' upbringing, in early twentieth-century Edinburgh, included an introduction to golf that was somewhat eccentric. The family played golf, especially, during their annual seaside holidays.

The three of us started off with three clubs between us – a driver, a cleek, and a putter – and no instruction of any kind. We simply imitated what we deemed to be the movements of other golfers. My father, who was a small man of robust physique but with relatively poor physical co-ordination, would address the ball with a swift, desperate, jerking movement; it never occurred to him that he might have a better chance of hitting it if he took a slow back swing. After pondering the ball for a moment he would jerk his club back a few feet and then, without any pause at all, jerk it forward to the ball. He would miss or top or slice the ball more often than not, but sometimes, by sheer good luck, he would land it a smart crack which would send it a fair distance. His gratification at such a lucky shot was immense. I believe he thought that all success in such physical activities was due entirely to good luck, and he had no awareness of how impossibly bad his golf was. He had the hands of a writer and scholar, with stubby fingers which looked most at home when curved about a pen. He was quite handy about the house in such things as mending fuses, and he fancied himself as a watchmaker and would pick away at a broken watch with a pin until he had rendered it beyond repair, but he was hopeless at anything that required delicacy of physical co-ordination. He was occasionally taken out fishing by a wealthy member of his congregation who had taken up the sports of the landed gentry, and on one occasion he caught the back of his coat with his very first cast. He was regarded as dangerous with a fishing rod, but not to the fish. He had great stamina, however, and until fairly late in life would walk for miles without fatigue.

My father, Lionel and myself playing golf together was, I suppose, something of a symbol of the attitude of the Daiches family to sport. With one set of three clubs between the three of us, we would pass the clubs around as needed, often to the amazement and sometimes to the annoyance of golfers coming up behind us. Often I would dash fifty yards to where my father was, to hand him the cleek after I had used it myself, while Lionel, who could not be bothered to go and fetch it after my father had used it, would make his slow progress down the fairway with a putter. We would lose balls frequently too; my father's propensity to wild slicing often resulting in the disappearance of the ball into a clump of whin bushes after his drive. Once we played with one ball as well as only three clubs between the three of us, taking alternate shots. This was at the very beginning of our golfing careers. The next year we acquired a mashie and a jigger, and a little later my father discovered that a putting green was really more his style. He became fairly efficient as a putter, and would often invite Lionel or myself to what he called 'a game of putt'. Lionel and I continued to play, on the Balcomie Golf Course at Crail, with one set of clubs between us. Eventually Lionel gave up golf altogether and I inherited the five family clubs, two of which I replaced with new ones bought at Thornton's, in Edinburgh, with bursary money.

I played occasionally with schoolmates on the Braid Hills course, and continued to play sporadically during my university days. I was never very good, but did acquire a modest competence at the game. I never had more than six clubs, and gave up the game completely when it became the fashion for golfers to carry a whole armoury of weapons around with them on the golf course. When I see golfers today going off to play with their enormous array of clubs, I think of the old men of Edinburgh in the 1920s who would go round the ancient and modest little course at Bruntsfield with a single club and then walk slowly home in the summer dusk, with the club held horizontally by the middle of the shaft, swinging to and fro as the arms swung . . .

Our time would be divided between the beach, from which we bathed daily (except Saturdays), and the rocks, where Lionel and I would spend hour after hour watching the marine life and catching the 'grannies' and other fish that inhabited the pools. Sometimes we would go for walks to Anstruther, four miles away, or to St. Andrews, ten miles in the opposite direction, or, more frequently, to the big beach at Balcomie, round at the other side of Fife Ness, where the sand was lighter and finer than the sand at Crail. There was a confectioner's, known as Mrs Aird's, where the young people would gather of an evening to buy ice cream or fish and chips, but our family was seldom there. True, we all had an ice cream a day, after bathing: that was a ritual, and the ice cream was bought from a stand by the beach. (It strikes me with amazement now that we should have wanted to eat ice cream after bathing in the chill waters of the North Sea.) But, quite apart from the fact that Mrs Aird's fish and chips would not have been kosher, having been fried in animal fat, we did not mingle with the 'fast' set that frequented such haunts: our holiday was open-air and active and innocent. We swam, walked, fished, played on the sand, occasionally played golf on the Balcomie golf course, or sat reading by the sea. Towards the end of August, as the evenings began to draw in, we would walk in the dusk along the Castle Walk, a picturesque path which began round the corner from our house and ran along the top of a field which sloped down to the rocks and the sea. There were wooden benches placed at intervals along the Castle Walk, and there my father would often sit in wet weather or in the evening after dark. He made friends with a Mr. Greig, Church of Scotland minister from Airdrie, and they would sit side by side at night talking of differences and similarities between their two religions while the fragrant aroma of Balkan Sobranie floated over the Castle Walk.[6]

Twentieth-century leisure time became increasingly machine-dominated. From their first appearance in 1895 in Glasgow, moving pictures progressed rapidly to amaze Edwardian audiences. At first people were content to be astonished by the spectacle itself; from 1903 enterprising producers developed stories in film-form, narratives that might, by 1914, last as long as half an hour.

Dove Paterson was one of the pioneers in Scotland of the travelling picture show. In 1908 he provided readers of the *Kinematograph and Lantern Weekly* with information about his career and his methods.

My living picture life has only just begun in earnest. Until three years ago I was quite unknown in "Screenland", though since the early eighties I had been before the public in one function or another, more especially the Scottish public, as an elocutionist and concert promoter. In this capacity I toured the United States and Canada in 1892–3 with the Royal Edinburgh Concert Company, and perhaps I then absorbed a little of the hustling propensities of the Yankee – which are very useful in making my picture shows a success at the present time.

At the time when the kinematograph first became a feature on concert programmes, I foresaw its drawing powers and great possibilities, and often wished that I might at some future time adopt what I quickly realised was to many 'the hen that laid the golden eggs.' This hope was destined to be realised in a curious and unexpected way. I had become a camera fiend, contributing snapshots to the local press and taking the 'shooter' with me on many Continental trips. About that time the illustrated lantern lecture was in great demand by the public, and on one eventful engagement at the Scottish National Salon in 1906, held in Dundee, I gave a Pictorial Trip to Belgium, with kinematograph pictures interspersed. The innovation was a marked success, and I lost no time in acquiring plant of the very best and latest type.

Fortunately, in my own son I had a very skilled electrician and lantern operator, who quickly mastered the bioscope, and as we worked in perfect harmony our entertainment soon became favourably known.

Our first big hit was at the Royal Horticultural Society's Show three years ago. Here I gave my first al fresco entertainment for three nights, drawing £357 for the Society. I hope to repeat my success with them on many occasions.

Another notable incident in my living picture life led to my present engagement, which started in October last year and looks like running on indefinitely. The proprietor of the Aberdeen Beach Zoo attracted my attention while amusing himself, when quite a lad, with a baby bear, and I engaged him to give a show at a youngsters' matinee: the booming I gave the 'baby' did us both good. The youthful animal trainer has now developed into a successful zoo exhibitor, and on acquiring the Alhambra Music Hall last year he very kindly remembered his first engagement and made me an offer for my show as a permanent feature of his, which has turned out to be a most successful venture, and he thanks the Electro-Graphic pictures accordingly.

My success I attribute to the following elements to be found in my programme: – The high ideal of giving only the best of everything, knowing that only the good lasts; changing subjects every week; providing an intelligent dialogue for every picture I show; demanding and commanding perfect silence and attention from the audience during dramatic stories; and joining with real gusto in the fun and acting in my comics. Every week a pictorial trip is given to some place of interest; the slides rest the eyes between the animated films, and also serve to give my voice a rest. I see that local pictures of the moment are made specialities.

I always welcome my audiences with a special curtain slide, and bid them au revoir by film. I tolerate no show of white sheet or 'blanking', but keep the screen continually aglow with hand-painted title-slides; in short, I endeavour to keep my audience in Pictureland when once the spell is cast. Should a break occur when running a film my operator flashes the following polite intimation. 'A film slip, please excuse a moment'. 'Ere the audience has time to read the request we are off again, the smart idea commented on, and the sympathy is never broken. The best possible music by the best possible musicians accompanies all my pictures. Being a methodical man and a strict disciplinarian, I insist on the sobriety of my whole staff. I have been a life-long abstainer, and Lady Nicotine claims none of my affections, and it is simply by adherence to those (some would think minor) details that I have been able to handle the pictures so successfully, and retain the favour and confidence of the public so far.[7]

Even in the era of the silent screen Scots showed a remarkable appetite for the medium. By 1914 there were fifty-seven cinemas in Glasgow alone. The memories of Mrs Ethel Kilgour of Aberdeen show the enormous popularity of the cinema with children.

I was initiated into the wonder of the cinema via the Star Picture House, known as the 'Starrie', in Park Street. The year was 1925 and the talkies hadn't been invented. I was too young to be able to read the captions and 'blurbs' on the screen, but from then on through my childhood years, the Saturday matinee 'tuppenny rush' was a must for me and my chums from the Footdee district.

I saw the genius of Charlie Chaplin, laughed at Harold Lloyd and Buster Keaton, and thrilled to the bravery of Tom Mix the cowboy star. When Tom Mix was chasing the Indians, the lady who played the piano accompaniment to all the films from her seat in front of the stage had to labour for her pay, as she had to keep in time with the galloping horses. There was always a moral in these films, for the 'goodies' always won – the 'baddies' never did.

The cinema itself was very basic. Seats were long wooden forms with backs from which most of the varnish had been worn off. The floor was of wood, so if the film broke down, as it frequently did, the noise of stamping feet was deafening. One side of the cinema had three or four very tall windows, and blinds had to be drawn before each performance. This task was done by the head attendant or 'checker', as they were called. He was dressed resplendently in a plum-coloured uniform, with lots of gold braid and a 'cheese-cutter' hat. I remember him very vividly as he looked so much like King George V, beard and all, and he had a very regal air as he walked slowly to each window and lowered the long navy-blue canvas blinds. As each blind was lowered, a thunderous cheer went up from the audience, as by this time excitement was at fever pitch. The last blind down, the lights went out and the piano accompaniment began.

In the programme, there was always a serial like the Red Phantom, with a cliffhanger ending which enticed the youthful audience back for more. During the films, the checkers had a busy time keeping order. If some of the kids got out of hand, a torch was shone on them, with the curt order 'Keep quiet or out you go!'

To freshen the somewhat fetid air, scented water was sprayed over the audience from a long brass-handled spray by one of the checkers. On Hogmanay, a special matinee was given and everybody got an apple and an orange on entry to the cinema. The checkers were so pelted with orange peel and apple cores, and indeed with orange juice rained down on them from the balcony, that the format was changed to an apple and orange going OUT.

When, in 1929, talking pictures began, we couldn't understand what the actors were saying, never having heard Americans speak, but soon we were saying 'OK baby' in a poor imitation of the stars who we so adored from our seats in the 'Starrie'. It was a great little cinema, jam-jar entry fee and all, and it was a form of escapism for so many children in a world so depressed between the wars.[8]

The popularity of the cinema with the working class demonstrated the way in which both their spending power and their leisure time had increased. Saturday afternoons free from work became increasingly common from the 1870s, and a massive programme of leisure-time provision in late Victorian times gave Scotland many of its parks, libraries, museums and art galleries.

The inter-war years saw a dramatic rise in outdoor activity holidays. The Scottish YHA was established in 1931, opening its first hostel in a row of cottages in Selkirk.

Cycling and rambling clubs flourished. Seaside holidays for the working class grew from the day trips of the late nineteenth century to actual residence for some fortunate families.

Developments in leisure from the 1870s involved, especially, the establishment of a national structure for soccer and the founding of a whole host of famous clubs. The creation of Queens Park F.C. in 1867 was followed by Rangers (1872), Hearts (1873), Hibernian (1875) – a club that required (till 1893) its players to be Catholics – and Celtic in 1887. Though the latter came relatively late to the scene, its development in the nineties of a stadium to hold 70,000 was clear evidence of the sport's popularity. Footballers became heroes to boys like Bob Crampsey. Even amid the restrictions of the Second World War Bob Crampsey managed to watch numerous matches.

Wartime internationals followed a predictable pattern for us which took the following shape.

We presented ourselves at Hampden Park about one o'clock. If the weather was wet, and it often was, we came by train. If it was a good day we came on foot, playing football all the way along the banks of the River Cart. It was quicker to come over Langside Monument Brae but much too steep and busy for football. We played a game called "Combination" with a tennis ball and when one of us brought off a dexterous flick or header or delivered a pass of outstanding accuracy, the correct form was to murmur "Helluva nice", one of our more daring phrases. I employed it more than the other two boys and when we fell out, they would sometimes threaten to denounce me at home for my use of it.

Once inside the ground, we got as near to the front as we could. Our great dread was that a six-foot-nine-inch Grenadier Guardsman would come and stand in front of us. Fortunately, these were thin on the ground and, on their infrequent appearances, very punctilious about letting us stand in front of them. The time dragged, not greatly helped by the community singing – number four on your songsheets, lads – although Elliott Dobie, the famous Scottish singer, tried hard to whip up national fervour as he stood white-sweatered on the rostrum. Of all the songs, only one, The Bonny Wells o' Wearie, stays in my mind. It lodges there because it was so dirge-like, an all-too-frequently apt prediction of our performance, and because I never heard it anywhere else although it was an annual inclusion in the Hampden repertoire. The singing over, pipe bands marched briskly across the ground, droning remorselessly before retiring in good order up the sloped running track at the side of the stand.

The teams were then presented to the Duke of Gloucester or General Montgomery or Lady Churchill or some such dignitary and while it was no doubt a considerable thrill for the players, we boys found the string of introductions irksome in the extreme.

At last came the National Anthem, even in wartime often exhausting the patience of the crowd, so that the roar of anticipation began to growl in the last two bars. Then the kick-off, and the English in their billowing white shirts which gave a curious impression of broadness, would run amok. They didn't always win, of course – they had lost 5–4 in a memorable match in 1942 – but now a year later they demolished Scotland. Their marvellous right wing of Stanley Matthews and Raich Carter shredded the Scots defence and behind them the half-backs, Cliff Britton, Stan Cullis and Joe Mercer, played the polished, intelligent football that we had been brought up to believe was purely and peculiarly Scottish. On that April day in 1943 we got off lightly at 4–0.

Of course we knew why we had lost, we muttered darkly as we hid in a passage at the Mount Florida end of the ground after the match. We were hiding because there was to be a Scottish Junior Cup semi-final that same evening and we didn't see why we should have to pay for admission twice. So we ate our sandwiches, skulked and kept watch. We had lost because all the best Scottish players were away at the war, knee-deep in jungle ferns, tossing on the North Atlantic or even at that very moment flying over the Ruhr.

The English side, it was well known on the other hand, were not allowed to be sent further than ten miles from Aldershot, so it stood to reason that they would win, didn't it? What had the comedian said in the last Alhambra pantomine? The English would fight to the last Scotsman.

It was a comforting notion and we cherished it fiercely but it owed more to wishful thinking than to reality. Most of the pre-war players of Rangers and Celtic were still available to the Scottish selectors even in 1943 since the war record of neither club was at all distinguished. Other noted Scottish internationals such as Tommy Walker of Hearts and Jimmy Carabine of Third Lanark were certainly on call for much the greater part of the war. We preferred the conspiracy theory to the actuality, not daring to admit that the English had thrashed us because they were far and away the better side.[9]

Amid the growth of organized leisure, the inventive play of children exploiting their environment continued. Mary Rose Liverani, her sisters and brother, found much to do in Glasgow.

Summer made of the slum children honorary citizens of the city of Glasgow. They were free to roam about at will and they did; they went walkabout, runabout and for tuppence, tramabout, to Queens Park, the Bluebell Woods, Rouken Glen, Milngavie and Linn Park, where they dragged ponds for minnows and tadpoles, threw bread to ducks, stood amazed at the beauty of swans, climbed trees, played Swiss Family Robinson, fell into burns and crammed their stomachs with unripe crab apples, gooseberries, raspberries and plums, finally staggering home at night clutching their distended abdomens.

Straps in hand their mothers waited at the doors with one eye on the clock and another on the street.

'Where have ye been a' this time! Ye've been away since nine o'clock this morning and look at the time now. It's nearly eleven o'clock.'

'But it's not dark yet. Ye cannae go to tae bed when its daylight. That's no for sleeping in.'

'Aye well, get something inside ye and get straight tae bed after ye've had a wash. Tomorrow ye're going tae take Jack and Sadie with ye' because ah want tae gie the place a reel good cleen ook.'

Part of the vast herring fleet that fished off Shetland in the 1880s.

Mussel fishers on the Eden, Fife, 1930s.

Women filling barrels with salted herring, Castlebay, Barra, 1925.

An Arbroath fishworker processing part of a haddock catch over a fire of oakchips, 1966.

At work in Montrose jute mill, 1957, prior to the industry's collapse.

Fife and Clackmannan Mine Owners Rescue Station - the first in Scotland, opened 1911.

Members of the guild of hammermen, Turriff, celebrating Queen Victoria's Diamond Jubilee, 1897.

A clipper (right) taking shape in this 1860s photograph of Hall's shipyard, Aberdeen.

Opening the Highlands to the car: the new road through Glencoe, 1926.

A tram on Perth Road, Dundee, just before the tram electrification boom around the turn of the century.

Aberdeen families enjoying an outing to Bay of Nigg, 1934.

An early twentieth-century photograph taken on an Aberdeen beach.

Henry Raeburn, leader of the 1921 Everest expedition, relaxing on Salisbury Crags, Edinburgh.

Old Tom Morris, four times winner of the Open Golf Championship, Custodian of the Links, St Andrews, 1867-1903.

Evacuees at St Andrews, September 1939: three thousand came on special trains from Edinburgh.

Rescuing possessions from bomb-damaged property in Menzies Road, Aberdeen, 1941.

Oh god, what utter agony to have young brothers and sisters when you wanted to play.

In the morning, after going the messages we strode through the streets with Jackie and Sadie half running, half falling along beside us, each clutching tightly a grudgingly extended finger. [They caught a tram to Milngavie . . .]

Milngavie was a little village on the outskirts of Glasgow, right at the tram terminus. A burn flowed by it and it was this we made directly for. The water in one part was only a few inches deep. Flat smooth stones covered the bed like a Roman road and we sat on these in our knickers, over dresses tucked up round our waists. The youngest ones took their pants off, but the heat was never strong enough to risk letting them lie naked. My mother was always warning us to keep our chests covered. We drank the water, washed in it, stared into it for hours, dug up stones to see what was underneath, splashed ourselves, jumped into the burn, played leapfrog and fell into it.

The time had gone and we would be for it.

"Gosh, ah think it's late, ye know," Margaret said, beginning to gather up our things. "We better get their faces and hands washed. Mammy'll kill us if we take them home all dirty. His dungarees are still wet."

"Here, run up and down Jackie," I told him, "and they'll dry a bit."

So as we got near the tram stop Jackie slowed down and hugged his knees together.

"Ah have tae go to lavatory" he cried. We all stared at him in horror.

"There's nae lavvy here ye wee pest, why did ye no tell us before when we were at the burn?"

"But ah didnae want tae go then," he wailed.

"Ah want tae go noo and ah have tae. It's comin oot."

"Oh try and haud it in," we pleaded with him.

"It won't take long tae get home."

"Ah did it," he said unrepentantly. "Ah told ye it was coming oot."

Margaret got hold of Jackie's dungarees and pulled the

seat of them, looking down and holding her nose. She sighed hopelessly.

"It's a big messy one. And look, here comes the tram. What'll we do? He'll smell terrible and everybody'll knows he's dirted his pants. Oh ah could kill you," she shouted to Jackie, giving him a little shake.

Robert and Susan moved off a little way, "You can go upstairs wi' him and we'll sit downstairs."

"Oh no you're not," Margaret shouted at her, balling her hand threateningly. "We'll all go upstairs and we can sit all round him and that might keep the smell inside."

So that was what we did. When we got home we complained loudly to my mother.

"That Jackie's never coming wi' us again, the dirty little pig. If he comes we're staying home." Jackie, however, remained defiant.

"Ah told ye," he said. "Ah told ye it was comin oot."

The street games were intensely active and required extraordinary stamina to keep at them all day. Once the interminable games of rounders, cricket, soccer, headies and juggling had been wrung dry of every last drop of sweat, a slight breather was taken and then the ropes were set up. French skipping for the older and more skilful of us. By the end of summer many parents were sighing for the shorter evenings of autumn and winter when children were home punctually for their tea and anxious to get to bed before 11 o'clock; doors were constantly being thrown open or banged shut, as just one, then another came hurtling inside to whine.

"Mammy, Tom Smellies hitting our Robert."

"Mammy, can ah have a piece an' jam?"

"Mammy, Susan won't let me have a go wi' the peever, she says, ah'm too wee, but ah know how tae play."

"Mammy, Mammy, Mammy," till my mother, maddened by the unending attacks on her peace, grabbed a broom and flayed about her like Goliath run amok.[10]

The dangers of modern streets have reduced the opportunities for many of these activities; the lure of modern technology has further diminished their popularity. Yet a glance at any primary-school playground today will show inventive, imaginative play still flourishes.

CHAPTER XIII

DEPRIVATION

Poverty and hardship have been a part of Scottish history from the earliest times. Although the last two centuries have generally been a story of increasing wealth and higher living standards for the majority of the population, there has never ceased to be an army of the poor and deprived for whom the success of the majority was a mockery. Over time, the size of that army has varied. In the eighteenth century, the general standard of living and expectations of most people were vastly lower than they are today – Scots were poor, but relatively few were so particularly poor as to stand out as deprived. In the nineteenth century, just as most people, including working people, became better off, the absolute numbers of those who were in the deepest poverty also increased, and their plight became worse when it was associated with the bad housing and appalling public health of the Victorian inner cities. In our own century the general improvement has been greatest, and the army of the deprived has shrunk again through the assistance of the welfare state: but problems of poverty are persistent – in the inter-war slums and the postwar housing estates they have again been associated with the towns.

It is worth recalling, therefore, that before the Industrial Revolution, the face of deprivation was seen most clearly in the least accessible parts of the countryside, where the ground was infertile and population pressed against the available resources. Thomas Pennant's visit to Skye in 1772 describes the grinding poverty of the Hebrides long before the days of the Highland Clearances:

July 22. "Skie is the largest of the *Hebrides*, being above sixty measured miles long; the breadth unequal, by reason of the numbers of lochs that penetrate far on both sides. It is supposed by some to have been the Eastern *Aebudae* of the antients; by others, to have been the *Dumna*. The modern name is of *Norwegian* origin, derived from *Ski*, a mist; and from the clouds (that almost constantly hang on the tops of its lofty hills) was styled, *Ealand skianach*, or, the cloudy island. No epithet could better suit the place, for, except in the summer season, there is scarcely a week of fair weather; the summers themselves are also generally wet, and seldom warm.

The westerly wind blows here more regularly than any other, and arriving charged with vapour from the vast *Atlantic*, never fails to dash the clouds it wafts on the lofty summits of the hills of Cuchullin, and their contents deluge the island in a manner unknown in other places. What is properly called the rainy season commences in *August*: the rains begin with moderate winds; which grow stronger and stronger till the autumnal *equinox*, when they rage with incredible fury.

The husbandman then sighs over the ruins of his vernal labours: sees his crops feel the injury of climate: some laid prostrate; the more ripe corn shed by the violence of the elements. The poor foresee famine, and consequential disease: the humane tacksmen agonize over distresses, that inability, not want of inclination, deprive them of the power of remedying. The nearer calls of family and children naturally first excite their attention: to maintain and to educate are all their hopes, for that of accumulating wealth is beyond their expectation: so the poor are left to Providence's care: they prowl like other animals along the shores to pick up limpets and other shell-fish, the casual repasts of hundreds during part of the year in these unhappy islands. Hundreds thus annually drag through the season a wretched life: and numbers unknown, in all parts of the western highlands (nothing local is intended), fall beneath the pressure, some of hunger, more of the putrid fever, the epidemic of the coasts, originating from unwholesome food, the dire effects of necessity. Moral and innocent victims! who exult in the change, first finding that place *where the wicked cease from troubling, and where the weary are at rest.*

The farmer labors to remedy this distress to the best of his power, but the wetness of the land late in spring prevents him from putting into the ground the early seed of future crops, bear and small oats: the last are fittest for the climate: they bear the fury of the winds better than other grain, and require less manure, a deficiency in this island. Poverty prevents him from making experiments in rural economy: the ill success of a few made by the more opulent, determines him to follow the old tract, as attended with more certainty, unwilling, like the dog in the fable, to grasp at the shadow and lose the substance, even poor as it is.

The produce of the crops very rarely are in any degree proportioned to the wants of the inhabitants: golden seasons have happened, when they have had superfluity; but the years of famine are as ten to one. The helps of the common years are Potatoes: it is difficult to say whether the discovery of *America* by the *Spaniards* has contributed to preserve more lives by the introduction of this vegetable; or to have caused more to perish by the insatiable lust after the pretious metals of the new world.

The difficulties the farmer undergoes in this bad climate are unknown in the South: there he sows his seed, and sees it flourish beneath a benign sun and secured from every invasion. Here a wet sky brings a reluctant crop: the ground inclosed only with turf mounds, accessible to every animal: a continual watch employs numbers of his people: some again are occupied in repairing the damages sustained by their houses from storms the preceding year: others are laboring at the turberies, to provide fuel to keep off the rigor of the severe season: or in fencing the natural (the only) grasses of the country to preserve their cattle from starving; which are the true and proper staple of these islands.

The quantity of corn raised in tolerable seasons in this island, is esteemed to be about nine thousand bolls. The number of mouths to consume them near thirteen thousand: migration, and depression of spirit, the last a common cause of depopulation, having since the year 1750 reduced the number from fifteen thousand to between twelve and thirteen: one thousand having crossed the *Atlantic*, others sunk beneath poverty, or in despair, ceased to obey the first great command, Encrease and Multiply.[1]

During the following sixty years, the growth of industrial towns and cities was more rapid in Scotland than anywhere else in the world, and the characteristic scenes of poverty became urban, especially affecting those who moved from the country to the town with too few skills to afford the cost of decent housing. Edwin Chadwick's famous *Report on the Sanitary Condition of the Labouring Poor* of 1842, though nothing like so detailed statistically for Scotland as it was for England, drew a fearful picture. The following describes Greenock 'notoriously the dirtiest town in the west of Scotland' in the words of a local doctor in 1772:

The great proportion of the dwellings of the poor are situated in very narrow and confined closes or alleys leading from the main streets; these closes end generally in a *cul-de-sac*, and have little ventilation, the space between the houses being so narrow as to exclude the action of the sun on the ground. I might almost say there are no drains in any of these closes, for where I have noticed sewers, they are in such a filthy and obstructed state, that they create more nuisance than if they never existed. In those closes where there is no dunghill, the excrementitious and other offensive matter is thrown into the gutter before the door, or carried out and put in the street. There are no back courts to the houses, but in nearly every close there is a dunghill, seldom or never covered in; few of these are cleaned out above once or twice a year; most of them are only emptied when they can hold no more: to some of these privies are attached, and one privy serves a whole neighbourhood. The people seem so familarized with this unseemly state of things, and so lost to all sense of propriety, that it is a matter of no small difficulty, in some of the back streets, to make your way through them without being polluted with filth.

Behind my consulting rooms, where I am now sitting, there is a large dunghill with a privy attached; to my knowledge that dunghill has not been emptied for six months; it serves a whole neighbourhood, and the effluvium is so offensive that I cannot open the window. The land is three stories high, and the people, to save themselves trouble, throw all their filth out of the stair-window, consequently a great part of it goes on the close, and the close is not cleaned out till the dunghill is full: the filth in the close reaches nearly to the sill of the back window of a shop in front, and the malarious moisture oozes through the wall on the floor . . .

Like other towns in Scotland, Greenock has a large pauper population; the great bulk of these (I would say three-fourths) are natives of other places, having come here in search of employment, and from destitution, disease, and other causes, have been thrown a burden on the community. A great number come from Ireland and the Highlands with the express purpose of making a settlement, that is, supporting themselves in the best way they can for three years, when they can have a legal claim for relief from the parish. There are many who, though not claimants for public relief, suffer much, especially during winter, from want of food and fuel. We still here and there find some remains of that spirit of independence which would rather suffer than complain, still it must be a matter of regret to think that many, feeling unable to maintain that spirit of independence, are induced from their destitution to commit crime, perhaps their first offence, or fall a prey to disease in its most malignant form. Last winter, when visiting in my district, I was informed by a neighbour that there were two sisters in a garret in great want; I found one of them sitting over the scanty remains of a wood fire; I learnt that at one time they had been in good circumstances, but had been gradually reduced; they generally suppported themselves by sewing, but owing to want of work, they had tasted almost nothing for three days; a neighbour had given them a few potatoes, and the other sister was out looking for a few chips with which to boil them; by the little relief they got, they were enabled to subsist for a week or two till they found employment. Such cases of endurance are seldom met with, but equal destitution is to be found in every close in the poor localities. Typhus fever last winter carried off many heads of families and left their children destitute. As I was passing one of the poorest districts not long ago, a little girl ran after me and requested me to come and see her mother as she could not keep her in bed; I found the mother lying in a miserable straw bed with a piece of carpet for a covering, delirious from fever;

the husband, who was a drunkard, had died in the hospital of the same disease. There was no fire in the grate; some of the children were out begging, and the two youngest were crawling on the wet floor; it was actually a puddle in the centre, as the sewer before the house was obstructed, and the moisture made its way to the middle of the floor by passing under the door. Every saleable piece of furniture had been pawned during the father's illness for the support of the family. None of the neighbours would enter the house; the children were actually starving, and the mother was dying without any attendance whatever.[2]

The responsibility for care of the destitute fell to the Scottish Poor Law, which mainly concerned itself with the widowed and elderly – neither the unemployed nor (before 1845) the temporarily ill could expect support, though in some places the Kirk Session stretched a point. The Royal Commission on the Scottish Poor Law in 1843 gathered evidence on poverty and poor relief from the entire country. Here they are listing 'cases' visited at Meigle and Newtyle, in Angus – a country area with traditions of textile manufacture. The poor are various both in their character and their relationship to the kirk session that grants or withholds assistance:

1. John Martin, aged eighty-nine. Was tailor. Has 8s. per month. Session pay his rent. Decent country house. Wife and fourteen children. Youngest a soldier, aged eighteen. Decent furniture, eight-day clock. Said he had no complaints to make. When he has any wants he is supplied.
2. Betty Petrie, widow, above eighty. Has 7s. a month, and a person is paid to attend her. Decent bed, and enough of furniture. Plenty of coals in a corner. Bad floor, but house warm. She is unable to go out. Says "her attendant is doing well for her." She, the attendant, is the mother of a large family, and the elder of the district pays her more liberally on that account.
3. Thomas Isles, aged eighty. Bed-ridden. Has 6s. per month. Rent paid for him. Common country house, warm enough, but not neatly kept. Has a wife and one child, who does for herself.

No appearance of want in the house. Eight-day clock, good fire, and plenty of potatoes.

4. Margaret Lundie, widow, aged seventy-five. Has two daughters at service. She is a pauper belonging to Coupar-Angus. Has 5s. per month. Rent 10s. per annum. Her daughter assists her. She gathers dung. Mrs Murray of Simprim gives her £1. in the year. Says "she is as happy as they that have mair gear. She sees things they can't see."

Newtyle. 1. Rachel Fergusson, widow. Eldest child five or six years old. She was left with ten of them. She will not have any assistance from the parish. She has a very clean house, and two clean beds, and has brought her children very well up. Mr Watson, to whom her husband was shepherd, allowed her to keep her house and little bit of garden ground and her cow's grass, and with that assistance she has brought her family very well up.

2. May Cowie. Has had fever. Lives with her mother. Clean bed and tolerable country house. Has had assistance from the session, and from Mr Watson.

3. Elizabeth McGregor, at Bannatyne. Is not sure of her age, but was shearing in the snowy harvest, and cannot be less than eighty. She has a very clean house. Has 6s. a month from the session. She cannot shear this year, but she has "some bawbees remaining of former times, and she bought two bolls of coal the other day with her own siller." She has a good chest of drawers, and chairs, and good clean bed. Plenty of crockery and cooking utensils. "She can wash her ain claes, and sort her ain mutches." She showed her wedding gown in perfect order, and quite clean, though it never had been washed. An inventory of all the goods and effects had been taken by the session. She says "they shall be very welcome to them when she is done with them, as she has naebody to gie them to." She came from Braemar, and has been twenty years in Newtyle. "She never drinks tea except upon Sabbath." She has plenty of good clothes, "the siller she gets maun serve her, and she gars't serve her, and pays her way too."

4. Mary Percy. A pauper belonging to Alyth, residing in Newtyle. Not at home, but house very dirty.

5. Agnes Stewart, in the village of Newtyle. Has five or six illegitimate children. Has occasional aid from session. House good, but dirty and ill kept. Session have put her boy to school. A daughter who lives with her weaves, and she winds her pirns, and they make 4s. 9d. a week between them. The father of her children never assists them. Has a son in Dundee, who does not assist her. Her boy at home makes 5s. a fortnight by weaving, which he gives to his mother.

6. Colin Brown. A shoemaker. A bad character in the village of Newtyle. Has been twice in jail lately. While he was there the session gave his family 2s. a week, and Mrs Watson gave them two and a half pecks of meal in the week. She gives them clothes and coals. His rent is £2. He can gain 8s. a week at his trade as a shoemaker, but he is a determined blackguard, and will never do any good.[3]

It was Glasgow, however, growing in population and in wealth as no city in Scotland had ever done before, that remained the most dramatic and squalid example of urban deprivation. Everyone wanted to reform it – evangelist, temperance crusader, socialist, municipal activist. In *Midnight Scenes and Social Photographs* an anonymous journalist calling himself 'Shadow' (Alexander Brown) attempted to describe the environment of slum poverty in 1858. His scene is Wednesday night: the 'Forbes Mackenzie' referred to was an Act of two years earlier which closed the pubs all day on Sundays and enforced 11 p.m. closing on weekdays.

As we escape from the Saltmarket, amidst a dense mass of human beings, we have the curiosity to look in upon the hovels of certain of the poor. Following a plain but respectable looking man up a narrow filthy close, we express to him our interest in exploring the locality. "Aye, sir," he says, "there's some queer places here, if you only saw them, but puir folks are glad to put their heads onywhere," – saying which, he turns into a dark and dismal looking entry. "Come on, sir," he continues, "don't be fear'd; I'll let you see whaur we live, if they're no gaun to bed." Hereupon we follow through a low, damp, earthy-smelling, subterranean sort of passage, with so many windings that we begin to fear we are about to reach that "bourne from which no traveller returns," when an aged woman, with a face deeply furrowed, hearing our steps, opens the door, bearing a candle in her hand. Before we have time to utter a word, she ejaculates, "Tam, the man, what's keep't you the nicht? – wha's that wi' you?" "He's jist a gentleman, Nelly, that wants to see the hooses, an' I thocht I wud gi'e him a fricht by bringing him oor way, through the lang passage." "We're jist gaun to bed, man, what's keep't you? Jenny's been in her bed the last hoor-an'-a-half, an' has to rise at four in the mornin'. Come in, sir, if you will," addressing ourself, "it's no a braw hoose to ask you till, for we're jist gaun to bed." As we enter full of apologies for so untimeous a visit, we are forcibly struck with the remarkable appearance of the domicile, and a group of half-dressed people of both sexes collected around the fire-place. Before us is a singular looking man, strongly tattooed by the wrinkles of advanced age; he is sitting upon a trunk, in a state of partial nudity. Another man, of middle age, somewhat similarly conditioned, makes his escape, as we enter, into an adjacent room, wherein being without a door, we observe places for two or three beds on the floor, into one of which he gladly hides himself from our ill-timed intrusion. "How do you manage," we say, "to live in such a place as this – there must be at least six or eight of you huddled together in these small ill-ventilated apartments?" "'Deed, sir," says the elderly dame already referred to, "we're nae waur than our neighbours, an' we dinna think onything aboot it." Hearing this, we glance again at the wretched hovel. It is small, ill-lighted, and worse ventilated. A dirty farthing candle stuck into the neck of a bottle diffuses a melancholy light throughout the room. In a corner is a window, near the roof, just enough grudgingly to illuminate a prison cell. On the floor, at convenient distances, and almost at our feet, are placed two beds, in one of which is a young woman, a lodger, but a few days ago returned from harvest operations. In an obscure part of the abode is a large filthy pail, apparently the urinal common to the entire household. The scene is a peculiar one; but the hour does not admit of prolonged inquiry or observation; and so, with many apologies and thanks for generous indulgence, we quit this so-called "home" of the

poor, with the kind welcome of the good old woman – "We'll
be glad to see you anither time, Sir." "Thank you, thank you,
ma'am," is our reply, as we retrace our steps through the devious
windings forming the entrance to this strange abode.

Again reaching the streets, and just as we are about to cross
to London Street, a virago, with her underlip characteristically
protruding, is scolding in a loud and violent manner a quiet-
looking man, her husband, to appearance a shoemaker. She
follows close upon his heels, shaking her right hand at his back,
and by sundry gesticulations labours hard to arrest the attention
of passengers: "Aye man, an' ye gang to Prince's Street, do you!
– you hidden villain! – you blackguard! you dinna think aboot
your aucht weans, do you! Aye man, an ye thocht I wasna
watchin'! – but I'll watch, you hidden villain! – I'll split your
head like a pea shod!" saying which, she passes under the shade
of the Tron Church, with a train of followers, who have a relish
for the scene. We are curious to follow. As she continues her
scolding and abuse along the street, the man utters not a word,
but, sinful-like, slouches along, bearing his flagellation with
wondrous equanimity, when the pair make their way towards a
dark narrow lane, and the man stops at the bottom of a stair,
still speechless. At this provoking silence she seems doubly
infuriated, and draws herself alongside of him, – "Aye man, I'll
stand by you, that I will – you hidden villain you! you thocht I
wasna watchin'! – aye man, but I'll watch!" At which the meek
but fallen son of St. Crispin retraces his steps towards the street,
still followed by his better half. At length he jilts her by entering
a dark close, thereby leaving her to drown her wrath in sober
reflection, while he, in all probability, drowns his in ale or
whisky.

Returning to Argyle Street, we are struck with the unusual
throng and noise of the street, when we remember the Laigh
Kirk bell has not long announced the memorable hour of
eleven. Small groups are everywhere collected about in the ample
thoroughfare. Artizans, with their hands in their pockets, are
helping each other to pipe-light by the aid of a fuzee, as they
loiter about a close mouth in rather a merry mood, after having
been ejected by a disconsolate landlord in reluctant observance

of "Forbes Mackenzie." Women of all grades of abandoned condition are alert after their prey. Virtue is now forbidden the streets, or endangered by insult and molestation. Drink, in many cases, has got possession of reason, and the moral dignity of the man is submerged in that of the bestiality of the brute. A few paces from us, and a respectable-looking young man, apparently inebriated, is way-laid by one of these poor wretches of women. True to the behest of a great law, herself ruined, she ruins others. In a moment she succeeds in reversing his course, and they both proceed towards the Gallowgate. We are curious to jot the history of the case. The woman is of the very lowest description, and as she passes a few of her idle sauntering companions, sunk to the lowest extremities of vice, she is cordi- ally saluted. Entering a close in the Gallowgate, and turning into a dark stair at the right, the woman knocks at a door, knocks and knocks again, apparently in quest of drink. Despairing of attention, she draws fresh encouragement from the fact that she hears the stealthy footsteps of some one inside, approaching her. "Granny! granny woman! it's me," she cries, "open like a dear!" "Wheest! wheest!" echoes a soft trembling whisper from a sepulchral-looking door of a cellar, "it's owre late the nicht to let you in, – we canna do't – is there ony body wi' you?" "It's jist a frien," is the earnest reply. "Na, na, I'm no gaun to do't," says granny, and forthwith the unlucky pair withdraw from the door, showering upon "granny" a goodly number of curses and abusive epithets.[4]

The reputation of Glasgow as the home of the worst concentrations of poverty in the northern half of Europe continued until well into the present century – indeed, for certain forms of deprivation it continues to this day, the old reputation of the inner city and the Gorbals having attached to certain peripheral housing estates, though we should not expect deprivation to take exactly the same form in the twentieth century as in the nineteenth.

One of the principal causes of poverty, then and now, has always been unemployment. It was endemic in Victorian Scotland, especially among the less skilled, many of whom were thrown out of work for months or even years at a time when the trade cycle dipped into slump – as it did every eight or nine years with varying degrees of severity. On such occasions the Scottish Poor Law provided no help: the unemployed were obliged to beg, or were relieved by *ad hoc* schemes of public works and soup kitchens financed by charitable appeals in the towns. The most severe and prolonged period of unemployment, however, came in the inter-war period of the twentieth century, when for almost twenty years the unemployment rate in Scotland exceeded ten per cent, and between 1931 and 1935 exceeded twenty per cent. In 1931–3 more than a quarter of the entire workforce was out of a job. Ways of relieving the unemployed at that time were a mixture of the Victorian and the modern – relief works, often not very practicable, were still being promoted, but unemployment benefit ('the dole') was being provided by the nascent welfare state at the 'Broo', and the old poor law ('the Parish') was still operating for those not able to obtain other forms of relief. By now it did admit the unemployed to benefit, but at an extremely low level of relief.

The following oral recollection of what it was like to be poor and unemployed in the 1920s and 1930s comes from Aberdeen; the woman who is speaking was a young mother at the time:

Most of the people along the street was unemployed, looking for jobs. When the snow came on they used to queue the whole night to try to get a job in the snow. They got 10d an hour and Alec'd work as long as they would let him. They never got home through the day and they got 6d for a pie and a cup of tea. There was dozens of men queued up all night and the foreman came out and said, 'You, and you, and you.' Frozen with cold they'd stand – and yet they'd say the unemployed was lazy.

Then Lady Cowdray at Dunecht House started a scheme. She had hundreds of acres of estates and she wanted these great stone walls built round every bit. The men had to live in bothies on the estate and they'd to keep their wives and families in Aberdeen besides that – and she was paying 10d an hour. She got some single ones, but the married men couldn't do it – and then they were called lazy because they didn't take the work. They'd to have 2 pairs of good dungarees and 2 pairs of boots. How could they afford it?

There was so many unemployed in the town. The Broo was only giving 21/- for the four of us. The Board of Health said it wasn't enough to keep you alive and that the Councils would have to help the unemployed themselves. They started a scheme to build the golf course at Hazlehead and you would get seven and six more on your dole for working three days a week. So of course they all did that. The Hazlehead golf course was built with sweat and tears. They were soaking up to their oxters with the peaty boggy ground. His feet was frozen. He used to come home exhausted. My brother gave him an old bike. We used it for years.

He got a job in Gibb's granite yard in King Street. He took awful bouts of malaria fever because he'd been in Egypt in the war. He used to shake all over. This day he took ill at his work and he came home. Next morning he got his books sent to him and when he went to sign on at the Unemployment Exchange they said he wasn't entitled to any money because he'd left his job without cause. Well, you can never beat authority. They put him to the Parish, and the Parish gave him a chit for 14/- to get food, but no money. We'd no money for rent or anything like that. Oh they were hard. He got that for 3 weeks and then he'd to go before a Board. They discovered he hadn't left this job without cause so they gave him the back money, but we'd to pay back what we got from the Parish. But that was the finish of the granite yard. There was always someone ready to take your place. They used to undercut one another – take it for a few shillings less. They'd have cut one another's throats for a job. But my husband wouldn't do that – he was determined he would never take a job at less than anybody else.

My father took a job as a jobbing gardener when Col. Davidson died, but he wasn't doing very much. He gave Alec a few weeks when he was busy one time and paid him better than anybody else. He gave him £2 a week. Then in 1937 Alec got into the gasworks, after trying for years and years. And he was only there a few weeks. He'd ulcers of the stomach for years and he got word to go into hospital. You got 18/- insurance money when you were ill, and they hardly paid it till you was back to your work again. After a fortnight I hardly had any money. I went to the hospital and Sister come to me as I was leaving and she says, 'You must bring a big tin of cocoa for Mr Watt tonight when you come in. The doctor's ordered cocoa.' You had to bring in all your extras and cocoa was an extra. They never got an egg unless you took it in. I hadn't a penny to buy a smattering of cocoa, so Alec says to me, 'Go to the Parish when you're going home.' I went in fear and trembling to the Parish. The clerk at the desk would hardly listen to me. He said, 'Go to the insurance offices and kick up a row there about your money,' and slammed down the hatch in my face. I sat down in a chair in the corner and cried. I didn't know what to do. And this man come along and he says, 'What's wrong?' He took me into the office and gave me tea. He rang up the Britannic offices and gave them a right telling off about leaving people starving. And he gave me 35/- right into my hand. He says, 'When your husband comes out of hospital, come in and we'll give you extras for him.' Well, they sent me 2 pints of milk every day, and they made his money up to 35/- a week the time he was off ill. That was the only kindness we ever had from anybody.[5]

Those who talk about 'the bad old times', and consider that we ought to be grateful that things are not as bad as they used to be, sometimes have a point. There is also a saying from the Orient that those who ignore the lessons of history will be compelled to relive them.

CHAPTER XIV

ILL-HEALTH

Children born in the 1950s could reasonably expect to live well into their sixties. Inhabitants of Scotland of a century earlier would have found this figure impressive; Scots of the mid nineteenth century had an average life-expectancy barely into their forties. The circumstances amid which people lived during the eighteenth and nineteenth centuries contributed to this likelihood of an early death. The travels of Captain Burt, a mid-eighteenth-century English visitor to the Highlands, brought him into intimate contact with conditions and customs he found entertainingly offensive.

I was one day greatly diverted with the grievous complaints of a Neighbouring Woman, of whom our Cook had borrowed a Pewter Pudding Pan and when we had done with it and she came for her Dish, she was told by the servants below stairs that it should be cleaned and then sent home.

This the woman took to be such an intended injury to her Pan that she cried out "Lord! you'll wear it out!" and then came up stairs to make her complaint to us, which she did very earnestly.

We perceived the jest and gravely told her it was but reasonable and civil, since it was borrowed, to send it home clean. This did not content her at all and she left us; but at the foot of the stairs, she peremptorily demanded her moveable; and when she found it had been scoured before it was used, she lost all patience, saying she had had it 15 years and it had never been scoured before . . .

Not only here, but in other parts of Scotland I have heard several common sayings very well adapted to the inclination of the people to save themselves pains and trouble; as, for instance

"A clean kitchen is a token of poor housekeeping" ... This happened to a friend of mine.

Some few years ago he thought it would be his job to continue long in the Lowlands; and accordingly he took a house which was then about to be left by a woman of distinction. The floor of the room where she saw company was clean, but the insides of the corner cupboards, and every other part out of sight were in a dirty condition; but when he came to the kitchen he was not only disgusted at the sight of it but sick with the smell, which was intolerable; he could not so much as guess whether the floor was wood or stone, it was covered over so deep with accumulated grease and dirt, mingled together. The walls near the servants' table, which had been white, were almost covered with stuff spit against it; and bones of sheep's heads lay scattered under the dresser ...

Some of the inns in these remote parts, and even far south of us, are not very inviting: your chamber, to which you sometimes enter from without doors by stairs as dirty as the streets, is so far from having been washed, it has hardly ever been scraped and it would be no wonder if you tumbled over clods of dried dirt in going from the fireside to the bed, under which there often is timber and dust that almost fill up the space between the floor and the bedstead. But it is nauseous to see the walls and inside of the curtains spotted, as if everyone that had lain there had spit straight forward in whatever position they lay.[1]

The industrializing and urbanizing of Scotland in the late eighteenth and early nineteenth centuries probably increased the likelihood of an early death. Of the many dreadful diseases likely to terminate life, popular opinion found cholera to be the most alarming.

The realization that the provision of clean water supplies was the best way of tackling cholera led Glasgow to an ambitious scheme to tap Loch Katrine. The scheme opened in 1859. When the next cholera epidemic swept Scotland in 1865–6, only fifty-three Glaswegians succumbed to it. By comparison, in the tiny Fife burgh of Methil, whose inhabitants still drank foul polluted water, sixty-three people lost their lives. Improved health in Scotland in the later nineteenth century owed much to the development of central and local government and to the growing body of officials enforcing a lengthening list of laws requiring the provision of drains, sewers, water supplies and the checking of housing and food supplies. The operation of free market forces had allowed dreadful disease to flourish; rates, taxes and public-authority intervention provided an improved environment and a greater life expectancy.

For people in pain the nineteenth century brought important developments in treatment too. At the beginning of the century James Hall traversed parts of Scotland. Whilst passing through the Banffshire burgh of Keith he stopped to watch a diverting spectacle:

> While here, I saw a number of people collected in the streets, as if some accident had happened. Upon inquiry, I found it was occasioned by a woman having gone three different times to Doctor Dougall, to have a tooth drawn; and as often run out of his house, her tooth-ache going away whenever she saw him come with his instruments to pull it out. Though an extremely good-hearted man, and always glad when he had it in his power to do good, he was so irritated, when he saw her running out a fourth time, that, holloing after her, and ordering her to be stopped, he followed her into the street; and, having, as it was dry, laid her down, there pulled out the tooth, and left her, with half a crown, to a person to take care of her.[2]

From 1846 dentists began to use ether to ease the trauma of treatment. Painful medical treatments – including operations – had to be born stoically – perhaps with the aid of alcohol. The most highly regarded surgeons of the early nineteenth century were those who could lop limbs or remove organs with the greatest rapidity.

In 1847 James Young Simpson, working in Edinburgh, began to use chloroform to render patients insensible whilst they lay on the rough wooden tables in the sawdust-strewn rooms that served as operating theatres. The carbolic spray developed by Joseph Lister (also in Edinburgh) in 1869 brought the further benefit of a dramatic reduction in loss of life due to operation wounds becoming infected.

The Victorian period also witnessed the creation of a number of medical institutions. Charity hospitals, infirmaries attached to poorhouses, and local authority hospitals (especially isolation units

for people with serious infections) were all constructed. In 1855 a
Royal Commission looked at the way people mentally incapable of
coping with life were housed and treated. It turned up some worrying
evidence. This is an account of just one of the many institutions it
visited.

12 MILLHOLME HOUSE, MUSSELBURGH.

MR. MACKAY, *Proprietor.*

Visited May 2, 1855.

Millholme House stands a little way back from the main street
of Musselburgh, from which it is separated by the mill-lead. The
buildings occupied by the patients consist of two dwelling-
houses, separated from each other by an intervening house, and
of some straggling out-houses behind. The premises are rented
at £66 a year. The principal dwelling-house is occupied by Mr.
Mackay and his family, and the female patients. The second
dwelling-house is occupied by the head attendant and his wife,
by three male patients, and several females. A garden of more
than half an acre extends in the rear of these two houses, and
serves as airing ground for the females.

The out-houses are occupied by male patients and are all of
one story only. The airing-ground is behind, and is extremely
small.

On the day of our visit the house contained –

Private patients, male,	4
Private patients, female,	2
Pauper patients, male,	23
Pauper patients, female,	30
	59

FEMALES – In the principal dwelling-house, at the back, and sunk
several feet below the level of the ground, are two or three small
rooms occupied by the worst class of female patients. One of
these rooms especially was in a wretched condition. It contained
a trough bed, with loose straw covered by a sheet; and three

other miserable-looking beds on iron frames. The brick floor was saturated with urine. This room is so damp and cold, that a fire is constantly necessary, even in summer, to make it habitable. It has only a small barred window.

The apartments of the better class of patients are tolerably comfortable, but some of them are very small and crowded. One patient sleeps in a closet which just holds a bed. Two others occupy respectively very small closets. The larger rooms are much crowded, and, as there are no day-rooms, the patients take their meals either in the grounds or in their sleeping-rooms.

In general the sleeping-rooms have fire-places, and fires are said to be lighted when necessary. The windows are mostly barred; some of those towards the street have also trellis-work, and darkened panes. There are no lavatories. Some of the females wash in their rooms, some in the court, others in the kitchen.

MALES – The sleeping-rooms of the pauper male patients are all in the out-houses, and are entered directly from the open air. They are mostly paved with bricks, but one or two are floored with wood. The bricked rooms are generally damp, especially one which is occupied by patients of dirty habits. Each room contains three, four, or five beds, according to its size; fires were burning in most of them. In the room occupied by the worst class of patients, there are five trough beds, containing only loose straw covered by a sheet. The beds of the other patients have straw mattresses, and appear more comfortable, with sufficient coverings, but they have each only one sheet. The windows are all barred. The bedrooms are not supplied with chamber utensils, but pails are placed in them at night. There are no lavatories; the patients wash at the pump, or, in wet weather, under a shed. The furniture is limited to benches. There are no separate day-rooms, and the patients take their meals as they best can, either in their sleeping-rooms or in the yard.

Three male patients sleep in a small dark room on the ground floor of the second dwelling-house, opening directly from the yard. The floor is flagged and damp, and is without any carpet or matting. A small fire is here constantly necessary. This room serves also as a passage, and is lighted by a glazed door.

The garden behind the house serves for the women's airing ground. It is about two-thirds of an acre in size, and is pleasantly laid out. The men's airing-ground is only about 30 yards long, and 20 yards broad, and is entirely taken up by a bowling-green and a walk around it.

There are no occupations for the men, except a little garden work. A few of the women sew. In one of the largest of the sleeping-rooms five females were thus engaged, under the care of an attendant.

Besides Mr. and Mrs. Mackay there are two male attendants, who receive £24 and £20 per annum respectively; and six female attendants and servants, at £8 per annum each.

For the season of the year the patients were sufficiently clothed, and appeared adequately fed. The diet consists of porridge and milk, or tea, for breakfast; broth and bread for dinner; and porridge and milk again at night; but there are no means of ascertaining the quantities allowed to each patient.

Restraint is in habitual use. One man, A. S., was handcuffed. A female, I. G., was in a strait-waistcoat. A shower-bath, which stands in an unenclosed outer shed, is occasionally used to quiet patients; it has a very high fall.

The rate of payment for pauper patients is £22 a year. Mr. Mackay has hitherto refused to receive any on lower terms, and one patient was removed to Mr. Aikenhead's on this account.

The private patients have tolerably comfortably bedrooms and are provided with a day-room.

The books kept are the Weekly Register and the Madhouse Register. Restraint is generally recorded, but not in the manner required by the statute.

A missionary attends once a fortnight.

There appears to be a disposition to treat the patients well, but the house is too full, and hence some of them are placed in damp and cheerless rooms, quite unfitted for occupation.

On the 26th May we again visited this house. On proceeding to the room of the worst class of patients, on the female side, we found I. G. standing in the middle of the floor on the damp bricks, in a strait-waistcoat, with no other clothing but her shift. A small fire was burning.

On the male side, we found A. S. lying in a trough bed on loose straw. The body of his shirt scarcely reached below the waist, and the sleeves did not reach the elbows. His arms were confined by handcuffs, and a strap was attached to the bed, to fasten him down at night.

On 31st May we again visited this house. I. G. was still in restraint, and on the floor were puddles of urine. A. S. was still in bed, strapped down, with his hands manacled.[3]

The consequence of the Commission was legislation in 1857 introducing better supervision of the system.

Despite the medical improvements of the Victorian period, typhus and tuberculosis, scarlet fever and measles, diphtheria and whooping cough were all frequently able to carry off human life. Angus Maclellan's experiences of illness on South Uist in the later nineteenth century show the problems of coping with the hardships of life in pre-welfare-state days.

When I was young (I was about 13 at the time) one of my brothers caught the fever on the Isle of Skye. He came home and when he got well after coming home, he went back to the Isle of Skye. After he had gone back my brother Hector who was at home fell ill.

We had a doctor called MacDonald who lived at Dremsdale. The doctor was sent for and he said that Hector had the fever. The doctor went away. Only a few days after he had gone 2 of my sisters fell ill with the fever. 3 of us were ill then. Then my father fell ill. I was happy enough as long as my mother was up, but unfortunately she herself fell ill and the 5 of them were ill together and there was no-one to look after them but myself. No-one was coming near them or near the house. I had to fetch peat from a good distance and I had cattle to look after, too, and I had no-one to help me.

Well, the doctor used to come fairly often. Every day that he came he used to say to me, "Don't be afraid at all, I don't believe you'll catch it. But put out every drop of water that's indoors at night and bring in fresh water."

I was alright as long as my mother was about but when she

herself fell ill my heart broke and I'm sure I wept enough tears to have washed my clothes with sorrow when I had no-one left to help me. They were allowed to have nothing but rice and milk. Well, we had only one cow to milk and I'm sure I went to milk her pretty often. Every time I went to milk her, I would get a jugful of milk from her and I used to go every day over to the head of the loch to get milk from the MacRaes house; they were very kind to me, their mother wouldn't think of putting a drop of milk in their tea, but kept it for me until I came for it. Things were hard enough for me; when I got wet with the rain, I had only the clothes on me to wear until they dried on me, and at last my skin broke out in a rash.

The first to recover was Hector. He got up and used to come to the fireside, that was all he could do. Then my sister got up. My mother and father were the last to recover; it was a very long time before my mother got up, I was wearing the same clothes for 6 whole weeks . . .

A few years afterwards these MacRaes were going to Benbecula. When they were making their flitting they had a servant girl, a cousin of theirs called Mary MacRae, and while they were flitting the poor girl fell ill in Benbecula and caught the fever herself and died.

After her death James MacRae and his brother Donald came over to take the thatch off the house so that they might take the beams and rafters to Benbecula. What happened but James fell ill at Loch Eynort. There was no bed or anything in the house, they had taken the bed away, he could only make his bed on the floor. One day my mother was baking and she had been churning. She told me I must go over to the MacRaes house with milk and bread and butter.

"You go over," she said, "to where James is, but take good care you don't go in: even if God saved you before take care you don't go inside."

When I reached the MacRae's house I went into the shack yard and whistled. No-one came out. I entered the house. I found only James; he was in bed in the kitchen and his bed was on the floor. He said "Oh, thank God there's someone who'll come in though I were dead."

"Are you thirsty?"

"Indeed I am."

"Oh well," I said, "I've plenty of milk."

When he had drunk it he said, "Oh, may your soul and the souls of your people be rewarded for that in heaven, but I hope to God you won't catch anything I have."

"I won't," I said ...

James said that the worst was over and he recovered all right, and I didn't catch the fever.[4]

In the second half of the nineteenth century surgery became more sanitized and more prevalent in Scotland's hospitals. Administrators and medical staff began also to attend more to the general level of care and support given to those admitted to hospital. One patient recounted her experience in a northern infirmary in the *Aberdeen Free Press* in 1895.

On account of the unsatisfactory state of my health, each visit saw Dr Orton more unwilling to operate, until at last, seven weeks after my admission, he saw I was gradually getting weaker, and that the only hope of saving my life lay in operating immediately. The day was fixed at last! Those days and nights of preparation seemed interminable. I suffered indescribable agonies! The starvation regimen which formed part of the preparation served to increase the pain unspeakably.

And now it was eleven o'clock. Half-past eleven was the time fixed for the operation. Nurses, sister, and house surgeon had just completed my preparation, and I was reading a note handed in by my husband, and wondering vaguely if this was to end all. I was silently committing myself and all so dear to me into the hands of the Great Physician, when Dr Orton came to see me. He held my hand tightly as if to say, "You may well trust me," and after ordering a little brandy for me he left the ward.

I fixed my eyes on the door. Presently a burly porter arrived with a trolley, which he drew up beside my bed. I was lifted from it and placed on this. The porter, accompanied by sister and two nurses, wheeled me through the ward, and along the corridor to the lift. Here the nurses left us to go to the theatre by the stairs. The lift was set in motion, and sister, the porter, and I went down, down, down. On landing on the ground floor I was wheeled along a narrow, winding passage to the theatre. Here in the gallery a crowd of students sat in rigid stillness! In the large bay window nurses and doctors were busy with sponges and antiseptic spray! I was wheeled to the centre of the area, where stood a long table about a foot higher than the trolley. Here were Dr Orton and two assistant surgeons, all in long, linen, sleeveless coats. The door was shut. I was placed on the table. The doctor who was to act as chloroformist stood by my head.

"Are you feeling nervous?" he asked.

"Not in the very least," I answered.

"What were your feelings?" I have often been asked since. I'm afraid I shall never be able to describe them. They were altogether so unreal!

"When I put this cloth over your face, take long, deep inhalations, will you?" said the chloroformist.

"Yes."

Then I saw an exhibition of the most lovely kaleidoscopic colours, and suddenly a distant chorus of the most heavenly music, compared with which the most perfect rendering of the "Hallelujah Chorus" would be tame and commonplace. Then followed a period of nothingness much as one experiences in a deep, unbroken sleep.

"How are you feeling, Mrs Hedley?" I opened my eyes at the sound of my dear nurse's voice. I was again in my bed in the far corner of the ward. I was entirely screened, and beside me stood the house surgeon, sister, and Nurse Chrystie. I was tortured with fearful sickness and burning thirst. I would have given my all for a drink of water, and yet all that was safe to give me was a small teaspoonful of warm water every three hours!

Of the first few days I remember very little, as I was almost continually under the influence of hypodermic injections of morphia. I shall never forget the first glorious sensation of convalescence. Whereas I had formerly awakened in pain, I now awoke with a lazy yawn, only to close my eyes again in refreshful slumber. Every day saw me a little stronger and much more hungry. No poor beggar ever pleaded more pathetically for a crust of bread than I. Yet full ten days passed before I was allowed a finger of toast. During these days none of my friends were allowed to see me, and except for the visits of doctors and sisters, I was alone with my "special." Never did nurse tend patient more patiently. Her movements were so quiet, her touch so gentle, her look and words so bright and hopeful – although she has told me since how she feared for me.

It was on the day I got my first solid diet (!) of toast that Nurse Chrystie was called to another ward to nurse a very critical case. One of my screens was removed, and I was left to the care of the ward nurses. Oh! how miserably lonely I felt, and nurse's eyes filled, as she told me of the summons!

Another fortnight completed my cure. On the evening of the twelfth day, wee Jeanie bought an evening paper, and sent it by a nurse to me. The child had noticed that I had given up buying one for some time, and had thought the reason must be pecuniary.

At this time a young girl was brought in to the bed next to mine, very ill. The doctors had no hope of her from the first. One morning I was awakened by hearing Jessie in breathless gasps crying out, "Oh! nurse, I'm dying." Her mother was sent for, and screens surrounded the dying bed. I could hear the mother say a paternoster and the feeble voice of the sufferer repeat – "Jesus, Jesus, I give Thee my heart and my soul. I am sorry I have sinned against Thee. Assist me in my dying moments!" This they continued repeating until a priest arrived, who administered the last sacrament. When the priest was gone, the mother, who seemed a very callous, stoical person, said, "Jessie, I doot I'll need tae gang hame, an' look aifter the denner." "Oh! dinna leave me, mother, I'm dyin'," pleaded the poor girl, but in vain. When she had left, I heard the girl say to sister, "Take me in your arms and kiss me. You have been very kind to me." Then there was stillness! The mother arrived too late!

Now, my friends came to see me, – my husband, my brothers, my sister, and my mother. The old interest in life, which had been greatly abated, came back again. Whereas before my operation my mirth was all assumed, now it was natural, spontaneous, uncontrollable!

The last day came. A cab was ordered to take me back to the home of my friend. I was assisted once more to the lift, and down, down I went, but this time on an easy chair, to be clasped in the arms of my husband on the ground floor.[5]

A range of treatments was available for purchase by people trying to avoid payments to doctors. Though some workers were covered by health insurance after 1911, Molly Weir's recollections show how, even in the inter-war years, the many who had to pay doctors' fees struggled to cure themselves.

If there was one field where we felt we excelled above all others it was in the matter of home cures. Doctors were only called in when all else had failed. Apart from the cost, we had great faith in the folk medicine which had been handed down to us from one generation to the next.

For whooping cough the favourite cure was to suspend the victim over a tar-boiler, or 'torry-biler', as we called them. During an epidemic of the 'whoop' it only needed a whiff of the boiling tar to send us rushing home. 'Mammy,' we would pant, 'the torry-biler's here. Do you want to haud Willie ower it to cure his whoop?'

Mothers would seize unwilling victims and drag them from the house – no-one was keen on having this cure himself, but all thoroughly enjoyed the sight of others getting it. Soon there would be a procession of mothers, patiently queuing to hold the spluttering child over the boiling, bubbling inferno, smoking like hell itself.

'Take big breaths, son,' they would urge. 'Draw it right doon into yer chest, and you'll no' cough any mair.' The victim, gasping at the sudden rush of tarry smoke which threatened to choke him, would cease coughing from sheer fright. Mothers would nod with triumphant smiles at each other, well satisfied that this free cure had worked once more.

Mind you, there were terrible tales of butter-fingered mothers who had allowed wriggling children to fall right into the bubbling pitch, later to be extricated coated forever in a deadly black embalming jacket. We'd never actually known anyone to whom this had happened, but the mere thought that it might have happened, and could do so again, was enough to make us stifle the slightest cough whenever we had occasion to pass the tar-boiler in company with an adult.

It was this added risk which made the sight of other children held high over the tar take on the excitement of a horror film. We would watch them with our breaths held in suspense until each little victim had feet planted safely on the pavement again. Only then would we resume our play, finding some of the soft tar to make 'torry-balls', which we rolled between our palms. Hardened in cold water, we used them like marbles for our games.

Some more fanciful mothers, with influential relatives, managed to get a card which admitted them to the gasworks, and swore by the effectiveness of the fumes there. The children were marched into the retort chamber, then instructed to climb upstairs and inhale deeply, to allow the gas fumes to circulate in their wheezing chests. It seemed to work, too, in spite of the envious sneers of those who couldn't get cards to take them inside the gasworks, and who declared it was just the diversion of the journey and the excitement of getting inside this impressive building which cured the weans.

One horrible scourge in our tenements was ringworm. I caught it myself, because a wee girl in my class at school fancied the tammy knitted for me by Grannie. She snatched it off my peg and pranced around the playground with it the whole of playtime one day, before I could grab it back. I jammed it firmly over my own curls and wore it in school the rest of the morning in case she would run away with it, for I knew Grannie would be mad if I lost it. What I didn't know was that the cheeky wee girl had ringworm and the infection had found a new home in my scalp! Home cures were no good this time and I was hauled off to the doctor, where every curl was cut off, then my head was shaved, and a bottle of iodine poured over it. I was taken to that surgery every Sunday, which was the one day my mother could spare from work, and more iodine poured over until the infection was killed. Oh the shame and misery of that shaved head! To be a skinhead in our tenements meant only one thing – ringworm! It shouted aloud as though I had carried a bell, and intoned 'Unclean, unclean', and left such a mark on my mind that I could never again be persuaded to let anybody try on my hats, nor would I even try one on in a shop afterwards, in case anybody with ringworm had been there before me.

Another head invasion, almost impossible to avoid in the tenements, was nits and head lice. The sight of fingers scratching at our heads was the signal for my mother to send us down without delay to the chemist for some quassia chips. These wee wood-shaving-like things were boiled up in water and the liquor strained off, and then a comb was dipped in the brew and drawn from root to tip of our hair. This went on for days, till all the eggs were tracked down, but unlike the iodine, which was drastic on hair roots, the quassia chips brew gave the hair a lovely gloss.

Borrowed combs were said to be the cause of spreading nits from one to another, and for a while we'd remember never to lend anybody our comb, then freedom from itch would make us careless – we'd lend our comb, and the quassia chips went on to boil again.

Worms was another affliction of our infants. It was quite usual to hear big brothers or sisters asking the chemist for a 'worm powder for my wee sister'. 'How old is she?' the chemist would inquire, unmoved at the thought of a human being having worms. I used to shudder at the thought of those wriggly things in anybody's inside, and wondered how they got there in the first place. It was whispered that pieces spread with oatmeal and sugar resulted in worms, but I liked this concoction so much I refused to believe such a tale.

We all believed implicitly that the huge jars on the chemist's shelves, filled with orange or royal-blue liquid, held the unborn babies till the mothers came into the shop to buy them. We'd stare intently at those bottles, imagining we could see the tiny infant shape swimming about in this glamorous liquid.

We were most interested in each other's purchases and could diagnose each ailment from the goods bought. Gregory's Mixture, declared by my mother as a marvellous cure-all, meant somebody's stomach was out of order. 'Enough to cover a sixpence' was the recognized dose. This was stirred in cold water and swallowed as rapidly as possible, for the smell was awful, and it helped to keep it down if the nose was held firmly as the nauseous drink was imbibed.

If the stomach wasn't too badly upset, and the discomfort could merely have been a touch of wind, then a pinch of baking soda in water was highly favoured by all of us. I quite liked this. It had a sort of flavour of puff candy, and the ensuing belches or 'rifts' were warmly encouraged, instead of being frowned upon as downright bad manners if heard at any other time . . .

We all shared the nightmare of toothache, and agreed with Rabbie Burns, strong language and all, that it was 'the hell o' a' diseases'. Apart from the fact that it cost two-and-six to have a tooth extracted, we were all terrified of the dentist, and only the punishing agony of a tooth rotten beyond the solace of our home-made remedies would drive us to his chamber of horrors. I quite enjoyed oil of cloves, the flavour strongly reminding me of Grannie's delicious apple tarts, but Sloan's Liniment had a heat and bite when rubbed inside and outside my cheek which brought tears to my eyes.

Adults swore to the relief afforded by a tiny drop of whisky dropped into the throbbing cavity, and once, when my own toothache had reached the unendurable stage, I was permitted a tiny drop of the golden brew. Not nearly so nice as cloves or myrrh, in my opinion, but strangely effective.

If the toothache developed into a gumboil, a favourite cure was heated salt inside an old sock laid gently against the swollen cheek. This was the cure, too, for a sore throat, and it was quite a performance heating the salt on a shovel, then guiding it into the sock with the aid of a big spoon, making all possible speed before the salt cooled. It was slapped against the sufferer's throat, and yells of 'It's too hoat!' met with the invariable reply, 'It has to be hoat to do ye ony good.' A scarlet neck, stiffly held away from a chafing collar, was mute testimony next day that the victim had been right. It had been too hot.

It was seldom that the hot-salt-sock cure was required a

second night. When asked how the throat fared the reply usually came surprisingly swiftly, 'Ma throat's fine noo.'

Rheumatism was an old people's disease, and anaemia a young one's trouble. Sometimes, when I was a bit anaemic after 'flu, I'd have to take Blaud's Pills. I found these so difficult to swallow that my mother was driven to try to break them on the kitchen table, using the poker as a cleaver. Those attempts dented our table for all time, and when the question of pills was raised as a cure for anything she would stare accusingly at the marks, and tell the story all over again of how thrawn I was at refusing to gulp down such a wee pill. But an uncle gave us a good laugh by coming to my defence with the suggestion that maybe I had a wee throat like a whale, which balked even at a tomato skin. 'She's certainly got a memory like an elephant,' retorted my mother, 'so maybe she's got a throat like a whale. Onywey, she's ruined my good table.'

For her own persistent affliction, blinding headaches, my mother found nothing better than a cloth dipped in vinegar, which I placed over her eyes as she stretched out on the bed. As the cloth dried, I'd dip it again and again in the saucer of vinegar, and soon she would drift off to sleep, soothed by this pungent bandage.

One old lady told me that when she was a wee girl her mother's cure for all the ills that God could send was the 'traycle' tin. This was a tin filled nearly to the top with black treacle, and it was put on top of the range to make it warm and runny. Into it went a big spoonful of Epsom salts, one of senna powder, one of Gregory's Mixture, and a pinch of sulphur. Then the lot was well stirred, round and round, and the whole family had a teaspoonful every night till the tin was empty. The taste was horrible, she told me, and the grit stuck to their teeth, but not a lad in the family ever suffered from pimples, and they all had clear and smooth skins, and required no other medicine throughout the year.[6]

Scottish medical schools were among the most eminent of the institutions that trained doctors. By the twentieth century women had won the battle to enter the profession.

Until the coming of the National Health Service in 1948 doctors had to charge many of their patients and manage their practices with a very careful eye on business matters. C. B. Gunn entered practice at the end of the nineteenth century.

In the Cowgate Dispensary, I extracted my first tooth, and in doing so made two mistakes. I set the patient, a half drunken Irishman, in a cane chair which was far too light in construction. Then, without any preliminary manoeuvres, but relying on force alone, I pulled the right upper molar as hard as I could. At first nothing happened; then, all of a sudden, I was flung violently back against the wall and the Irishman, as violently, was thrown in a heap on the floor, the ruins of the chair on top of him. But my hand still grasped the forceps, which in turn still grasped the tooth!

At Newburgh I soon became accustomed to the routine of daily duty. At nine each morning the Dispensary opened. Thither I proceeded, to dispense medicines and drugs to all and sundry. Thereafter I saddled the grey mare, and as a rule rode "west." This meant towards Abernethy and the adjoining region, which lies in the county of Perth.

In the afternoon we "did" the town, each independently visiting his own part of the practice without overlapping. Before starting, I devoted another hour to the Dispensary; the last attendance there was from six to seven o'clock. On all these occasions advice was given, as well as drugs made up.

It was a strenuous life, and work seemed never ending. My salary as Assistant was £80 per annum. All the night duty was discharged by me, at all seasons and in all weathers.

When on horseback one could not carry lights, but had to trust to the horse's instinct in avoiding dangerous parts of the road. There was no tar macadam, nor electric torches, then, and the risks were many. Occasionally mists descended, and so obscured the atmosphere that one became bewildered and lost. Sometimes, on finding the wall of a cottage, I had to dismount, tap at the window, and ask the suddenly aroused inmates where I was.

All maternity instruments were carried in one's many

pockets; and on stormy or snowy nights a riding-cape covered all. It was never possible to make up sleep, for on returning in the morning, after bath and breakfast, one had to resume the daily round, the common task. I often wore my riding-boots and spurs throughout the day, and folks remarked that the Assistant slept in them.

Looking back, I am inclined to think that these Fife maternity cases were unduly protracted and severe, and that this was possibly due to local conditions of existence, as many of the mothers spent their days sitting at the handlooms weaving linen, and took little other exercise. When I went first to Newburgh one might hear at the mouth of every wynd the rattle of the shuttle; now there is not one surviving, their place having been taken by steam-power in mills.

Three dogs accompanied me on my daily rounds on horse-back: Nell, a greyhound, Dizzy, a Scotch terrier, and Jock, a wire-haired mongrel. Dizzy and Jock invariably behaved well, and passed their time in the open while I was engaged with a patient; but, despite all my efforts at discipline, the greyhound never failed to obtain entrance, not merely to the house, but to the sickroom, where, with one swift silent leap, she would ensconce herself on the bed. Her interest in my professional methods never diminished!

So our daily cavalcade proceeded: greyhound Nell ever in the front line, myself next on the grey mare, the Scotch terrier scampering alongside, and wire-haired Jock all over the place, chasing every rabbit and cat we encountered. The nightly clatter of our hoofs on the causeway of the long High Street wakened the douce Newburgh burgesses, who doubtless turned in their warm beds with the drowsy comment: "There's the Assistant away by." Often I walked the midnight echo against the lofty cliff of Clatchart, as I rode eastwards in the silent night.

I was ever a light sleeper, and would usually wake on hearing, at first distantly, then nearer and nearer, the ominous plod-plodding of some ploughman's horse steadily approaching the doctor's house. The messenger's purposeful tread down the short avenue followed; then the noisy jangling of the bell. Up would go the blind to ascertain the kind of weather, and whether or not there was a moon; then a hurried dressing, unlocking the stable door, rousing the sleepy horse; on with saddle and bridle, and so away on my lonely ride ...

Among my duties in the Dispensary were 3 which caused me much trouble; pills, plasters and ointments. These had to be manufactured by hand. For pills, breadcrumb and treacle was added [to] the medicament, the whole mass rolled out, chopped small and rolled into the shape of pills. Ointments were made in the kitchen where the housekeeper placed a large pot of melted lard on the fire ...

[One] doctor ordered 6 leeches to be applied to a man's stomach, the patient's wife [said] 'he could na' swallow a' the leeches raw, so we just fried three'.[7]

George Gladstone Robertson worked in quite a different area – the Gorbals district in Glasgow. He began practice there in 1923 and remained for fifty years.

Prior to the introduction of National Insurance in 1912 most doctors in the industrial parts of Glasgow kept a chemist's shop alongside their consulting rooms. Although the 1912 Act insisted that these shops be given up by the doctors, the practice of charging an inclusive fee for medicine and service had become so standard that the majority of doctors continued to dispense medicine to their private patients. Insured persons obtained their medicine on prescription from authorised chemists.

On arriving in the consulting rooms after a round of visiting, my first task was to make up medicines for the private patients I had seen in their homes and leave it, correctly labelled, in the hall to await collection. The better-off patient did not pay cash, but was sent a quarterly account. The poorer patient paid cash when money was available and, if not, asked that the fee be charged to account. More often than not this resulted in the fee never being paid at all. Generosity to the dependants was rewarded by the growth of one's panel of insured patients, but as the doctor had to pay for the medicine out of his own pocket some care was needed if he were to make ends meet ...

The tenements in which the people lived, or in many cases,

simply existed, were almost universally four storeys high. A great number had been built initially as large houses, but were now divided up into tiny apartments. One of the most squalid blocks was at 197 Centre Street. On each landing a passage went to right and left and four homes were entered from each narrow corridor. A small gas jet beside the stairway provided the only means of lighting this stench-laden cavern and as I climbed the worn steps, usually to answer some call in the hollow early hours of a long dark winter's night, I would creep through the shadows and hear the sounds of snoring, children crying or screaming; the never-ending squabbling between husbands and wives. In this building there was a fifth level of attics, making about thirty-six houses in all. Over two hundred people were crowded together in this miserable and hellish tenement.

The eerie sounds and the flickering shadows of the gas light were only minor obstacles with which I had to contend on my night visits. Men, and sometimes women, too drunk to crawl through their own doorways, lay in the passages. Some I managed to avoid, but more often than not, I would stumble and trip over a sprawled figure to be greeted on some occasions by a stream of oaths from the body I had jerked back into consciousness. This was humanity living at its lowest level and the drunks strewn in untidy heaps, many of them lying in their own vomit, would soon become a shameful symbol of the Gorbals and bring a stigma on Glasgow which the city would find difficult to erase.

In many cases the total possessions of a family would be worth little more than a five-pound note and sometimes a father, mother and six children would all be living, cramped together, in a single apartment. The birth-rate was high, but so, too, was the incidence of death, especially among the very young. However, despite the squalor and the utter state of hopelessness which stared thousands of people directly in the face, the enlarging of families went on as baby after baby was born into a life surrounded by misery and perpetual torment.

In one three-apartment flat in another part of Centre Street I delivered a woman of her twenty-second child. She was married to her second husband and on the second or third day after the birth of a child was always up and about and out to work in a greengrocer's shop as if nothing untoward had happened. Even after her twenty-second baby she rose from her bed on the third day and went back to work. In all she had twenty-six pregnancies – there were four miscarriages. To her, childbearing and the ultimate delivery were no joyous and wondrous occasions. They were merely mechanical happenings, bereft of love; duties which she, as a woman, was called upon to perform.

Most doctors were on their own or had one assistant to help out. Partnerships were rare. The older and more successful practitioners could afford to be selective and largely confined their attention to families of regular patients who could pay them for their services. A young doctor, like me, trying hard to make a way for himself, had to go wherever he was called. As a result things could become extremely exhausting.

The proportion of late or night calls was always high; not because the baby or child had turned ill late at night, but because it was then that the parent became worried or developed a bad conscience over previous neglect during the day. In many cases a husband would arrive home about 11 p.m. after an evening's hard drinking. His wife would immediately set about upbraiding him for wasting his time and neglecting the children. In order to hammer home her feelings she would point to the baby, who, due to the surrounding row, would almost certainly be awake and crying through fright and the pain of teething troubles. This provided a cue for the husband that he would 'bloody soon get her a doctor' and off he would stumble to the nearest telephone.

If, in answering the phone, I protested that he should have sent his request earlier or added that he had not yet paid for the last late call I had made to his house, I would normally be subjected to a stream of obscenities along with threats of complaints being made to medical executive bodies, the police or the Press – sometimes all three.

For a time I always went out to the first, second and even third late call, but eventually one's sense of what was fitting and reasonable led to refusal, such as when I had been hauled out of the house at 11 p.m., again at midnight, probably around 2 a.m. and was then being asked to attend to another baby at 4 a.m.

The strain of losing so much sleep was becoming too great, but the act of actually refusing to make a call brought on a mental strain. Even after replacing the telephone receiver and returning to my bed my conscience would keep on nagging me over what I had done and sleep was again denied me as I lay wrestling with the problem . . .

At that time I was losing a baby nearly every week due to broncho-pneumonia; the babies were almost equally divided between those occurring at home and in hospital. My colleagues in hospital never tired of advising me to keep the babies in their own homes if possible as the hospital mortality rate was extremely high.

Deaths from this form of pneumonia were far more numerous than all my other deaths put together. Why was pneumonia so common among babies and why did almost fifty die each year? It was well known that the mortality rate of babies in the city suburbs was much lower than in the Gorbals–Tradeston–Hutchesontown area, but despite the poverty in many of the homes there was no reason to suppose that the young children were being starved. Indeed, I often thought that the very fat babies succumbed the more easily. The more I thought about the problem the more puzzled I became until I suddenly realised that perhaps, as in my own case, the resistance of these babies to germ life had been lowered by lack of sleep.

In the small single apartment house, of the type that abounded throughout the Gorbals, the baby was living among constant noise and in artificial light until late at night. In many cases when a mother went out visiting at night she took her baby with her and this, too, meant that its hours of sleep were being reduced . . .

Theoretically, people without means could apply to the parish for medical aid when a doctor appointed by the parish would call on them. However, the demands on this doctor's time were so great that he could only afford to spend a few minutes with each patient.

In this connection I well remember a sick call I made to Mrs McGill. She told me that a month previously she had been forced through lack of money to call in the parish doctor to attend to her baby. She went on to say that she had 'awful' faith in my bottles of medicine – something I never had myself – so when the baby was no better after taking the parish doctor's bottle for a few days she turned in desperation to an empty bottle lying on her shelf, prescribed long since by me.

She filled it up with water, swilled it around and began giving a teaspoonful three times a day to the baby, which, she assured me, did the baby far more good than the parish doctor's bottle.

This practice of removing patients from their doctor's register seemed an unjust one as the Approved Societies had remaining in their coffers considerably over a hundred million pounds contributed by these very people who were now so light-heartedly discarded. I remember writing indignantly to journals at the time, before I quite came to appreciate that were it not for the Government's National Health Insurance and the many names remaining on my list I might well have become as destitute as any.[8]

Whereas improved living conditions probably played the predominant role in reducing disease in the nineteenth century, in the twentieth century the development of effective treatments has proceeded at an accelerating rate, even permitting, upon occasion, the prolongation of life beyond, perhaps, what the patient himself would wish.

CHAPTER XV

CRIME

The transformation of the economy produced a much larger and more urbanized society, whose potential for violent upheaval alarmed the well-to-do. Large gatherings of labourers wandered across the countryside constructing canals and railways. The arrival of these navvies was a matter of acute concern to local people perturbed by the visitors' numbers and their readiness to drink and fight. The inhabitants of slum areas in the cities seemed, to the comfortably off, to be a population prepared to resort to lawlessness. Some mid-Victorian slum clearance was, in part at least, motivated by the desire to remove a threat to respectable lives. Inevitably, at a time when welfare was grudgingly dispersed at minimum levels and in humiliating circumstances, crime overwhelmingly meant theft. In 1830, 93 per cent of crimes tried before Edinburgh High Court were committed against property, not against people. Such crimes were more common in the bleak conditions of winter than during that part of the year when employment was more readily available. The development of properly paid police forces was one of the features of nineteenth-century life. Armed with sticks, they were dressed in uniforms that had a naval rather than a soldierly look, in the hope that this would avoid stirring against them the resentment felt against troops who were quite often deployed against gatherings or demonstrations. It was some time before the working men recruited into the police could be cured of the working class' fondness for heavy drinking. Dismissals for drunkenness among the early police forces ran at high figures.

It was not easy for the individual criminal to conceal himself in the predominantly rural Scotland of the mid eighteenth century. Members of little communities knew one another too well for crime to be easily concealed. Captain Burt, a military engineer who worked in Scotland at this time published a large number of letters he had somewhat self-consciously written to a friend in London. This particular letter, written from Inverness, describes the trapping and punishment of a murderer.

Some Time ago a Highlander was executed here for Murder, and I am now about to give you some Account of his Education, Character, and Behaviour.

This Man was by Trade a Smith, and dwelt near an English Foundry in Glengary, which lies between this Town and Fort William.

The Director of that Work had hired a Smith from England, and as it is said that Kings and Lovers can brook no Partners, so neither could the Highlander suffer the Rivalship of one of his own Trade, and therefore his Competitor was by him destined to die. One Night he came armed to the door of the Englishman's Hut with intent to kill him; but the Man being for some Reason or other, apprehensive of Danger, had fastened the Door of his Hovel more firmly than usual, and, while the Highlander was employed to force it open, he broke a Way through the back Wall of his House and made his Escape, but, being pursued, he cried out for Assistance; this brought a Lowland Scots Workman to endeavour to save him, and his generous Intention cost him his Life.

Upon this several others took the Alarm and came up with the Murderer, whom they tried to secure; but he wounded some of them, and received several Wounds himself; however, he made his Escape for that Time. Three Days afterwards he was hunted out, and found among the Heath (which was then very high), where he had lain all that Time with his Wounds rankling, and without any Sustenance, not being able to get away because a continual Search was made all round about both Night and Day, and for the most Part within his Hearing; for it is more difficult to find a Highlander among the Heather, except newly tracked, than a Hare in her Form.

He was brought to this town and committed to the Tolbooth, where Sentinels were posted to prevent his second Escape which otherwise, in all Probability, would have been effected.

Some Time afterwards the Judges, in their Circuit, arrived here, and he was tried and condemned. Then the Ministers of the Town went to the Jail to give him their Ghostly Advice, and endeavoured to bring him to a Confession of his other sins, without which they told him he could not hope for Redemption. For besides this Murder, he was strongly suspected to have made away with his former Wife, with whose Sister he was known to have had too great a Familiarity. But when the Ministers had said all that is customary concerning the Merit of Confession, he abruptly asked them, if either or all of them could pardon him, in Case he made a Confession; and when they had answered – "No, not absolutely", he said, "You have told me, God can forgive me." They said it was true. "Then," said he, "as you cannot pardon me, I have nothing to do with you, but will confess to Him that can."

A little while after, a Smith of this town was sent to take Measure of him, in order to make his Irons (for he was to be hanged in Chains), and, while the Man was doing it, the Highlander, with a Sneer, said – "Friend, you are now about to do a Job for a better Workman than yourself; I am certain I could fit you better than you can me."

When the Day for his Execution came (which by a late Law, could not be under Forty Days after his condemnation), and I had resolved to stay at Home, though perhaps I should have been the only one in the Town that did so; – I say having taken that Resolution, a certain Lieutenant-Colonel, who is come into these Parts to visit his Friends, and is himself a Highlander, for whom I have the greatest Esteem; he came to me, and would have me bear him Company, declaring, at the same Time, that although he had a great Desire to see how the Criminal would behave, yet he would wave all that, unless I would go with him; and, therefore, rather than disoblige my Friend, I consented, but I assure you with Reluctancy.

The Criminal was a little Fellow, but a fearless Desperado; and having annexed himself to the Clan of the Camerons, the Magistrates were apprehensive that some of the Tribe might attempt his Rescue; and therefore they made Application to the

Commanding Officer for a whole Company of Men to guard him to the Place of Execution with greater Security.

Accordingly they marched him in the Centre, with two of the Ministers, one on each side, talking to him by Turns all the Way for a Mile together. But I, not being accustomed to this Sort of Sights, could not forbear to reflect a little upon the Circumstance of a Man walking so far on Foot to his own Execution.

The Gibbet was not only erected upon the Summit of a Hill, but was itself so high that it put me in mind of Haman's Gallows.

Being arrived at the Place, and the Ministers having done praying by him, the Executioner, a poor helpless Creature, of at least eighty Years of Age, ascended the Ladder. Then one of the Magistrates ordered the Malefactor to go up after him; upon which the Fellow turned himself hastily about; says he, "I did not think the Magistrates of Inverness had been such Fools, as to bid a Man go up a Ladder with his Hands tied behind him." And, indeed, I thought the great Burgher looked very silly, when he ordered the Fellow's Hands to be set at Liberty.

When the Knot was fixed, the old Hangman (being above the Criminal) began to feel about with his Feet to find some Footing whereby to come down beside the other, in order to turn him off, which I think could hardly have been done by a young Fellow the most nimble and alert, without getting under the Ladder, and coming down chiefly by his Hands. Thus the Highlander, feeling the Executioner fumbling about him, in a little Time seemed to lose all Patience; and turning himself about, with his Face from the Ladder, and his Cap over his eyes, he cried out upon the Trinity, which I daresay he had never heard of before he was committed Prisoner for this Fact, and then jumped off the Ladder. And though his Hands were free, there did not appear in them, or any other part of his Body, the least Motion or Convulsion, any more than if he had been a Statue.

It is true, I could not compare this with other Things of the same Kind, but I thought it a very bungling Execution, yet liked the Cause of their Unskilfulness.

His Mother, who, it seems, is a very vile Woman, and had

bred him up in encouragement to Thieving and other Crimes, was present, lying on the Heath at some little Distance, when he leaped from the Ladder; and at that Instant set up such a hideous Shriek, followed by a screaming Irish Howl, that every Body seemed greatly surprised at the uncommon Noise; and those who knew the Woman loaded her with Curses for being the Cause of this shameful End of her Son, who, they said, was naturally a Man of good Sense.

To conclude this Subject. The Smith who had made the Irons (I suppose frighted at the Execution) had run away, leaving his Tools behind him; and one of the Magistrates was forced to rivet them, there being none other that would undertake so shameful a Work for any Reward whatever.[1]

During mid-Victorian times executions ceased to be spectacles available to a gawping public. Aberdeen's last public execution was held in 1857 (when a man was hanged for murdering his mother-in-law).

By the early years of the nineteenth century criminal activities included the gruesome work of the 'resurrectionists' who dug up newly-buried corpses to sell them to surgeons eager to demonstrate features of human anatomy to the students of the growing medical schools. In Edinburgh, two Irishmen, William Burke and William Hare decided to move beyond stealing the bodies of those who had died naturally. Among its numerous accounts of the activities of these two, the periodical *Courant* included these two descriptions.

In June last, an old woman and a dumb boy, her grandson, from Glasgow, came to Hare's, and were both murdered at the dead hour of night, when the woman was in bed. Burke and Hare murdered her the same way as they did the others. They took off the bed-clothes and tick, stripped off her clothes, and laid her on the bottom of the bed, and then put on the bed-tick, and bed-clothes on top of her; and they then came and took the boy in their arms and carried him to the room, and murdered him in the same manner, and laid him alongside his grandmother. They lay for the space of an hour; they put them into a herring barrel. The barrel was perfectly dry; there was no brine in it.

They carried them to the stable till next day; they put the barrel into Hare's cart, and Hare's horse was yoked into it; but the horse would not drag the cart one foot past the Meal-market; and they got a porter with a hurley, and put the barrel on it. Hare and the porter went to Surgeon Square with it. Burke went before them, as he was afraid something would happen, as the horse would not draw them. When they came to Dr. Knox's dissecting rooms, Burke carried the barrel in his arms. The students and them had hard work to get them out, being so stiff and cold. They received £16 for them both. Hare was taken in by the horse he bought that refused drawing the corpse to Surgeon Square, and they shot it in the tan-yard. He had two large holes in his shoulder stuffed with cotton, and covered over with a piece of another horse's skin to prevent them being discovered.

When they first began this murdering system they always took them to Knox's after dark; but being so successful, they went in the day-time, and grew more bold. When they carried the girl Paterson to Knox's, there were a great many boys in the High School Yards who followed Burke and the man that carried her, crying 'They are carrying a corpse'; but they got her safe delivered. They often said to one another that no person could find them out, no one being present at the murders but themselves two; and that they might be as well be hanged for a sheep as a lamb. They made it their business to look out for persons to decoy into their houses to murder them. Burke declares, when they kept the mouth and nose shut a very few minutes, they could make no resistance, but would convulse and make a rumbling noise in their bellies for some time; after they ceased crying and making resistance, they left them to die of themselves; but their bodies would often move afterwards, and for some time they would have long breathings before life went away.[2]

In 1828 they were arrested, Hare turned Crown witness and escaped execution; Burke's death was witnessed by a crowd of 25,000. His body was then dissected by a surgeon who was a rival of the man whom Burke and Hare had supplied.

Until the early nineteenth century, dealing with crime relied heavily on the deterrent effect of fearsome punishments. Yet Scottish law was more lenient than English. A Scottish thief was not liable to capital punishment until he had been caught offending on at least three occasions.

Large-scale disturbances required the military to deal with them. In burghs the task of keeping the peace fell on a variety of town officers, guards and watchmen. In Edinburgh Henry Cockburn bewailed the passing of the City Guard in favour of full-time police.

In 1817 our streets were deprived of one of their most peculiar objects. The City Guard of which Scott has given so good an account in his *Heart of Midlothian*, after subsisting since about the year 1696, was abolished in November 1817. The police had made them useless; but I wish they had been perpetuated, though it had been only as curiosities. Their number was liable to be increased or diminished according to circumstances. At this period they amounted, I conjecture, to about 200, regimented like ordinary soldiers. They were all old, hard-featured, red-nosed veterans; whose general history was, that after being mauled in the wars, commonly in a Highland regiment, they brought their broken iron bodies home, and thought themselves fortunate if they got into this fragment of our old burgher militia, where the pay was better than nothing, and the discipline not quite inconsistent with whisky, while the service was limited to keeping the peace within the city. Naturally disliked by the people, they were always asserting their dignity by testy impatient anger. This excited the mischief and the hostility of the boys, by whom their small remains of temper were intolerably tried; and between the two there never ceased to be a cordial and diverting war.

Their uniform was a red coat turned up with blue, a red waistcoat, red breeches, long black gaiters, white belts, and large cocked hats bound with white worsted ribbon. They had muskets and bayonets, but rarely used them for their peculiar weapon was the old genuine Lochaber axe – a delightful implement. One saw Bannockburn in it. One of these stern half-dotard warriors used to sit at each side of the prisoners at the bar of the Court of Justiciary as guard; with his huge hat on his old battered head, and his drawn bayonet in his large gnarled hand. They sat so immoveably, and looked so severe, with their rugged weather-beaten visages, and hard muscular trunks, that they were no unfit emblems of the janitors of the region to which those they guarded were so often consigned. The disappearance of these picturesque old fellows was a great loss.[3]

Scotland's cities contained 'bridewells'. Here a variety of petty criminals and vagrants were confined and put to work. Proper prisons were ill-equipped to cope with large numbers. Cramped and squashed dungeons housed some criminals – notably debtors – denying them fresh air, exercise and employment. The jails in smaller burghs were far from secure as is demonstrated by this reminiscence of the early nineteenth century.

In my own days, a merchant of Inverness, named Chisholm, managed affairs better. He was on slight evidence convicted of receiving a few stolen handkerchiefs, and thereupon sentenced to death. The laws were then enforced with great severity, and every one sympathised with their neighbour doomed to die for so trifling a crime. Probably this had something to do with his escape; however this may be, he was confined in the "Thieves' Chamber", and perhaps out of respect or under pretence of illness, was allowed to hang sheets around the bare stone walls. A friend supplied him with some instruments, and with these he busily employed himself, when safe from intrusion, by loosening the stones of the wall, behind the sheets which were hung up a distance from the wall, and the bottom of which, lying upon the floor, prevented the mortar and rubbish from being seen by the keepers, who we must suppose, were anything but anxious to be over officious in their surveillance. The night before the day fixed upon for his execution, he removed sufficient of the stone work to enable him to pass his body through the aperture, using his sheets as ropes by which he descended to the street, and effected a safe retreat, passing the first night after his escape in a peat stack at Dores, and from thence taking refuge among his clansmen in the wilds of Strathglass.

Search having been given up, he emigrated to America, and

soon after he was joined by his family, where, on account of his exemplary conduct, he rose eventually to affluence and distinction; his son, who attained the high office of a Judge, died only a few years ago in that country, upon which occasion the gentlemen of the bar went into mourning for six weeks. Another merchant of the name of Tolmie, involved in the same charge, was sentenced to be whipped through Inverness, his ears to be cut off at the cross, and then banished. I well remember he was a fine lad, and general sympathy was also felt for him. By stratagem he contrived to banish himself before the other part of the sentence was carried into effect.

The diet of the prisoners were as bad as the jail, accommodation was wretched, and penal inflictions unnecessarily severe. The prison discipline, however, was lax, and those who had friends were not only allowed to see them, but to partake of any supplies which they may bring. I know, on one occasion, the debtors were visited by some friends, and one of the former being a good hand at the fiddle, a dance was agreed upon, which was kept up with plenty of good cheer until morning, and it is a fact that the officers on being invited partook both of the refreshment and joined in the dance. I was one of the guests who was invited to this jail ball. These things were winked at in those times. The destitute criminals, however, used to have bags attached to strings, which they let down from their places of confinement, and in these, friends or charitable persons put in either money or provisions they might happen to have; and market days were, on a count of extra supplies, gala days to the prisoners.

One celebrated character, Peggy Raff, used to keep a stall, just opposite the jail, so that parties disposed to give the incarcerated provisions were at no loss to procure them. Peggy had always plenty of good oatmeal bannocks, cheese, and in season, boiled salmon, the latter she sold at 1d. per lb., and the other et ceteras proportionably cheap. Many a respectable farmer and country gentleman have I seen buy of Peggy, and retreat to an inn where they would get the best beer for 3d. a Scotch pint, whisky being then hardly known and less cared for.[4]

By the early nineteenth century, prison reform was very much in the air. English reformers like Howard and Romilly visited Scotland. Their views did not greatly impress Sir Walter Scott. He wrote in 1828:

A certain Mr. MacKay from Ireland called on me – an active gentleman, it would seem, about the reform of prisons. He exclaims – justly I doubt not, about the state of our lock-up houses. For myself I have some distrust of the fanaticism even of philanthropy. The philanthropy of Howard, mingled with his ill-usage of his son, seems to have risen to a pitch of insanity. Yet without such extraordinary men, who call attention to the subject by their own peculiarities, prisons would have remained the same dungeons which they were 40 or 50 years ago. I do not, however, see the propriety of making them dandy places of detention. They should be places of punishment and that can hardly be if men are lodged better and fed better than when they were at large. As to reformation, I have no great belief in it, when the ordinary class of culprits, who are vicious from ignorance or habit, are the subjects of the experiment.

The state of society now leads to such accumulation of humanity that we cannot wonder if it ferment and reek like a compost dunghill. A great deal, I think, might be done by executing the punishment of death, without chance of escape, in all cases to which it should be found properly applicable; of course these occasions being diminished to one out of 20 to which capital punishment is now assigned. When once men are taught that a crime of a certain character is connected inseparably with death, the moral habits of a population become altered and you may in the next age remit the punishment which it has been necessary to inflict with stern severity.[5]

Judges of the time had punishments other than prison to inflict on those who escaped execution. Transportation to one of the colonies was the most important of these. The loss of the American colonies brought a temporary setback to this type of sentencing. But an alternative was soon found. In 1787 a convict ship arrived in Botany Bay, Australia. Vessels continued to dump their human cargoes in different parts of Australia till the last ship sailed for Western Australia in 1867.

By this time changes in both policing and punishments had been forced upon the authorities by Scotland's changing society. The rapidly growing population produced crowded city streets that seemed to well-to-do observers to be hot-houses stimulating the growth of crime. First in burghs, then in rural areas, the response to this sense of a population potentially out of control was to finance full-time police forces. By the 1840s such forces were common across Scotland.

In Edinburgh James McLevy, who had begun work as a night-watchman, became one of Scotland's earliest detectives. Till 1860 he used common sense, careful observation and detailed local knowledge to trap a succession of criminals. The following account is one of the many triumphs gleefully recorded by McLevy.

The Breathing

One night in 1832, I was at the station in Adam Street, at that time a very disreputable part of the town – it is better now – in consequence of the many bad houses and whisky-shops in the vicinity. There were often rows there, chiefly occasioned by the students, many of whom lodged in the neighbouring streets, so that when our men were called upon it was generally to quell a quarrel, or carry off some poor degraded wretch of a woman for some drunken violence or pocket-picking. On the occasion to which I now allude the call upon us was different. The time was late, – past twelve, – and the streets were being resigned to the street-walkers and collegians. All of a sudden a shrill scream of a woman's voice reached my ear, and, running out, I heard a cry that a man of the name of M'—ie, who lived in Adam Street, had been robbed, or attempted to be robbed, on his own stair. Then there was a shout, and a pointing by two or three people, – "They are down to the Pleasance". On such an occasion it has always been my habit not to take up any time by questions for an account of external appearances because the answers are tedious, and there is more to be gained by time in a rush in the proper direction, trusting to what I may call "criminal indications", than by ascertaining what kind of a coat or hat a man wore, or the length of his nose, or height of body, and so forth. So I noted the index, and took to my toe-points as fast as I could run, down in the direction indicated, but as lightly as I could, for fear of my tread being carried in the silence of the night on to the ears of the runaways. I may mention, too, that I stopped several sympathisers, who were inclined to join, but who, I knew, would only scare, and do no good.

I had the pursuit, if such it may be termed, all to myself, but was immediately "called up" by one of those rock-ahead incidents which are so tantalising to our class, – no other than two roads, each holding out its recommendations to me, the one that the robbers would certainly take to the deep haunts of the Old Town, where the fox-burrows are so inviting and the difficulty of unearthing not easily surmounted; and the other, that they would seek the outskirts, and so get down to the valley between the Pleasance and Arthur's Seat, where they might skulk in the deep darkness of the night, and so escape.

A minute or two would turn the scale, and I must decide even almost as I ran. I have often quivered in this dilemma, and seldom been wrong in my choice; yet I can't account for one out of ten of these instantaneous decisions. I really believe I have often been swayed by some very trivial incident, perhaps the shuffle of a foot, perhaps a gust of wind not heard as such, but simply as something working upon the ear. The barking of a dog has resolved me, the shutting of a door, or even a greater silence in one direction than another, nay, to be very plain, and perhaps weak, I have sometimes thought I was led by a superior hand, so directly have I been taken to my quarry. It was so now. It was just as likely the fellows would go north to the Old Town, or south to the Gibbet-Toll, – no gibbet now to scare them. I turned to the left, down the Pleasance; even as I ran, and about halfway between my turn and Mr. Ritchie's brewery, I met one of our men on his beat, coming south, pacing as quietly as if no robbery could have been suspected in his well-watched quarter.

"Met two fellows in a skulk or a run?"

"No one; but before I crossed the foot of Drummond Street,

I thought I heard the sound of quick feet, but it stopped in an instant, and I then thought I might have been mistaken."

"Then stand you there as steady as a post, but not as deaf. Keep your feet steady, and your ears open."

I had got just a sniff, and it is not often I have needed more. They had, no doubt, gone that way, and, on observing the officer, had gone into a burrow. I stood for an instant, – no common-stairs here, no closes, no cul-de-sac, no hole even for the shrinking body of a robber. The first glance brought me near my wit's end, but not altogether.

I have always been led on by small glimpses of Hope's lamp till I got nearer and nearer her temple, and never yet gave up till all was dark. I stepped to the other side of the street, where there are some bad houses. No door open, every window shut, and no light within that could be observed. I could walk with the lightest of feet, and proceeded noiselessly along the narrow pavement till I came to Drummond Street, where there is the recess in which the well stands. I had no hope from that recess because it is comparatively open, and, dark as the night was, they could scarcely have skulked there without the man on the beat seeing them. Yet I was satisfied also that they could not have gone up by Drummond Street. I may mention that I could hear when almost every other person could discover nothing but silence; nay, this quickness of the hearing sense has often been a pain to me, for the tirl of a mouse has often put me off my rest when I stood in great need of it. I require to say nothing of my other poor senses here; they were not needed, for there was nothing to be seen except below the straggling lamps, in the pale light of one of which I saw my man standing sentry, but nothing more.

Expecting nothing from the recess, I crossed to the angle, rather disappointed, and was rather meditative than listening, foiled than hopeful, when my ear was arrested by one or two deep breathings, – scared robbers are great breathers, especially after a tussle with a victim. I could almost tell the kind of play of lungs; it speaks fear, for there is an attempt to repress the sound, and yet nature here cannot be overcome. On the instant

I felt sure of my prey, yet I tested my evidence even deliberately.

There was more than one play of lungs at work, – I could trace two, – and all their efforts, for they had seen the man pass, and had probably heard our conversation, were not able to overcome the proof that was rushing out of their noses, (as if this organ could give out evidence as well as take it in,) not their mouths, – fear shuts the latter, if wonder should open it, – to reach my ear, just as if some great power adopted this mode of shewing man that there is a speaking silence that betrays the breakers of God's laws. Now certain, I hastened over to the man on the beat, and, whispering to him to go to the station for another man, took my watch again. I knew I had them in my power, because if they took themselves to flight, I could beat them at that trick; so I cooled myself down to patience, and kept my place without moving an inch, quite contented so long as I heard the still half-suppressed respirations.

In a few minutes my men were up, coming rather roughly for such fine work. I took each by the coat-neck, –

"Steady, and not a whisper! They are round the corner, – batons ready, and a rush!"

By a combined movement, we all wheeled round the angle, and before another breath could force itself, we had the two chevaliers in our hands, – even as they were standing, bolt-upright against the gable of the house that forms one side of the recess. Like all the rest of their craft they were quite innocent, only their oaths – for they were a pair of desperate thimblers, whom I knew at once – might have been sufficient to have modified the effects of their protestations.

They were, indeed, dangerous men. They had nearly throttled M'—ie, and in revenge for getting nothing off him had threatened to murder him. My next object was to get them identified by the people who had raised the cry, for if they had dispersed we might have been – with nothing on them belonging to the man – in want of evidence, though not in want of a justification, of our capture of two well-known personages. Fortunately, when we got to the station some of the women were there who identified them on the instant, whereupon they became, as sometimes the very worst of them do, "gentle lambs", and were led very quietly to their destination in the High Street. Remitted to the Sheriff, their doom was fourteen years.

"And the breath of their nostrils shall find them out."[6]

By the early twentieth century a professional police force walked the streets of Scotland. Scottish prisons had been transformed by a huge building programme that provided most of the jails still in use. Peterhead, for example, was built in 1886. Control over prisons was shifted from local authorities to the government by an act of 1877. A further reform – in 1898 – swept aside the various means of occupying prisoners with useless labour (like the treadmill) and encouraged more purposeful activities. In 1912, the medical officer at Glasgow Prison, James Devon, published an account of Scottish prisons. Devon held views on the possibility of reforming prisoners which would have horrified Sir Walter Scott.

Once prisoners are within the prison their condition is much more comfortable than it had been when they were under the charge of the policeman. They are taken one by one and questioned as to certain details that are noted for purposes of identification and for statistical records. Then comes the bath. The prisoner removes all his clothing and an inventory of it is taken. When he leaves the bath his own clothing has been replaced by a dress provided by the State. His clothing is disinfected and placed aside in a bundle, against the time of his liberation. He now receives a copy of the prison rules, which he must obey; a Bible, which he may study; a hymn-book; an industry-card, on which his earnings will be noted; and he is passed on to prison. His life there is one of monotonous routine whether his sentence be short or long.

The prison surprises visitors by its quiet and by the conspicuous cleanliness which is its characteristic feature. Yet it is not surprising that people should be able to keep the place clean and tidy, when they have little else to do and no opportunity for making it dirty and untidy. The cleanliness and tidiness of a prison is different from that of any household. It is not the cleanliness and tidiness of healthy life. It is part of the prisoner's work to keep his cell and its furniture in order.

One thing visitors cannot miss seeing, yet do not observe, though it is of much more significance than the cleanliness they admire: the good temper and tractability of the prisoners. That a prisoner should be clean is wonderful; that people who have been committing breaches of the peace, assaults, thefts, and have been generally a nuisance or a terror to the public, should be moving about at work or at exercises quietly and peaceably, should be so obedient and tractable that one warder can look after twenty of them and seldom have anything to report to their discredit, is far more wonderful. These people are sent to prison because they cannot obey the law, but while in prison they are not rebellious; so that it is reasonable to infer that there has been something in the conditions of their life outside which has led them into misconduct, and not that they are inherently incapable of behaving themselves.

The modern prison is built on a simple plan. Roughly it may be described as two blocks of cells joined by a gable at each end and roofed over; a well being left between the blocks and lighted from the roof. All the cells have windows in the outer, and doors in the inner, walls. Balconies run round these inner walls, from which access is had to the cells in each flat. The cells in which the prisoners are confined are apartments measuring about 10 ft. by 7 ft. by 10 ft. high. The partitions and roofs of the cells are of whitewashed brickwork, and the floor of stone and asphalt. Each cell has a little window in the wall near the door glazed with obscured glass, and on the outside of these windows a gas bracket is placed. At night the cell is lit by this arrangement, which diminishes the amount of light and fixes its source in a corner. It is designed to prevent any person from attempting suicide by inhalation of gas.

A prison cell does not contain much furniture. The bed is a wooden shutter hinged to the wall, so that it can be folded up during the day-time. When not in use the bedding is rolled together and placed in a corner of the apartment. Convicted male prisoners who are under sixty years of age are not allowed a mattress during the first thirty days of their imprisonment; they just lie on the board. I do not suppose that anybody imagines that a man is more likely to lead a new life if he is made to sleep on a bare board, than he would be if he were allowed a mattress. It is intended to hurt, and it will hurt the more sensitive in a greater degree than those of a coarser constitution. It is a part of the system, and will go with it when people wake up to the fact that it is a senseless thing to set about to irritate and annoy others.

Of late years it has been discovered that prisoners were as little likely to escape if their cells were well lit as they would be their cells being ill lit. The windows have consequently been enlarged and nobody has been the loser.

In Scotland the diet prescribed is a very simple one. In quantity it is ample for the needs of the great majority of the prisoners. Indeed, a fair proportion receive more than they are fit to consume. The medical officer may reduce a diet to prevent waste; or he may increase a diet, if in his view the prisoner requires more food. As I believe that nearly every man knows his own needs a great deal better than the diet specialist, a request from a prisoner for more food is never refused provided he is consuming all he gets. A request for a change of food is quite another thing; but a man who for gluttony would gorge himself with the diet provided for prisoners would be a curiosity.

The food is excellent in quality, but there is not much variety. There are three meals daily. Porridge and sour milk with bread form the morning and evening meals, and the dinner usually consists of broth and bread. It is a simple diet and is sufficient. The death-rate in prisons is small. The improvement in the health of broken-down and habitually debauched persons during their term of imprisonment is marked.

The clothing of prisoners, as regards cutting and material, resembles nothing seen outside. The untried male is officially clothed in brown corduroy, and when convicted he exchanges this for white mole-skin. The surface of the cloth used to be decorated with broad-arrows, so that the prisoner looked like a person in a prehistoric dress over which some gigantic hen had walked after puddling in printer's ink; but this has been discontinued.

The cut of the clothing seems to be designed to save cloth, and so long as the prisoner is kept warm he does not concern himself about the unfashionable character of his clothes. As for the women's dress, being a mere man I cannot describe it; but ladies who visit the prison seem to be agreed that it is plain and neat. It is certainly strikingly different from anything they wear.

It is a rule that all convicted prisoners shall wear prison clothes. There are not very many of them whose own clothing is clean enough for them to wear.

Persons whose sentences exceed fourteen days may have books from the prison library with which to beguile their time. The books provided resemble the clothing, in respect that it is greatly a matter of chance as to whether they suit the person who gets them. I have seen an illiterate lad from the slums hopelessly wrestling with an elementary manual on Electricity and Magnetism. I suppose this would be regarded as an educational work. The library is carefully selected with the intention of excluding all pernicious literature – certainly the sensational is passed by.

The untried prisoner may have newspapers and magazines sent in to him as well as books, unless, indeed, the Visiting Committee refuse to permit this. He can choose suitable literature for himself provided his friends are willing to send it to him, but immediately he is convicted he has no choice in the matter. The State is his librarian.

Of late years lectures have been given to prisoners, and occasionally concerts have been provided for them. The lectures have been on all kinds of subjects. Some of them have dealt with travel and have been illustrated by limelight views; others have dealt with sanitation, physiology, and the treatment of common ailments; others have taken the form of cookery demonstrations; and the prison audience is invariably more appreciative than most audiences outside. They enjoy anything that breaks the dullness of their routine life. No sensible person expects that the lectures will make them travellers, or physiologists, or cooks, though an interest in these subjects may be kindled by the lecturer. Few people are ever lectured into a change of life, but anything that prevents them from sinking into apathy, from brooding on the petty incidents that go to make up their lives in prison, from beating against the bars of their cage, is beneficial.

There are those who protest against making the prison too comfortable and who seem to believe that people want to go there. There need be no fear of this. A cage is a cage even though it be gilded, and they are few indeed who seek imprisonment. Occasionally you have some saying they prefer the prison to the poorhouse. I have worked in both places and wholly agree with their preference, but that is not a testimony to the desirability of life in prison, but a reproach to the poorhouse. Those who support efforts to lessen the monotony of prison life are not moved by any desire that the prisoners may have a good time. For my own part, I am not concerned to make their lot less mechanical merely for their sakes, but for the sake of the community of which they are a part. I believe that imprisonment has been shown to have a bad effect on those who suffer it, and as some day they are to be turned loose on the community, it is advisable to prevent them being liberated in a condition that would make them more dangerous to their fellow-citizens, or more troublesome, than they were before their arrest.

Outside the block of cells is an airing-yard, which consists of a space round which two narrow paved walks run. On these the prisoners take their exercise, each walking for an hour daily for the benefit of his health; separated by a space from the prisoner in front and the prisoner behind him, and watched by a warder lest any conversation or sign of recognition takes place between him and his fellows. The elderly or physically defective prisoners walk round the inner ring, where the pace is slower.

Some of the female prisoners undergo a course of instruction in Swedish drill. Their opinion is expressed in the name by which the exercise is known. It is called the "Daft hour," and they enjoy it. As to its usefulness from an industrial standpoint, the less said the better. It does no harm and it is a pleasant break in the day. In short, the prisoners are better employed in going through the drill than in doing something worse.[7]

The reforms of the Victorian period did not solve all the problems of keeping law and order; they did not even end government readiness to use the military. Unrest in Glasgow at the end of the

Great War saw tanks and troops deployed in the city, to control and intimidate protesters. In depressed working-class areas like the Gorbals, where Ralph Glasser grew up in the 1920s, there was an atmosphere vividly captured in this extract from his autobiography.

We grew up with violence. It simmered and bubbled and boiled over in street and close, outside the pubs, at the dance halls in Bedford Street and Ballater Street and Crown Street, sometimes in gang raids from adjacent slum areas: Kinning Park, Hutchestown, Govanhill, Kingston. Seldom did such attacks find the defenders unprepared. Like the raiders they would be armed, with bicycle chains, knuckle-dusters, chisels, open razors, or the fearsome Razor Cap – razor blades embedded in the peak of a cloth cap with their cutting edges projecting, and swung in a scything motion across an enemy's face and neck.

More often, violence settled private accounts, transgression of codes, the spilling over of grievance or spleen. It was so closely intertwined with everyday life, its inescapable rough edge, logical, cathartic, that its occurrence, like rain and cold and frequent shortage of food, was recognised with equal fatalism. That it could also be an instrument of cool business calculation never occurred to me, until one day in the slack summer season a ruthless enactment in our street brought a harsh awakening. I saw that the smooth face of successful business could conceal a use of violence and terror as merciless, as detached and as passionless as anything in the annals of the Borgia or the Medici. It darkened the sun. It was a reminder from the Furies.

With two older brothers Meyer worked in his father's joinery workshop, part of an old stables in a lane behind Warwick Street, a few minutes from our tenement. With its cobbled floor and high blackened rafters, it was a place of saturnine gloom, in which a half-light was provided by three gas mantles.

Early one evening I went there to collect Meyer on my way to the Baths. As we rounded the corner into our street we heard shouting from a little group on the pavement outside Meyer's close a few doors away from mine.

'Fuckin' hell!' Meyer ran ahead. Two heavily built young men were scuffling with an older man in shirt-sleeves who, as we came near, fell to his knees on the wet pavement. Blood from his nose and lips had made dark streaks on his collarless shirt. Like a penitent before inquisitors he held up his hands in supplication. It was Mr. Fredericks – middle-aged (old to us), white hair thinning, narrow-chested, afflicted with the almost universal bronchial cough. With his wife and consumptive daughter he lived on Meyer's staircase. Like many of us in the garment trade, he was out of work in this off-season.

'It's the fuckin' menodge men,' Meyer muttered.

The street was unnaturally quiet. Here and there a face peeped out from shop doorway or close mouth. This was a time, the code said, when it was safer to see nothing. To be known to have watched could be interpreted as participation, support for one of the contestants, and retribution might follow. It was a time not to be involved.

The words 'menodge men' carried terror for the tenements – more than 'the factor' or rent collector, and perhaps comparable to the black shadow that hovered round the sheriff's men who came to distrain on property for non-payment of rent or, since there was seldom anything worth distraining, to put you out on to the street.

A menodge – a local word, probably from the French 'menage' – was in its origins a thrift system. It became for a great many people the only way to buy clothes, bedding, household equipment, furniture, on credit. You began by making payments, usually through a neighbourhood collector working on commission, or perhaps sixpence a week to a 'warehouse', in effect a retailer selling at a high mark-up to people lacking the ready money to buy at a normal shop. When your 'menodge book' showed a stipulated credit balance you went to the warehouse and chose goods to that value. In the interim the money held in your name was of course at the interest-free disposal of the warehouse. If you undertook to continue weekly payments of a stated figure you could become a credit customer and take away goods up to a certain 'loan' value. Concealed in the price of the goods was a high interest rate on that loan. From then on, as in the 'loan shark' system exploited by the Mafia in America, you were encouraged to be in debt for evermore.

Since you would not be in the menodge at all if you could afford to buy elsewhere for cash, you were a captive customer in every sense. One-and-three-ha'pence a week was a common loan repayment figure, high for most people even when in work, impossibly so when they were on the dole and bringing fifteen shillings a week.

Almost by definition menodge customers had no reserves, so when life hit them hard, through illness or unemployment, and the one-and-three-ha'pence could not be found, they could do nothing but hope, miserably, that the menodge men, 'the frighteners', would not come to their door and make a public example of them.

There was a dreadful irony in that. People became menodge customers from a desire to remain respectable, to pay their way and avoid the great indignity, 'going on the parish', the pauper's way. And so the others, those who were on the parish, showed little sympathy for them when the frighteners did come. They stood back and watched, not with satisfaction but allowing themselves a breath of comfort, as if they said to themselves: 'There but for the grace of God – or our better judgement – go we! They shouldn't have been so stuck-up, they should've gone on the parish like the rest of us.'

The label Rachmanism had not been invented then but the form of customer discipline was familiar and, from a narrow point of view, effective. For the menodge or credit warehouse the purpose was twofold – so to terrorise the defaulter that he would put his debt before every other need, even food and coal, and to send a terrible warning to everyone else. For the latter reason the defaulter must be attacked and humiliated publicly.

These frighteners, we would hear, were acting for Great Universal Stores in Cathedral Street, a forbidding factory-like building of blackened sandstone with broad, flat-arched windows, beside the railway lines at the back of Queen Street Station. Seeing it I always thought of 'the dark Satanic mills'.

As we ran up, Mrs. Fredericks was standing at the close mouth, shaking with distress, wiping away her tears with a soiled black apron. Then she too held out her hands in appeal. The men stood over her husband's crumpled form, dour messengers from the Inferno, seemingly pondering what further suffering to inflict.

"For God's sake have pity on us! We're at our wits' end! Please give us time – till he's in work again. It's not our fault. We want to pay but we can't!'

One of the men kicked Mr. Fredericks in the ribs and he howled in pain and toppled on his left side and lay groaning and gasping for breath. With a cry she tried to push past, reaching out to him. The other man put out a foot and she fell heavily to the ground.

I had seen Meyer in the ring, a figure of poised, scientific intensity, showing no emotion. In these few seconds it seemed that his whole frame shook as with a fever. His face had gone dead white. I was afraid for him.

'Fuckin' bastards!' He leapt between them and with a shoulder lunge and a trip kick, toppled the one on his left. The other, turning, slow to react, accustomed perhaps to meek submission, had time only for a few snarled words, the beginnings of an automatic response: 'Fuck off! This is none o' yewr . . .'

Meyer, swivelling like a dancer, chin tucked in, shot out a left to the solar plexus and, as the man grunted and bent forward, hurled his weight behind a straight right to the jaw that toppled him like a falling log. The back of his head hit the pavement with a sullen, bony thud and he lay still.

Turning as the first one got to his feet, Meyer ducked a wild swing and delivered a straight left to the jaw; and as the other rocked back, followed with a lightning right hook to the head and another straight left to the chin, his whole frame lunging behind it like a battering ram. The man's knees sagged and he subsided vertically like a collapsing building and lay inert.

I glanced round. Every furtive face had disappeared. We stood in an icy desert.

We helped the couple to their feet and led them to their house.

'It's no good,' Mrs Fredericks muttered through sobs, 'They'll come back. They never give up.'

'I don't understand,' Meyer said. 'They can't get money out of you if you haven't got it.'

We both knew that that was not the point. The supreme purpose of sending in the frighteners was *pour encourager les autres*.[8]

The men with whom Ralph Glasser's friend had clashed returned with reinforcements. Faced with the alternatives of joining them or being badly beaten, Meyer enlisted in the army to escape.

Street gangs flourished in early twentieth-century Glasgow. For a while their character was partly shaped by attachment to a particular religion as well as a particular territory. By the 1960s, they were in decline; here a journalist investigates.

There are about 150 YY Shamrock, hard children who hang around Dundas Street and Parliamentary Road, an area of betting shops, cheap cafés and cigarette kiosks near Queen Street railway station and the main bus station, before Sauchiehall Street begins. The core, 30 to 40 strong, stopping women in the street and cadging cigarettes, jumping on the back of moving scooters, are mostly unemployed, sporadically violent and dangerous – but still with the bravado which is only the steel-plating of the very immature young.

Peter is 17, and produced a new, stolen breadknife as credentials the second time I met him. He has short, fluffy hair and a large area of acne spots along his jaw. He scratches himself when he talks to you, and his arms push into the air in short jerks. He has a job as a pipe insulator, but gets away early and is usually in Dundas Street by the afternoon. He says his mother and father are happily married, that he had a happy childhood, and is happy now. He has served one short borstal sentence for breach of the peace, and been fined once for breach of the peace and once for theft of a scooter.

He says he joined the Shamrock 18 months ago because he couldn't walk down the town without being attacked by other gangs. 'Now we're the top and we don't need to protect ourselves. Carrying weapons is just a habit, like smoking or drinking. Everybody wants to be a big name. It's fighting for the sake of fighting. You feel good inside when you're chasing them and all, and batter them with bottles and slash them with razors. They deserve it. They wouldn't feel sorry for me if they set about me, so I don't feel sorry for them.'

Peter hates queers, men who interfere with children, smartly-dressed toffs, and the police. 'Most of these toffs, their old man's a lawyer. Not many people start off poor and get money. The Glasgow police have been watching these Yankee movies too much, driving about in their Jaguars and sunglasses. They all want to be Yanks. "Put your hands up against the wall," they say in an American accent.

'I'd like to go to elocution lessons to learn how to talk, and buy clothes and just go about drinking and all that. I'd like lots of birds, not just one. With money you can go anywhere with nobody to stop you. The coppers aren't going to tell you to move on and pull you up in front of birds all the time. I'd like to be a guy who is in charge of the underworld, a big top nut, or Lee Marvin. He is cheeky. I like him; he is a kind of rough diamond, but he is always smartly dressed.'

The meeting place of the Real Mental Shamrock used to be a bar nicknamed 'Munnie's', in Castle Street. I was introduced by a drunk called King, who claimed to be a member of the team and offered to protect me – for money, of course. His personality had deteriorated too far for him to belong to any group, and I never saw him again. But when he tried to make me frightened of the Shamrock it was because *he* needed to believe they were dangerous: the power he attributed to them was the only mental weapon he had left against whatever other powers threatened to overwhelm him. Later, a barman at 'Munnie's' said: 'You're frightened and I'm frightened. But they're frightened too. The difference is that they don't admit it.'

'Munnie's' was closed down by the time I left Glasgow, although it may since have reopened. The Shamrock drank in the pub during the Glasgow Fair holiday at the end of July, and by the beginning of the second week their money had run out.

They owed the pub over £30, and stock was missing: they had stolen bottles over the counter behind a barman's back, and he, through fear or stupidity, had sold them rounds of drinks at something like quarter-price. One night after closing time they broke into the pub and got away with a few bottles of sherry and spirits. Half of it was stolen from the empty house where they dumped it overnight, and next morning they sat in the pub discussing how to move the remainder in a van with no brakes. Two policemen, whom you learn to smell in such a setting, were standing a few feet away. The following night the Shamrock broke into the pub again. Their profit from the two operations was about £20.

It is hard to be objective about the Real Mental Shamrock. I liked them, the way you tend to like most of the people you talk to at length, particularly if you sympathise with them because they are mentally or economically depressed. I was lucky to meet them when they had even less money than usual, and were grateful for the drinks I bought them. But they gave me a lot more, relatively, than I gave them. Once in the team you share what you have, and it is only when group finances are nil, and there is no dole or wages due to anybody, that they turn to thieving. Their technique, as the 'Munnie's' incidents showed, is less than immaculate.

The real test of your attitude towards people like the Shamrock is how you react when you are threatened by them. One night in George Square a group of them were arguing about a petty incident with the Fleet, going over the rights and wrongs of something too trivial to loom in anybody's mind. Then one lashed out at me, blind drunk, shattered by some anger he did not understand: 'You, standing there smiling, wanting your story. You'll get it all right, but it'll be what happened to yourself you'll be writing about.'

I had been smug for 10 days, proud of making contact with the gang and getting them to trust me, shaking my head over their sad backgrounds. Now the aggression was turned on me, and my pride was hurt because the rest of the gang were watching and I could think of nothing to say or do.

Immediately, anger made me look at the other side of the

coin: other people with the same backgrounds as the Shamrock did not use weapons or thieve or waste time as if it was water. They were Shamrock because they were weak and selfpitying, not because they had no choice. So one of these yobs, a bit of dirt, ignorant and worthless, was threatening *me*, and if I had been able to get him beaten up or destroyed or put inside I would.

Any relationship I made with the Shamrock was artificial and shortlived. Any understanding I gained would not generate enough tolerance to let them threaten my pride or comfort. Until I gain the tolerance there will be the Shamrock, and me, and the gulf between us. And the police? What do they think?

'We are aware that there is a group called the Shamrock operating in the city,' said Sir James Robertson, Chief Constable of Glasgow. 'We have had occasion to deal with members of the group on a variety of charges.

'Our attitude must be repressive. Violence must be treated severely. I could not have any sympathy for violent manifestations of protest against society.'⁹

The old street gangs have vanished, to be replaced by gangs of hooligan football supporters. Theft may no longer be motivated by the most desperate poverty; the temptations and pressures of modern materialistic society mean that it continues to flourish, nevertheless.

CHAPTER XVI

TRAVEL

For the traveller of the mid eighteenth century, moving across the Scottish landscape was no easy matter. Few bridges spanned the numerous rivers. Moorland, moss and mountain were traversed by winding poorly-surfaced tracks. Men taking animals to markets in the south found it easiest to walk them there, meandering through mountain passes, fording rivers, seeking suitable grazing along the way. The main network of roads were maintained by the inhabitants of the parishes through which they passed. The giving of six days' unpaid labour was a source of much resentment to men of an age (between fifteen and sixty) liable for it. The results of their grudging efforts were all too often most unsatisfactory. Wheeled traffic found it difficult to struggle over these bumpy and uneven roads. Increasingly, this system of 'statute labour' was converted into money payments of around threepence a day voluntarily until 1845, thereafter compulsory till the system vanished in 1883. The resulting funds were used to hire full-time workmen.

Even within burgh boundaries eighteenth-century streets were all too often bumpy and badly drained. For the well-to-do, one of the easiest ways of travelling during unpleasant weather was not by wheeled vehicle, but in a sedan chair. Sir J. H. A. Macdonald, who was born in Edinburgh in 1837, could recall this mode of transport in its declining years.

> At every corner of the residential streets there was kept, in the area below, the sedan-chair, that was freely used to convey ladies from house to house. And at the corner there stood, or sat on a little bench, the chairmen, who acted also as porters.
>
> They wore the old-fashioned leather slings over their shoulders, in which the staves of the sedan-chair rested, and

these formed their official insignia, by which they were known as licensed porters. They were for the most part Highlanders, and little people like myself often had friendships with them and got rides on their shoulders. They had, by custom I suppose, a monopoly of carrying coal from cart to cellar, and the moment a coal cart was seen to enter their street they came running along with their creels, something like those of the Newhaven fish-women, but more square and strong, and in these they carried the coal to the cellar below. Free Trade, I was told as a boy, brought all this to an end, and when the sedan-chair was no longer in use the chairmen gradually disappeared, although they lingered on for many years, with the chair straps on their shoulders. There were a number of them still in the Seventies, and they sat on forms at the corners.

Although it was gradually dying out, the use of the sedan-chair was not uncommon when I was in child's frocks. It was a very pleasant way for a lady making a call on a friend or going out in the evening, she entering the chair, as she did, within her own lobby, and leaving it in the entrance hall of her friend's house, free from the dust or rain without, or the wind which threatened her elaborately dressed ringlets. I have seen my brother with his sister on his knee, going out to a children's party by chair, and I have even seen ladies coming to call by chair in the afternoon, in dresses with very short sleeves, and very long gloves coming far above the elbow, or long mittens.

The chairmen carried their passengers very pleasantly, except when there had been too many drams during the day. It was so easy a mode of conveyance, that it was still employed in my boyhood's years for conveying patients to the infirmary. But the drams were a serious drawback, and caused many a discomfort, and sometimes much alarm. During the day the chairmen did other work, conveying goods to retail shops on barrows, and too often they got a glass when delivering. My father used to tell of two Highland chairmen who regularly brought chemical stores, that came by waggon from London, to the druggists' shops, and for whose refreshment one of the bottles on the shop shelf, supposed to contain chemical solution, was filled up with whisky.

The sedan-chair could not hold its own when cities grew large. The great distances that had to be traversed made it no longer a convenient mode of moving from house to house.[1]

The most sustained and systematic road-building efforts of the mid eighteenth century took place in the Highlands and were funded by the government. From the 1720s to the 1760s, fear of Jacobite uprisings led to a major civil engineering enterprise executed by units of the British army. These military roads and bridges are commonly named after the first soldier to command their construction – General Wade. In fact, more than three-quarters of the work was supervised by his successor, Major Caulfield. Once road-building had ceased, road maintenance continued to be funded by the Government. By the early nineteenth century, a new source of concern about the Highlands had emerged that was to stimulate a fresh programme of road and bridge building.

The movement of the population out of the Highlands led to the creation of a Parliamentary Commission to try and halt the decline. The Commissioners hired the great road engineer, Thomas Telford, to survey the situation and supervise new works. In 1845 a typical group of Highland roadmen were seen by the banker, John Eddowes Bowman. It was at Glencoe that he and his companion, John Dovaston, encountered them. Bowman noted in his diary:

I passed ten or twelve Highlanders repairing the road, and another seated on a tuft of heather, at a little distance from the road, reading. Just beyond them, a large and very broad green caravan, like those which contain wild beasts, was standing in the road without horses, on which was painted, 'Highland Roads and Bridges, No. 27'. A stout and rather short Highlander with swarthy complexion and black hair, and having more of the Celtic character than I had yet seen, was fetching water to boil his oatmeal and seeing me look at the caravan with some attention, set down his iron pot, and asked if I had any wish to see the interior. It appeared from my informant, that the great military roads are kept in repair at the expense of government, and the caravans furnished by it for the temporary lodging and accommodation of the workmen, the country being so thinly inhabited, that much time would be lost, in going to and from the widely dispersed huts. The respective parishes, however, are not wholly relieved from the charge, as every male in each house pays six shillings per annum, or gives three days' labour. There is not a single turnpike gate upon any of the military roads throughout the Highlands.

It is probable that the man was an overseer. At each end of the caravan were six oblong open boxes, which were the beds or berths of the workmen; they were placed one above another at right angles, the ends for the feet all meeting together, and only half the depth of the opposite ends, or head of the bed. In the middle of the caravan was a stove, so contrived that it would boil a pot; furniture of any kind there was none, not even a bench; I saw nothing but a bag of oatmeal and a few bed clothes. I expressed some surprise, and his civil and open demeanour emboldened me to ask if they had no animal food, bread, or potatoes? Nor was it lessened when he said that their sole food was 'porridge', or oatmeal and water, seasoned with a little salt. Upon such simple food do these hardy people labour hard and brave the rigours of a Scotch winter.[2]

Telford's road-building programme petered out in the late 1820s. Its decline aggravated the existing problem of unemployment in the Highlands. In 1846, the area was struck by an even bigger disaster. Blight ravaged the potato crop upon which so many Highlanders had become dependent. Road-building resumed as a means of providing work in return for meal. In Wester Ross, Osgood Mackenzie, the third son of the Laird of Gairloch, was a small boy at the time. Many years later, in old age, he looked back on this time and recorded his memories of it:

I cannot say I can remember my first coming to Gairloch, as I was then only about two years old, but there were soon to be very trying times there, during the great famine caused by the potato blight. I have quite clear recollections of my own small grievance at being made to eat rice, which I detested, instead of potatoes, with my mutton or chicken in the years 1846–1848, for even *Uaislean an tigh mhor* (the gentry of the big house) could not get enough potatoes to eat in those hard times. Certainly things looked very black in 1846–1848 in Ireland and the West of Scotland, though, but for the potato blight, when should we have got roads made through the country? My mother never left Gairloch, not even for a day, for three long years when the famine was at its height.

In Ireland a very stupid system was started – namely, the making of roads beginning nowhere in particular, and ending, perhaps, at a rock or in the middle of a bog. It was thought that working at an object which could never be of any use to anyone would be so repugnant to the feelings of the greater portion of the population that only the dire stress of actual starvation would induce them to turn out for the sake of the trifle of money, or one or two pounds of maize meal, which constituted then the daily wage. My mother was totally opposed to this ridiculous plan in our district, and also against merely giving miserable doles of meal, which were barely sufficient to keep the population alive. Her plan was to pay all the able-bodied men a sufficient wage in money or food to enable them to do good work themselves and to support their dependants. So with the help of Government and begging and borrowing (I think) £10,000 she and my uncle undertook the great responsibility of guaranteeing that no one would be allowed to starve on the property. Thus the Loch Maree road was started, and this was about the only thing which could possibly open up the country.

I, as a small boy, had the great honour conferred on me of cutting the first turf of the new road. How well I remember it, surrounded by a huge crowd, many of them starving Skye men, for the famine was more sore in Skye and the islands than it was on our part of the mainland. I remember that tiny toy spade and the desperate exertions I had to make to cut my small bit of turf; then came the ringing cheers of the assembled multitude, and I felt myself a great hero. I must have driven or motored past that place thousands of times since that day, but I never do so, even if it be pitch dark, without thinking of the cutting of the first turf, and the feeling of great gratitude to the Almighty for His having put into the hearts of my mother and uncle the strong determination to carry through the great work. Nor did they cease with the finishing of the Loch Maree road, but went on with local roads, such as from Kerrysdale to Red Point, Strath to Melvaig, and Poolewe to Cove; and instead of the little narrow switchback road from Slatadale to the Tigh Dige, an almost entirely new road was made from Loch Maree to Gairloch through the Kerry Glen. After the good example of the Gairloch trustees, other neighbouring proprietors followed suit, and the lairds of Gruinord and Dundonnell in course of time made a road the whole way from Poolewe, via Aultbea, Gruinord, and Dundonnell, to join the Garve and Ullapool road at Braemore. This gave the whole of the coast-line from the mouth of Loch Torridon to Loch Broom the benefit of more or less good highways, which are all now country roads. How well do I remember the first wheeled vehicle, a carrier's cart, that ever came to Gairloch, and the excitement it caused.

My uncle says: "There being no need of wheels in a roadless country in my young days, we had only sledges in place of wheeled carts, all made by our grieve. He took two birch-trees of the most suitable bends and of them made the two shafts, with ironwork to suit the harness for collar straps. The ends of the shafts were sliced away with an adze at the proper angle to slide easily and smoothly on the ground. Two planks, one behind the horse and the other about half-way up the shaft ends, were securely nailed to the shafts, and were bored with holes to receive four-foot-long hazel rungs to form the front and back of the cart and to keep in the goods, a similar plank on the top of the rungs making the front and rear of the cart surprisingly stable and upright. The floor was made of planks, and these sledge carts did all that was needed for moving peats, and nearly every kind of crop. Movable boxes planted on the sledge floor between the front and back served to carry up fish from the shore and lime and manure, and it was long ere my father Sir Hector paid a penny a year to a cartwright. The sledges could slide where wheeled carts could not venture, and carried corn and hay, etc., famously."

My readers will perhaps wonder how we got our letters before the Loch Maree road was made. Well, there was a mail packet, a small sloop which ran between Stornoway and Poolewe and carried all the Lewis and Harris letters for the south, and which was supposed to run twice a week, though, as a matter of fact, she seldom did it even once. There was a sort of post office at Poolewe, to which the Gairloch and Aultbea letters (if there were any) found their way, and the whole lot was put into a small home-made leather bag which Ian Mor am Posda (Big John the Post) threw on his shoulder.

With this he trudged, I might say climbed, through the awful precipices of Creag Thairbh (the Bull's Rock) on the north side of Loch Maree, passing through Ardlair and Letterewe, and so on at one time to Dingwall, but latterly only to Achnasheen. Imagine the letters and newspapers for the parish of Gairloch and Torridon (part of Applecross), with about 6,000 souls, and the Lews, with a population of nearly 30,000 inhabitants, all being carried on one man's back in my day.

The only possible way of getting baker's bread in those days was by the packet from Stornoway, and a big boy, John Grant, came over to us at Gairloch with bread and the letters once or twice a week. How well I can remember him standing, usually dripping wet, shivering in the Tigh Dige kitchen, while the cook expressed lively indignation because the bread-bag was soaking wet. That lad served me as a man very faithfully for many years as grieve after I bought Inverewe in 1862.[3]

In lowland Scotland decently surfaced major roads were slow to develop in the early and mid eighteenth century. The first Scottish Act (for Midlothian) sanctioning the building of a privately financed 'turnpike' road was passed in 1713. The next did not come until 1751. It was in the latter part of the century that a flurry of road building took place, stimulated by economic expansion and eased by the improved road-building techniques of engineers like Telford and Macadam. Though turnpike roads were welcomed by the well-to-do, the ordinary inhabitants of areas through which they ran did not necessarily regard them with pleasure. Many objected to being stopped at the barriers (spaced at six-mile intervals along the turnpikes) and required to pay. In the Duns and Kirkcaldy areas, for example, rioters attacked both the bars across the roads and the tollhouses where lived the keepers who were charged with exacting payments from passers-by. But the turnpikes did at last allow wheeled traffic to speed across Scotland and down into England. A network of stage-coach services sprang up offering travel at around 10 mph. Elegant coaches built of ash or elm carried six people inside on unsprung horse-hair seats, and twelve people on top, huddled on bare wooden planking. Such journeys were not cheap. Travellers catching the 6.55 a.m. Edinburgh 'Defiance' for the twelve-hour trip to Aberdeen paid £2.10s. for a single-fare inside seat and £1.16s. for an outside accommodation. Joseph Mitchell, Chief Inspector of Highland Roads and Bridges in the early and mid nineteenth century, was a frequent user of this form of travel.

At four o'clock p.m. of the 9th of August set out for the north on the top of the mail. Dr. Johnson remarked that nothing afforded him greater pleasure than rapidity of motion. Had he been in Her Majesty's mail this night he would have had ample enjoyment. In thirty-five minutes we reached Queen's Ferry, a distance of nine miles, and were in Perth (including the half hour or more at Queen's Ferry) in 4½ hours, forty-two miles. The Edinburgh coachman seemed to have inspired his brother of the Highland road, for there was no lack of driving through the vale of Athole. Down we swept one hill, and the impetus brought us half up another. The quick turns were taken, sometimes within six inches of the stones placed to define the edge of the road, or the corner of a bridge; still, neither these, nor the bolting or kicking of some of the horses, nor the darkness of the night, diminished our steady pace of ten or twelve miles an hour. It was very dark till about two in the morning, and being an old traveller, I dozed, well protected by great coats between two less prudent passengers. I like to ride outside, if well protected, on a summer night, the pure morning air being so fresh and grateful . . .

In the early days coaching was very slow and imperfect. The coachman's drive was limited to one stage of ten or twelve miles; thereafter he tended his horses, and prepared them for their return journey. His reward was sixpence from each passenger. The roads throughout the country became very much improved between 1830 and 1840, and coaches improved also and became numerous. A few years after 1840 coaching in Scotland was brought to its greatest perfection.

A great impetus was given to it by an association of some county gentlemen, chiefly Mr. Ramsay of Barnton, Mr. Barclay of Ury, Lord Glen Lyon, afterwards Duke of Athole, and others. They started a coach between Edinburgh and Aberdeen. Their coaches were luxurious and handsome, the horses beautifully matched and of the first character, harness in good taste and of the best quality. The drivers and guards in their uniform of red coats and yellow collars were steady and respectable men, great favourites on the road, obliging, full of conversation and local knowledge, and several of these played with no mean talent on the bugle and cornet. Time was kept to a minute, and so complete and perfect was the whole establishment that a highly paid veterinary surgeon was employed to tend the horses and see that they were properly looked to.

Soon after a "North Defiance" was established between Inverness and Aberdeen, on the same principle, and then the mail and other coaches were obliged to follow suit, and travel with equal speed and punctuality. But, true to red-tapeism, the cramped form and colour of the mail coach never changed, and until the last it retained the iron skid instead of the screw break.

But on a fine day on the box-seat outside of these coaches nothing was more enjoyable than sweeping through the country at ten or twelve miles an hour. The guards, particularly on the Highland and North roads, were good, obliging fellows.[4]

It was water transport that offered the most effective means of shifting bulky goods cheaply. As the Scottish economy expanded, so Scottish engineers of outstanding ability, like John Rennie and Thomas Telford, tackled the problems of improving water transport. Much of Scotland was not really suitable for canals, but nevertheless a canal-building boom in England in the 1760s and 1770s inspired efforts in Scotland. The Forth–Clyde Canal finally opened in 1790. The Crinan and Monkland Canals were completed. The Caledonian Canal initially opened in 1822 but was in such poor shape that a further two decades of investment and effort were needed before sizeable vessels could use it. By the end of the

eighteenth century the growth of coastal shipping and of trade with
the Empire (as well as with the traditional Baltic and Low Countries
ports) meant that harbourworks were needed to provide shelter, and
deep-water anchorage. At all the major ports, harbour building and
channel dredging went on throughout the nineteenth century to
accommodate an increasing number of vessels, and to allow the
entry of bigger and bigger ships. Nowhere was this more important
than on the Clyde. In the mid eighteenth century the Clyde estuary
was so shallow that large vessels were unable to sail up as far as the
city of Glasgow. A programme of jetty-building to narrow the river,
and of dredging, scoured and deepened the waterway so that, by
1870, the largest vessels could reach the city.

The nineteenth century witnessed a revolution in ship design
and propulsion. Vessels of the 1800s were timber-built and driven
by sail. Most ships of the 1900s were constructed of metal and
powered by steam. By then the Clyde ship-building yards dominated
the world. Sail's last throw took the magnificent form of clipper
ships, especially those built in Aberdeen. The *Thermopylae*, finest of
all clippers, managed to cover 380 miles in a single day's sailing.
But not even this vessel could stand up to the challenge of steam.

But though the Victorian traveller could choose from a variety
of water transport, and would find vessels powered by steam as well
as by sail, journeys could still be uncomfortable, as this personal
recollection of a voyage in mid-Victorian times by one W. Roberton
demonstrates.

I went on deck, and saw every kind of lumber for the Highlands
taken on board. Old beds, old tables, old chairs, old boxes, old
hampers, old every thing, were knocked about in great confusion;
but the principal part of the cargo consisted of tar barrels. These
were rolling in all directions, and perfuming the boat and all in
it in a way I did not by any means like. There was a number of
patriarchal-looking rams – some with astonishingly tortuous
horns, and some with none – cooped up forward; and as to the
number of wild, savage-looking fellows, with large whiskers,
unshaven beards, and dirty faces, and gaunt but sagacious-
looking dogs, their name truly was legion. All this was soon
seen, and I must say it did not prepossess me with any favourable

opinion of the comforts of the "Arab". The longest voyage I had ever before made was from Newhaven to Kirkcaldy, and I was therefore not aware of all the manifestations of a disagreeable one in prospect, that presented themselves to more experienced eyes than mine.

After losing a couple of hours of good daylight, everything was got on board, but certainly not in a ship-shape condition, and we started for Oban. I like to see everything going on around me, and instead of again going below to the cabin, I mounted up to a cross plank resting on the two paddle-boxes, which I heard them call "the gangway", and found a good-looking quiet man standing there looking right before him, and not taking the least notice of anything but the head of the vessel. I went up to him, and remarked it promised to be a good night.

"Oh yes," he said, "it's a good night." He then looked down to where the tar barrels were crowded about the deck, and cried "Take you there, M'Innes, some planks and confine these sheep well forward, the shepherds will help ye. You, Beaton, get some hands and stow away these tar barrels, and make things snug for the night."

"Ay, ay, sir," sounded from below.

"You are the captain of the 'Arab'?"

"Yes."

"She is a good boat," I ventured to say.

"Yes, sir, she's a good boat," shortly.

"Is the wind fair, captain?"

"It will do very well if it keeps this way."

"You do not expect a change; do you, captain?"

"Well, sir, it is difficult to say when to expect a change and when not. I do not expect any change to signify."

I observed that he looked at the moon, which was surrounded by a bright golden ring. The clouds were scudding past her very fast, and a black cloud stood right ahead of us, which I would have willingly steered clear of, if that were possible. I saw the captain every now and then looking to see that his orders about the tar barrels had been carried out, and I confess that a sort of disagreeable idea began to creep upon me that we were to have a stormy passage round the Mull of Cantyre. I kept up on the gangway to see how matters were likely to go, and I began to perceive a decided heaving under me. This suddenly increased, and the steamer gave a plunge that made my heart start to my mouth. Still the reflection of the moon shone brightly on the water, and there was plenty of laughing and talking on all sides of me, which made me think, at all events, that there was no danger.

The plunges became more frequent, and by and by the vessel began to go down sideways, and then come up with a sudden spring that was very unpleasant to me. Shortly after this a bell rang, and I saw a man making his way towards me, and with much ingenuity avoiding the many obstacles that lay in his path. He would dive under one thing, round another, and lightly step over a third. I am quite certain that I saw him make a stepping-stone of the body of a recumbent Celt, almost without being noticed. At last he reached me and said –

"Tea is ready, sir; will you be pleased to take some?"

"Well, I suppose I had better."

"This way, if you please, sir," and away he went in the same eel-like manner as he came, but every moment looking back and saying, "This way, if you please, sir."

I soon found following him a matter of no small delicacy and difficulty. Every place that was not taken up by tar barrels and other unsavoury lumber was occupied by human be-ings, who lay about in inconceivable places, and I found myself tumbling and floundering among them, kicking this one, trampling upon that, and leaving behind me a track of "oich-oichs" and gutteral benedictions which I did not pretend to understand. My first feeling on getting into the cabin was one of dislike to everything I saw. There was a smell of fish, flesh, and fowl, combined with a close and oily atmosphere, and the fumes of toddy and bilge water which prejudiced me against the display I saw of dish covers, cups, and plates, surrounded by a goodly row of weather-beaten, rugged faces, seemingly intent upon some expected event of considerable interest.

"This way, sir, if you please," said my friend the steward. An intolerable heat came over me, and the perspiration came streaming out of every pore. The steward came past, and I said to him –

"The room is too close; will you open the window?"

"All battened down for the night, sir."

"Steward, what can the matter be with me? I feel very uncomfortable."

"Perhaps you are getting sick, sir," without even attempting to throw a grain of compassion into his voice; "a little brandy might do you good, sir."

"Bring me some"; and forthwith it came, but I cannot say that I experienced much relief from this sovereign remedy for sea sickness.

The rest of the tea-party still lingered about the table, as if there yet remained something to be done, and my helpless state, for I may now call my state helpless, attracted their attention. They instantly began to prescribe.

"A pottle of porter did me goot once," said one.

'I think ale's petter," said another.

"Goot room [rum] is about the pest thing I know," said a third.

"If you tak my advice," said a gaunt old fellow, with a pair of threatening eyebrows, "ye'll gie a rub to the pit of your stomach wi' a little turpentine and wanager."

"Well, chentlemen," said a round-faced jolly little Celt, "I wadna gie a drap of good whusky for them aal put together."

"Ferry goot observation, sir," responded on all sides.

At this time a fine old man, with a shrewd intelligent face, came quietly up to me, and advised me to lie down on the sofa, and keep very quiet in whatever position I felt most free from the intolerable feeling of sickness and nausea I had. The good old fellow, God bless him, helped me to the vacant sofa himself, and made me snug there.[5]

The spread of the railway system hit hard at older forms of transport. Long-distance stage-coach services dwindled and the shrinking revenues of the turnpikes led to the ending of the system in 1879. Local authorities took over responsibility and travellers no longer paid for their journeys. Steam-hauled railway traffic arrived in

Scotland in 1826 with the opening of the Monkland–Kirkinkilloch line. In the next twenty years it spread across the country at an amazing pace. Passengers first travelled in steam-hauled trains in 1831, rolling along the tracks of the Glasgow–Garnick Railway in open wagons. To many early travellers, the prospect of a railway-journey was a matter for apprehension and excitement, as this Edinburgh inhabitant noticed.

It may interest the reader to get an idea of travelling in the early Forties, if I say a few words about my first railway journey, when I was five years old. My father had to go to Madeira with a delicate half-sister of mine, and he took my own sister and me to London, to live with my uncle, the Adjutant-General, during his absence. Well do I remember the excitement as we watched for the railway omnibus that was to take us to Haymarket terminus. The building of the station above ground was then exactly as it is now. Luggage was passed down to the level of the platform by a steep shoot of wood, which shone with the polish of many a portmanteau. With what eager glee I watched a great lady's trunk chasing her own bandbox down the shoot, and how chagrined I was when the bandbox seemed to me to take fright and slid over the side of the shoot on to the floor, just as it was on the point of being crushed flat against the last heavy package that had gone down. Railway travelling was then very different from what it is now. Ours was the important train of the morning, but more than two hours passed before we descended the tunnel to Queen Street, and completed the distance of 47½ miles over one of the most level lines in the country, except at the Glasgow end. It will hardly be believed, but – as I saw when I was older – there was a blackboard at every station, on the Edinburgh and Glasgow line, on which this rather Irish notice appeared in bold white letters: *"Passengers are advised to be at the station in good time, as the Company cannot guarantee that the train will not start before the hour stated in the Company's Time Tables"*! The failure to guarantee would rather be the other way in the twentieth century.

Travelling by steamer to Liverpool, we were taken on from there by train to Birmingham, which we reached in the middle of the night, being turned out on to the line outside of the city, the passengers' luggage, which was put on to an open truck, being pushed along the cinder track in front of us, we following on foot through the tunnel into the station, where I remember being taken into the great dining room, and gazing in wonder at the long line of dishes with all sorts of cold meats. They looked to me like a hundred, having never been in a public dining room before. We were, after waiting sometime, put into another train and carried on to London, arriving early in the morning, after forty-six hours travelling, little better in time than could be done by a fast mail-coach. What a contrast to the present day, when the traveller can leave Edinburgh at 7.45 in the morning, be in London from 4.10 to 11.35, and be back in Edinburgh at 7.10 next morning. Contrast this with the positive utterance of Sir Henry Herbert in the House of Commons in 1671: "If a man were to propose to convey us regularly to Edinburgh in coaches in seven days, and bring us back in seven more, should we not vote him to Bedlam?"

When railways were established, and in daily use, there were thousands who vowed that they would never put a foot in a railway carriage, and there were a few of those thousands who never did so.

What many people thought about railways in those early days is illustrated by a scene witnessed when my father, being in bad health, travelled to Malvern, and my stepmother, for his sake only, took her place in the train. I see her still, sitting in the carriage, as we children were taking leave of her. She had her handkerchief tightly pressed to her eyes, so that she might see nothing, and begged us not to make her uncover them. A more abject picture of terror and dejection I never saw. Four years after this I went on a journey with her and all the fear was gone, and she should chat and laugh like others. I remember her amusement, and that of other ladies in the compartment, when I showed her with schoolboy pride my skill in throwing sweetmeats into the air and catching them in my mouth. All feeling of looking for catastrophe was gone.

In my childhood's days I remember well hearing the denunci-ations of railroads – their dangers, their tendencies to injure health, their ruinous effect on trade, their causing all cows within reach of the railway line to refuse to be milked, their ruin of the horse-breeding trade, and many other imaginary calamities which were certain to follow their introduction.[6]

By the early twentieth century the extensive network of lines was helping transform life in Scotland. The atmosphere of a busy railway station is well-recorded by the writer and academic David Daiches in his account of Waverley Station, Edinburgh, in the 1920s and 1930s.

It had been horse cabs when I was very young, but the taxi soon established itself in my gallery of exciting and anticipated objects, and the very smell of its exhaust set the heart beating faster. The leathery smell inside, the straps hanging down from the adjustable, rattling windows, the little folding seats that could be pulled out for us children to sit on – how thoroughly delectable these things were! And then to watch as the taxi came into the precincts of the station, marked by the appearance of hoardings covered with advertising posters – Stephen's ink, Oxo, Bovril, Virol ('growing girls need it'), Pears' soap, the Pickwick, the Owl and the Waverley pen, that come as a Boon and a Blessing to men. These were signposts to adventure, indications that we were nearing the actual station, with its infinite glories. People have complained of the typical British railway station, with its noise, its dirt, its apparent confusion; but as a child I found it magnificently thrilling (an attitude I have never wholly lost). Porters rushing about with barrows heaped with luggage, the noise of trains arriving and departing, carriage doors slamming, the guard blowing his whistle, engines letting off steam, uniformed boys with trays strapped to their chests shouting 'Chocolates! Cigarettes!', trolleys with newspapers and confectionery being wheeled along the platform, everywhere the sense of movement, bustle, excitement and romance. And to know that one was going off oneself in a train, out beyond Haymarket tunnel, across the Forth Bridge, beyond, beyond – such knowledge made the railway station the most perfect spot on earth. Waverley Station, Edinburgh, was an especially good station; it was large, busy, noisy, with a great number of platforms and trains departing for almost every possible direction.[7]

City travel expanded in the late nineteenth century to include not only horse-drawn vehicles and bicycles, but also trams. Glasgow was the only city to invest in an underground railway. A six-and-a-half-mile system that took five years to build opened in 1896. For nearly forty years it was powered by steam-driven cable, then electric traction took over. Tramways, however, were a feature of all the major cities. They first appeared in the 1870s, the cars being pulled by horses. During the 1890s lines began to be electrified. Trams became a means of transport that ordinary people could afford. The network of lines helped to knit together the different parts of Scotland's cities. The sight of tram rails being ripped up and cars burned in the 1950s was a matter of regret to many. The actress Molly Weir who grew up in Glasgow could recall the trams in the inter-war years before buses and cars had driven them into decline. She found these vehicles endlessly fascinating.

One of the most dramatic stories told to me by my mother was of an accident to me in babyhood, when a tramcar was pressed into the rescue operation. I was about nine months old at the time and my mother had stood me up on the sink-ledge by the window while she cleared up the bathing things before putting me to bed.

The china bath, washed and dried, was beside me on the draining board, and when I turned round at the sound of my father's key in the door, my foot went through one handle, and I crashed to the floor. The bath broke into a dozen pieces, and an edge cut through the bridge of my nose like a knife.

My mother used to shudder as she described the blood as 'spurting up like a well', but my father, quick as lightning, seized the two cut edges of my skin between his fingers, bade my mother throw a shawl round me, and before she knew what was happening had dashed down two flights of stairs, kicking over the basin of pipe-clay water and the stair-women in his flight. He leaped on to the driver's platform of a passing tramcar.

"Don't stop till you get to the Royal Infirmary," he ordered.

The driver was so impressed with his urgency that he did exactly that, and all the passengers were carried willy-nilly to the doors of the infirmary. To me the most impressive part of the story was that the tramcar wasn't even going near the infirmary on its route. It should have turned at right angles at the points long before then. I was astounded that a tramcar should have been used in this way as an ambulance for me, and that the driver had dared vary the route from that marked on the destination board. It was maybe this thrilling piece of Weir folklore which started my love affair with tramcars. When I was a little girl I only had the penny for the homeward tram journey, when my legs were tired after the long walk into the town for special messages. It would have been impossibly extravagant to ride both ways. That luxury was only indulged in when travelling with Grannie, and the journey to town then seemed so different from the top deck of the tram, the landmarks so swiftly passed compared with my usual walking pace . . .

The most sought-after seating was in the front section of the upstairs deck. This was a favourite meeting place for the youngsters, for it felt just like being on the bridge of a ship, and it was cut off by a door from the main top deck. We could sing or tell stories if we felt like it and were sure we were disturbing nobody. The driver, whom we'd forgotten, could hear every word, for we were sitting directly above his platform with only an open staircase between us. He didn't mind the singing at all, but if a foot-thumper kept up a steady drumming in time to the rhythm of the ditty he'd shout up to us to be quiet, or he'd come up and throw the lot of us off. This was enough to silence us, for it would have been a terrible waste to have been thrown off before the stage we'd paid for had been reached. We all loved riding in trams and quite often went right to the terminus to get our money's worth, and walked back the odd quarter-mile to our homes.

At one time fares weren't paid for in cash, but in little bone tokens which were bought in bulk at the tramway offices in town. I don't know why this precaution was taken, unless it made the conductor's bag lighter, or foiled a would-be thief, or a dishonest employee. Their colours fascinated me and I longed to save them up and use them at playing shops, but the tram rides they bought excited me even more, so I never possessed more than one at a time.

When I was very small the routes were indicated by the colour of the trams. When colours were replaced by numbers we thought we'd never get used to them. How could we be expected to remember the No. 25 went to Springburn and Bishopbriggs when all our lives we'd travelled in a red car to our homes in these districts?

You could see colours a long way off, but you had to be fairly close to see a number and the queues teetered uncertainly trying to decide which number suited them, and delayed the tram's departure. This infuriated the conductress, who would shout "Come on youse. Whit are youse waitin' fu? The baund to play?"

Sometimes our mothers sent us to the terminus to get coppers for a sixpence, from the stock carried by the conductor. But, of course, if we'd been cheeky about his trolley attempts we could say goodbye to any thought of getting our money exchanged. There was nothing for it but to wait for the next tram, and stand admiringly by, hoping our compliments on the trolley finesse would soften the conductor and we'd get our coppers.

When the old cars were moving, these trolleys could be temperamental especially if the driver was new. There would be a lurch, and the trolley would come bouncing off the overhead wire in a shower of sparks, and swing wildly back and forth as the car slithered to a halt. This was a nerve-racking experience for the timid, and there would be shouts, "The trolley's off – the trolley's off" and all eyes would fasten anxiously on the conductor as he swung it towards the overhead wire again.

There was no danger, but it made us all uneasy to feel we were sitting there unconnected to that magic overhead wire. If this happened three or four times in the course of a journey, there would be alarmed tut-tutting from the women, and contemptuous opinions from the men that the driver had "nae idea how to drive a caur". "Aye, he must be new," somebody would murmur. "He juist hasnae got the hang o' it". Even with trams there were plenty of back-seat drivers.[8]

Yet the cost of travel meant that many people continued to walk considerable distances, just as they had in earlier times. Alexandra Stewart, who was born in 1896 and brought up in Glenlyon in Perthshire, recalled how people walked many miles as a matter of everyday life:

A lot of adults nowadays would consider our daily journey to and from school "a long walk". There wouldn't be many would walk eleven miles to and from Aberfeldy, all on the same day, to hear Gladstone make a political speech. Father did. He was a great Liberal, although the laird, Sir Donald Currie, was a Conservative M.P. There would be even fewer would walk 28 miles to Glen Almond one day and 28 miles home the next, leading a cow. Father did, at an age when some people have taken early retirement.

A cousin, Charlie Allan, had the farm at Tulchan, which is a mile or two down Glen Almond from where the river leaves the Sma' Glen. He sent father a note to say that he could have a white cow that was at Tulchan if he could come and get it. There was no public transport between Glenlyon and Glen Almond – the railways were far to the east or the west, there were no buses; beasts that could not be taken by train were still herded for long distances by drovers, and small towns like Aberfeldy had their own stockyards and meat markets. My father couldn't even take his bicycle one way, because he could hardly lead both a cow and a bicycle on the way back.

The emphasis on speed takes something out of life – and more if you replace animals with engines; like the old ploughman who said that he didn't know what loneliness was until he was put on a tractor, since before that he had always had the company of two wise horses. The faster you go, the more blurred is what you see. All his life my father seemed to preserve the doting eye that poets share with little children. I don't believe he was ever bored in his own countryside from the early days as a herd boy. There was always something to watch, some association to

remember, changes in light and sound and fragments of poetry
and local lore to think about. A well-stored mind is its own good
company and long hours spent walking were not time wasted as
they could be to mechanised armies nowadays who can't enjoy
what they are passing because they've timed themselves to be
somewhere else as soon as possible.

From Woodend to Tulchan is a marvellous walk – all the
better then when the roads were smooth and white and soft as
velvet to bare feet in the cart tracks, free of the noise of engines
on the ground or in the air, and no smells of petroleum or
rubber to get up your nose. I like to think of my father setting
out on a bright morning in the late spring, a long lifetime ago
– the dew still on the grass, for he was an early riser.[9]

Until the recent past ordinary people walked ill-protected from the
rain. When, in 1760, the citizens of Inverness first saw an umbrella,
it aroused intense interest. This event was recalled in 1842 by an
elderly inhabitant of the town.

It is now 82 years since the natives of Inverness, were astonished
at the appearance of an umbrella, which was used in a procession
on "St Crispin's day", the 25th of October. Whether it was
imported by some daring navigator from China, or from what
part of the universe the umbrella came, we can scarcely imagine;
certain it is, that one of the knights of the awl held the umbrella
over the king of the Crispins, although the day was fine and dry.
This procession was very grand, and almost all the inhabitants
of the town and parish were out to witness it, yet the principal
object of astonishment was the umbrella, which totally eclipsed
"My Lord King Crispin" in his robes, supported by train-
bearers, various pipers leading the van, and numbers gaily
dressed in the national costume.

Mr Fraser of Farraline was the first gentleman known to
possess an umbrella in this place, where they are now so plentiful
that the poorest old wife is seldom to be seen without one, and
on a wet market morning in front of the Exchange the extended
canvases resemble the closely-placed shields of the ancient infantry when warding off a shower of hostile darts and arrows.

Previously to the introduction of umbrellas, "Come under my plaidie," was an invitation which necessity as well as gallantry required of the husband towards his spouse, and of the lad towards his lassie, when a shower occurred; unwelcome in the former case, but not always so in the latter.[10]

By the 1900s Scottish roads were beginning to be used by the form of transport that was to end the age of the tram and erode the habit of walking – the motor car. W. S. Speed's father served as a coachman to a family in Fife. When they bought a car he had to learn to drive. W. S. Speed too, became a chauffeur and retained vivid memories of these early motoring days:

Prior to the First World War, the motor car was gradually beginning to take the place of the horse, and like many young men at that time father decided to learn to drive. Considering the hardships attached to working with horses, exposed to all kinds of weather, it was no wonder horsemen took kindly to this new form of travel. It was also with some regret, however, that they accepted the change-over, because in spite of those hardships, there was something akin between man and horse which was absent in the association between car and driver. Very few cars were to be seen on the roads yet and as far as I can remember there would only be a few hundred in our country alone.

Being invariably chauffeur driven, and as good manners were essential to a private servant, there was always great consideration given to horse-drawn vehicles which were still very much in the majority.

Drinking and driving was almost unheard of in those days for one or two very good reasons. Firstly, roads were more difficult to negotiate, so it was imperative that the driver was constantly on the alert as, apart from meeting candle-lit vehicles, hazards like flocks of sheep on a blind corner were quite a common event. Also no such fineries as windscreen wipers, self-starters, syncromesh or dipping headlamps had as yet been introduced, not to mention many other gadgets which the driver now takes for granted. However, I think the greatest deterrent to drinking and driving was the fact that any chauffeur, not necessarily under the influence, but just having the smell of alcohol on him, promptly got his notice . . .

As tyres in those days were more or less in their experimental stage, it was not unusual to have a puncture on about every fairly long distance run. In fact you were lucky if it was only one. I've had three in one day and as wheels were not detachable then, the second and third meant changing a tube which necessitated jacking up the offending wheel, levering off the tyre and fitting the inner tube. The first punctured tyre was simpler, as all cars then carried what was called a Stepney and was really a complete rim with tyre inflated which was then clamped alongside the offending wheel. It was a bit awkward to drive with it but it usually got you home. In those early days of motoring it was no uncommon sight to see cars stopped by the wayside, bonnets up and perspiring chauffeurs trying desperately to coax life back into their engines. Alternatively, if the unsuspected trouble was underneath, a common source of trouble in those early stages, a pair of legginged legs protruding from the vehicle conveyed to the world at large that the driver was taking a worm's eye view of parts of his charge, trying to locate the trouble . . . I began my driving career with a 1914 Ford, the famous "Tin Lizzie". One had to start it by hand of course, as self-starters were still unheard of, and it could kick like a mule. It possessed three foot pedals, brake, gear and reverse. In conjunction with the hand lever, the gear pedal, when depressed, gave you low gear. High gear was obtained very simply by releasing the pedal and hand lever simultaneously. Having only two forward gears, there was obviously a big gap between the speeds, but it was surprising the gradients one could take in high gear, and the low one, when required, apart from starting off, could enable you to climb almost any incline, not too surprising when you realise the engine was 21 horse power. An example of the climbing ability of the Tin Lizzie was shown about this time, when an intrepid motorist drove on to the top of Ben Nevis, the highest mountain in Scotland. The road of course being non-existent in places, had to be planked in parts, but nevertheless, the enthusiastic driver got to the top. It was a truly remarkable feat and was a great advertisement for Ford, boosting the latter's sales considerably.

Often when I am driving a car now in comfort in all kinds of weather along the marvellous motorways, I think how father would have delighted in it all, and how he would have revelled in all the modern niceties of present day motoring.

Apart from the lack of windscreen wipers, heaters, indicators, I think the non-existent self-starters were the most missed in those early days. To stall your engine at a crossing on a wet night and have to get out to crank your charge into life again, under the stern glare from the policemen on point duty while the traffic, such as it was, stood still, was a most exasperating and humiliating position to be in, as I knew from personal experience.

Night driving was a particular hazard as most cars still sported paraffin side and tail lamps, of course, only one of the latter in each case. Although the later models possessed electric ones, headlamps were still unable to dip. One of the cars in my charge was a Straker Squire 1914 model, an open tourer with all brass fittings. Its huge brass headlamps were lit with acetylene gas, but, with this difference, whereas most were self-contained, like the smaller type on bicycles in those days, these were fed from a generator housed outside on the running board. One advantage was that while darkness began to fall, the driver could lean out and turn on the water so that it could drip into the lower chamber which contained the carbide. A mile or two further on, the driver could then stop and light the headlamps which the gas had now reached, applying a match at the same time to the paraffin side and tail lamps.

I sometimes amaze my motorist friends of the present day when I tell them that the tail lamp was as a rule fastened by a bracket to the outside petrol tank which usually had a capacity of ten or twelve gallons. I often wonder what might have happened had there been a leak but, in all the years I drove such vehicles, I never once heard of a fire being caused by that practice. We never seemed to realize we were sitting on the veritable top of a volcano!''

Nothing has been more dramatic than the transformation of travel in the twentieth century. Horse transport and steam railways survive as leisure interests, tourist attractions, and anachronisms to be peered at when displayed in the centres of the expanding heritage industry. Motor transport has swept all before it, altering the Scottish landscape and revolutionizing our way of life.

CHAPTER XVII

THE HIGHLANDS AND
THE CLEARANCES

The Highlands have always been a distinctive part of Scotland, never more so than in the eighteenth century when Lowlanders were wont to describe them as barbarous and to call the Gaelic language 'Erse' or 'Irish'. Gaelic at that time was spoken throughout the Highlands as far south as Loch Lomond and Dunkeld. The fact that so many Highlanders (by no means the majority) had joined in the Jacobite risings further served to distance them from a Lowland Scotland increasingly loyal to the House of Hanover as the century progressed, and the crushing of the '45 rebellion was often portrayed as the turning point in Highland history: before that, a traditional society, brave, rebellious and poor; after it, a society dragged into the modern world by improving lairds and outside interests. The truth was more complicated – long before the adventure of Prince Charles Edward the Highlands had been commercially exploited for cattle and timber, often by the very Jacobite clan chiefs who were to join the rebellion, sometimes by outsiders. The second half of the century saw an acceleration of that change, but such an acceleration took place in the Lowlands as well. The defeat of Jacobitism probably had a minor effect on the social history of the Highlands: the relentless pressures of the market would have brought about a fundamental change in land use and society whatever the political régime.

Nevertheless it was in the third quarter of the eighteenth century that the Highlands became a major attraction to outsiders for the sake of their scenery, which was just beginning to be appreciated as wild and romantic, and for the curiosities of local society.

The two most famous early visitors were Dr Samuel Johnson and his biographer, James Boswell: Johnson was more interested in the people than the scenery, but unwilling to allow his companion to get away with a sloppy description of either. The following extract from Boswell's account of the journey shows how strange the southerners found the north and the northerners. An account of nineteenth-century Europeans in East Africa would have given no sharper sense of discovery and difference:

We passed through Glensheal, with prodigious mountains on each side. We saw where the battle was fought in the year 1719. Dr Johnson owned he was now in a scene of as wild nature as he could see; but he corrected me sometimes in my inaccurate observations. "There," said I, "is a mountain like a cone." JOHNSON: "No, Sir. It would be called so in a book; and when a man comes to look at it, he sees it is not so. It is indeed pointed at the top; but one side of it is larger than the other." Another mountain I called immense. JOHNSON: "No; it is no more than a considerable protuberance."

We came to a rich green valley, comparatively speaking, and stopped a while to let our horses rest and eat grass. We soon afterwards came to Auchnasheal, a kind of rural village, a number of cottages being built together as we saw all along in the Highlands. We passed many miles this day without seeing a house, but only little summer huts, called *shielings*. Euen Campbell, servant to Mr Murchison, factor to the Laird of Macleod in Glenelg, ran along with us to-day. He was a very obliging fellow. At Auchnasheal, we sat down on a green turf-seat at the end of a house; they brought us out two wooden dishes of milk, which we tasted. One of them was frothed like a syllabub. I saw a woman preparing it with such a stick as is used for chocolate, and in the same manner. We had a considerable circle about us, men, women and children, all McCraas, Lord Seaforth's people. Not one of them could speak English. I observed to Dr Johnson, it was much the same as being with a tribe of Indians. JOHNSON: "Yes, Sir; but not so terrifying." I gave all who chose it, snuff and tobacco. Governor Trapaud had made us buy a quantity at Fort Augustus, and put them up in small parcels. I also gave each person a bit of wheat bread, which they had never tasted before. I then gave a penny apiece to each

child. I told Dr Johnson of this; upon which he called to Joseph
and our guides, for change for a shilling, and declared that he
would distribute among the children. Upon this being announced in Erse, there was a great stir; not only did some
children come running from neighbouring huts, but I observed
one black-haired man, who had been with us all along, had
gone off, and returned, bringing a very young child. My fellow
traveller then ordered the children to be drawn up in a row; and
he dealt about his copper, and made them and their parents all
happy. The poor McCraas, whatever may be their present state,
were of considerable estimation in the year 1715, when there
was a line in a song,

> And aw the brave McCraas are coming.

There was great diversity in the faces of the circle around us:
some were as black and wild in their appearance as any American
savages whatever. One woman was as comely almost as the figure
of Sappho, as we see it painted. We asked the old woman, the
mistress of the house where we had the milk (which by the bye,
Dr Johnson told me, for I did not observe it myself, was built
not of turf, but of stone) what we should pay. She said, what we
pleased. One of our guides asked her, in Erse, if a shilling was
enough. She said, "Yes." But some of the men bade her ask
more. This vexed me; because it showed a desire to impose upon
strangers, as they knew that even a shilling was high payment.
The woman, however, honestly persisted in her first price; so I
gave her half a crown. Thus we had one good scene of life
uncommon to us. The people were very much pleased, gave us
many blessings, and said they had not had such a day since the
old Laird of Macleod's time.[1]

This view of the Highlanders as a simple, aboriginal people, somehow analagous to the American Indians, easily slid into a view that
they were backward and incurably lazy, and perhaps needed to be
brought into the modern world by the tactic of the short, sharp
shock. Needless to say, this paid scant regard to the Highlanders'
hostile environment, but it became of real importance when the

Highland clearances began on a large scale in Sutherland in the second decade of the nineteenth century. The Countess of Sutherland, Lady Stafford (and her husband, Lord Stafford, later the Duke of Sutherland) wished to increase the rentals of their estate by turning the inland straths, like Strathnaver, into sheep farms and moving the peasantry to, as they assumed, more profitable and demanding occupations as fishermen on the coasts. This was how Patrick Sellar, the principal factor responsible, described the Gaelic-speaking population of the Highlands:

There is no one thing to be imagined more deeply affecting or afflicting, than the absence of every principle of truth and candour from a population of several hundred thousand Souls, the sad remnant of a people who once covered a great part of Europe, and who so long and so bravely withstood the invading strength of the Roman Empire. Their obstinate adherence to the barbarous jargon of the times when Europe *was possessed by Savages*, their *rejection* of any of the several languages now used in Europe, and which being Sprung or at least improved from those of the greatest nations of antiquity, carry with them the collected wisdom of all ages, and have raised their possessors to the most astonishing pitch of *eminence* and *power* – Their seclusion, I say, from this grand fund of knowledge, places them, with relation to the enlightened nations of Europe, in a position not very different from that betwixt the American Colonists and the Aborigines of that Country. The one are the Aborigines of Britain shut out from the general stream of knowledge and cultivation, flowing in upon the Commonwealth of Europe from the remotest fountain of antiquity. The other are the Aborigines of America equally shut out from this stream; Both live in turf cabins in common with the brutes; Both are singluar for patience, courage, cunning and address. Both are most virtuous where least in contact with men in a civilized State, and both are fast sinking under the baneful effects of ardent spirits.

The Aborigines of America receive this poison in exchange for the few products of their industry which they give to Europe in barter for it. The Aborigines of Britain owe their misfortune to causes totally different and which I shall endeavour briefly to explain.

He continued by denouncing those Highlanders on the Sutherland estate and elsewhere who eked out their legal incomes by indulging in illicit whisky distillation:

> These are hard truths, but they certainly are truths, and there is another truth still more afflicting, which is that the poor smuggler gets the least share of the profit, and pays the dearest for it. His life becomes a continued struggle, how by lies, chicanery, perjury, cunning, midnight journeys, the midnight watching of his wife and family, debasing artifices, and sneaking to his superiors, he can obtain thro' theft a miserable livelihood. Debauchery and beggary follow the total absence of principle, *essential to his trade*. His children trained up in deceit, exceed their father in turpitude, and the virtue of a Scotch Highlander is exchanged for the vices of the Irish Peasantry. If ever there existed an evil crying for the prompt interference of men in power, it is this rapid demoralization of a brave people, for the basest, the most nefarious and the worst purposes. Lord and Lady Stafford have in their own power its correction on the Estate of Sutherland, at least the diminution of it to a very great degree as well as the turning of the sentiments of the people and the infusing into them some portion of that stream of knowledge before alluded to, and which had been so successfully communicated in the highlands of Banffshire to the fathers of Sir William Grant and Sir W. Garrow.[2]

He concluded by recommending the eviction of such nests of smuggling and distilling tenants, and the total re-employment of the population on the coasts as crofters and villagers compelled to fish. The result was the notorious Sutherland clearances, which stirred up such hatred and resentment against Sellar and his employers that the memory lingers to this day. It was certainly very vivid to Angus Mackay, cottar, of Strathy Point, when he gave evidence at the age of eighty to the Napier Parliamentary Commission in 1884. Some account should be made for the fact that he

was an old man, and his memory of distant times perhaps invested
the land of his childhood with a glow of prosperity it never really
had: but the bitterness and vividness of his account of what had
happened seventy years before, and its effects on Highland society,
brook no contradiction.

Where were you brought up yourself?
— In Strathnaver.
When did you leave Strathnaver?
— I left when young and came to Strathy Point, when the
sheep commenced.
Do you remember the time?
— Yes, I was very nearly drowned that day.
Is that what makes you remember it?
— Yes. I will remember it as long as I live. I got a terrible
fright.
Were you old enough to remember the circumstances of the
people at the time?
— It would be a very hard heart but would mourn to see the
circumstances of the people that day. He would be a very cruel
man who would not mourn for the people.
What condition were they in before they left?
— If you were going up the strath now you would see on
both sides of it the places where the towns were — you would
see a mile or half a mile between every town; there were four
or five families in each of these towns, and bonnie haughs
between the towns, and hill pasture for miles, as far as they could
wish to go. The people had plenty of flocks of goats, sheep,
horses, and cattle, and they were living happy.
Do you remember yourself quite well that these people were
comfortably off at the time?
— Remarkably comfortable — that is what they were — with
flesh and fish and butter and cheese and fowl and potatoes and
kail and milk too. There was no want of anything with them;
and they had the Gospel preached to them at both ends of the
strath. I remember of Mr McGillivray being there as a preacher.
But what I have seen since then! There was a beggar like
myself, a woman living in Strathnaver, and she went round the

shepherds; and when she came back were was one Gordon in this low country asked her 'had she news from Strathnaver', 'I shall tell you my news from Strathnaver.' 'What is it?' 'The wood has been taken off the crofters' houses and it was sent to Alt-na-barra for a house of revelry and drunkenness. The manse which the godly ministers of old occupied is now occupied by a fox hunter, and his study is the dog kennel. The house which yourself had, and the great big stone at which you were wont to pray, the crow now builds its nest upon the top of it.' Now I consider at that time the Gospel was preached at both ends of Strathnaver, and in the middle of the strath; and in several other towns the elders and those who were taking to themselves to be following the means of grace were keeping a meeting once a fortnight – a prayer meeting amongst themselves – and there were plenty gathering, so that the houses would be full.

I am sure those good practices have not been altogether forgotten?

– I hope not.

You are quite satisfied yourself that these people were far better off then than their children are now?

– Oh yes, I am quite satisfied of that. The thing that frightened me when I was nearly drowned that day was this: my father and mother and my brother went away, having got notice that if anything was upon the ground at twelve o'clock they would be fined. They rose in the morning and went away with cattle, sheep, a horse, two mares, and two foals, to the place they were to live in after, and left me and my brothers who were younger sleeping in the bed; and there was a woman came in and said – 'Won't you wake up, Sellar is burning at a place called Rhistog.' We got such a fright that we started out of bed and ran down to the river, because there was a friend of ours living upon the other side, and we wished to go there for protection. I took my brother on my back, and through the river I went; and the water was that deep that when it came up upon his back he commenced crying and shaking himself upon my back, and I fell, and he gripped round about my neck, and I could not rise nor move. We were both greeting, and took a fright that we would be drowned. There was a poor woman coming with her family up the strath, and she saw us and jumped into the river and swept us out of it.

Did you see any burning houses yourself in Strathnaver?

– No, I did not. I was naked when I went to the river; and when they took me out of it my friends took such care of me that they dried me and put me into a bed.

How old were you when this happened to yourself?

– About eleven years of age.

How old was your brother that you were carrying?

– Three years of age.

Do you know that a number of houses were burned at that time?

– Oh! yes, yes.

Many houses?

– All from the river Owenmalloch and another river coming into Strathnaver on the east side, down to Dunvedan Burn.

The houses were burning?

– That is said, but I cannot say; I saw nothing because I was in bed.

But you were told at the time?

– Yes.

Were the people very willing to leave Strathnaver?

– You would have pitied them, tumbling on the ground and greeting and tearing the ground with their hands. Any soft-minded person would have pitied them.

Were there a great number of people removed at that time?

– I cannot give the number, but yon was the first removal in Strathnaver.

What was the notion of the people at the time as to the real cause of all?

– I cannot say who was the cause, but this is my opinion – Sellar was factor, Roy was clerk, and William Young was head factor, and they had Lady Stafford under their own control, and the factors were something troubled gathering their rent, and they just blindfolded Lady Stafford and said – 'We will give you £100 or £200 out of that and move the people out of the place and give the money to you all at once,' and the people were removed.

Who got the place after the people were removed?

– Sellar got it, but in five years' time we had a second removal.

Who got the place from which you were removed the second time?

– I believe Sellar. I was in Caithness herding at the time, but I suppose it was just Sellar who got it.

Would you like to go back to Strathnaver?

– What would I do there? Nothing at all. I want nothing but raiment and daily bread, if the Lord provide that for me.

Was there, to the best of your knowledge, and from what you have been hearing since then, any cause whatever for removing these thousand people from Strathnaver?

– I never heard any cause for it.

Any good cause?

– No, I never did; no reasonable or lawful cause about it at all.

You stated that your father and mother and the family went away with the stock of cows and horses in the morning?

– Yes.

So as to reach their new place of abode?

– Yes.

And that they left you and your brother in the house lying asleep on the bed?

– Yes.

How do you explain that your father and mother left their two sons alone in the house in bed asleep when they went away themselves?

– Because we were weak and young, and they were sure we would sleep to nine or ten o'clock, when they would be back again. My father was back before I was ten minutes out of the river.

How far had your father to go; how far was the new place from the old?

– About a mile and a half to the place called Wood of Skail, which was an uncultivated piece of ground until then.

What sort of place was it; was it worse than the old place?

– It was a place that never was laboured before.

Was he assisted to build his house?

– No, he had to build his house with feal and no stone at all.

Did the proprietor give him any stones to build a new house?

– No.

Did he give him any compensation for the old house he left?

– Nothing in the world.

How long was he in this new place?

– Five years, when he got a second removal.

Why did he get the second removal?

– To Strathy Point, to the worst place there is in the district.[3]

Clearances, mainly of congested and poverty-stricken crofting communities to be replaced by more profitable sheep farms, continued all over the Highlands until around 1855, with a large number following the years of potato famine after 1846 when the estates of bankrupt lairds (who often acted with generosity to their near-starving tenants in that crisis) passed into the hands of trustees with no other plan than to recoup their losses. The harrowing nature of one such clearance on Skye is brought to life in the description of Sir Archibald Geikie, a geologist working on the island at the time:

One of the most vivid recollections which I retain of Kilbride is that of the eviction or clearance of the crofts of Suishnish. The corner of Strath between the two sea-inlets of Loch Slapin and Loch Eishort had been for ages occupied by a community that cultivated the lower ground where their huts formed a kind of scattered village. The land belonged to the wide domain of Lord Macdonald, whose affairs were in such a state that he had to place himself in the hands of trustees. These men had little local knowledge of the estate, and though they doubtless administered it to the best of their ability, their main object was to make as much money as possible out of the rents so as, on the one hand, to satisfy the creditors, and on the other, to hasten the time when the proprietor might be able to resume possession. The interests of the crofters formed a very secondary consideration. With these aims, the trustees determined to clear out the whole population of Suishnish and convert the ground into one large sheep-farm, to be placed in the hands of a responsible grazier, if possible, from the south country.

I had heard some rumours of these intentions, but did not realise that they were in process of being carried into effect, until one afternoon, as I was returning from my ramble, a strange wailing sound reached my ears at intervals on the breeze from the west. On gaining the top of one of the hills on the south side of the valley, I could see a long and motley procession winding along the road that led north from Suishnish. It halted at the point of the road opposite Kilbride, and there the lamentation became loud and long. As I drew nearer, I could see that the minister with his wife and daughters had come out to meet the people and bid them all farewell. It was a miscellaneous gathering of at least three generations of crofters. There were old men and women, too feeble to walk, who were placed in carts; the younger members of the community on foot were carrying their bundles of clothes and household effects, while the children, with looks of alarm, walked alongside. There was a pause in the notes of woe as the last words were exchanged with the family of Kilbride. Everyone was in tears; each wished to clasp the hands that had so often befriended them, and it seemed as if they could not tear themselves away. When they set forth once more, a cry of grief went up to heaven, the long plaintive wail, like a funeral coronach, was resumed, and after the last of the emigrants had disappeared behind the hill, the sound seemed to re-echo through the whole wide valley of Strath in one prolonged note of desolation. The people were on their way to be shipped to Canada. I have often wandered since then over the solitary ground of Suishnish. Not a soul is to be seen there now, but the greener patches of field and the crumbling walls mark where an active and happy community once lived.[4]

In the final part of the nineteenth century there began a movement of crofters' resistance which culminated in the passing of the Crofters' Holding Act of 1886 that made further clearances illegal, gave the tenants the right to hand on their holding to their children, and fixed rents through the arbitration of a land court. The so-called 'Battle of the Braes' in 1882 was a critical incident in that development: a community on Skye made an attempt to resist Sheriff Ivory and a band of policemen brought in from Glasgow to arrest six crofters. What follows is not exactly an eye-witness account – Norman Maclean was a boy in the village who did not get up early enough to see what happened, and the vivid reported speech need not be taken literally: but it conveys the excitement and confusion of the day:

There were six men to be arrested, and the Inspector of Police detailed six policemen to arrest each of them at the same time. The sheriff-officer led off and showed the houses to be entered. Swiftly and methodically the little groups of police made for each house. As two of the accused resided in one house, it had ten police assigned for its attack. The two men were putting on their clothes when the police walked in. Mary Nicolson, the wife of James Nicolson, had the big pot on the fire with water just coming to the boil, and she was on the point of adding the meal to make the morning porridge. Slowly and deliberately she detached the big pot of boiling water from the chain and hurled its contents at the nearest policeman. With a quick movement he averted his face, and the hot water spent itself on his clothes. "Thank you," said he, "the hot water is very welcome as a change from the ice-cold rain with which I am soaked." The men offered no opposition. The other four accused crofters were seized half-dressed. In less than half an hour six dazed, breakfastless prisoners were brought to Ivory and his coadjutors, and placed in the centre of the host. In ones and twos the people rushed up the brae to the road and menaced the invaders. Stones began to be thrown. The word of command was given and the police set out for Portree.

Only two of the three townships had as yet assembled their people for the defence of their kindred and their homes. The boy from Achnahanaid had passed on his warning to Sam Nicolson, who ran like the wind to Peinchorran. But most of the houses were still wrapped in silence; and sleepy voices bade Sam begone. But the clamour he made roused them. Time, however, was lost, and the question arose on all sides: "Where are the Peinchorran men?" Just as the invaders began their march back with their prisoners, Sam came running along the road from Tor-na-cro. "They are coming," he cried. "They will be too late," said Alasdair.

It was then that Angus MacBhannain took charge. "Run to the Cumhag and stop them there," he called out to the crowd, and himself led the way. His wife, Mary Ann, a sister of James Nicolson, ran beside him. Sam took command of the boys and girls. "To the Cumhag," he cried, and led the way. But as he had been running for half an hour through Peinchorran, he was soon outstripped. The police kept to the road, and the people ran straight to their goal across Alt na golag and through the croft of Eoin 'ic Domhuill 'ic Ian 'ic Eoin, and gathered on the steep slope above the pass before the police arrived. When the invaders reached the south end of the pass, they were met with a fusillade of stones and clods. Sam had some twenty boys and girls under his command. They filled their pockets with sharp flints.

"They have no guns," cried Sam; "let us charge them: throw the stones and then run back up the brae."

And this they did, hurling down the slope like a mountain torrent. Stopping where Sam stopped, a rain of stones descended on the police. Sheriff Ivory, the sacred representative of Queen Victoria, the embodiment of law and order, was hit with a clod on the jaw. For Sam never missed the target. The Sheriff's teeth were set on edge and he held his jaw with both hands. His deputy, Spiers, was struck with a clod in the face. The men and women were gathering large boulders to roll down on the invaders when they entered the pass. The fusillade of stones from the light infantry commanded by Sam never ceased. The women were foremost, and Widow Nicolson raised to heaven a ceaseless litany of imprecations. "May the curse of heaven be upon you, ye sons of Belial; may the fires of hell consume you, ye whelps of Satan."

Angus MacBhannain, while the Inspector of Police and Sheriff Ivory stood discussing the situation, suddenly called out, "They are coming at last," and the whole body of the defenders looked south, and there, a quarter of a mile away, were the Peinchorran men running to the help of their comrades. Sam described the scene to me afterwards. "You remember the Battle of Bannockburn," said he, "when over the ridge there came the Scots camp followers, and the English thought they were a new army and broke and fled. So it was here. The Inspector ordered half his force to charge up the brae with their batons; and the rest with the prisoners to rush at the double through the pass."

This they did. Drawing their batons, half the police ran up the slope and attacked the stone-throwers. The head of Widow Nicolson was cracked as she poured out her maledictions. Murdo the Bard, well in the rear, threw ineffective missiles. The youngsters broke and fled. Sam stood his ground and got a blow that stunned him. From the top of the narrow pass the men came running to save the women. Then, at the word of command, the escort of the prisoners rushed through the pass into the open, and the rearguard ran after. The pass was forced and the Battle of the Braes was won by Sheriff Ivory and the forces of law and order.

It did not last more than a quarter of an hour or so. Sam said it was the most exciting quarter of an hour in all the world; and that it would have ended quite differently if the Peinchorran men had only arrived five minutes sooner. "For the Peinchorran men," said he, "are great fighters, especially Cluny and Ronald and Donald Somhairle. But when they were half through Ewen's croft the last of the police were through the pass and Angus could only roll one big boulder down on them, and it missed."

The Peinchorran men were received with jeers. All they could do was to go up to the top of the hill, to the spot where the boys had kept watch, and there gaze at the retreating police so long as they were in sight. I remember that morning so well. When I looked out of the window at nine o'clock, there was the group of men gesticulating on the top of the hill while the rain was driving in sheets from Ben Lee. And there they decided that in the evening they would march to Portree, storm the jail, and free the prisoners.[5]

In the event, the crofters lost their nerve and thought better of storming a gaol now protected by armed soldiers. The incident (probably not untypical in itself of Highland reactions when men

were arrested for trespass or non-payment of rents) attracted attention in the Scottish press, and snowballed into a movement for
crofters' rights.

The Highlands for the next century were protected by the
ensuing legislation from clearance, eviction and arbitrary increases
in rent. Unfortunately changes in the law did not themselves stem
the migration to the Lowlands or to Canada, Australia and New
Zealand by crofters in search of a more rewarding way of life. The
population of the Highland counties dropped more rapidly in the
next seventy years, when clearance was illegal, than it had done in
the previous seventy, when clearance had been allowed.

CHAPTER XVIII

THE OUTSIDERS' HIGHLANDS

When Boswell and Johnson visited the Highlands in 1773, they were like explorers in an unknown land. When Queen Victoria came in 1842 she was part of a well-established trail of tourists and sportsmen who had 'discovered' the romance of the north. The royal couple fell completely in love with Scotland, and ultimately decided to build a holiday home for themselves at Balmoral. They thus became the first monarchs since before the Union of Crowns to visit Scotland on a regular basis, and their infectious enthusiasm for everything Highland greatly reinforced the fashion for recreation in the hills. From this point onwards, the Highlands increasingly came to be appreciated, and therefore to 'belong', to the visitor, the outsider and the incomer, as well as to the Gael. The tourist often seemed simply not to notice the condition and problems of those who lived there: but that is usually the case with tourists, who come to enjoy pleasures, not to see miseries.

Victoria and Albert completed the construction of Balmoral in 1848. This is the Queen's entry in her journal of her 'first impressions of Balmoral':

Balmoral, Friday, September 8, 1848
We arrived at *Balmoral* at a quarter to three. It is a pretty little castle in the old Scottish style. There is a picturesque tower and garden in front, with a high wooded hill; at the back there is wood down to the *Dee*; and the hills rise all around.

There is a nice little hall, with a billiard-room; next to it is the dining-room. Upstairs (ascending by a good broad staircase) immediately to the right, and above the dining-room, is our sitting-room (formerly the drawing-room), a fine large room – next to which is our bed-room, opening into a little dressing-

room which is Albert's. Opposite, down a few steps, are the
children's and Miss Hilyard's three rooms. The ladies live below,
and the gentlemen upstairs.

We lunched almost immediately, and at half-past four we
walked out, and went up to the top of the wooded hill opposite
our windows, where there is a cairn, and up which there is a
pretty winding path. The view from here, looking down upon
the house, is charming. To the left you look towards the beautiful
hills surrounding *Loch-na-Gar*, and to the right, towards *Ballater*,
to the glen (or valley) along which the *Dee* winds, with beautiful
wooded hills, which reminded us very much of the *Thüringer-*
wald. It was so calm, and so solitary, it did one good as one
gazed around; and the pure mountain air was most refreshing.
All seemed to breathe freedom and peace, and to make one
forget the world and its sad turmoils.

The scenery is wild, and yet not desolate; and everything
looks much more prosperous and cultivated than at *Laggan*.
Then the soil is delightfully dry. We walked beside the *Dee*, a
beautiful, rapid stream, which is close behind the house. The
view of the hills towards *Invercauld* is exceedingly fine.

When I came in at half-past six, Albert went out to try his
luck with some stags which lay quite close in the woods, but he
was unsuccessful. They come down of an evening quite near to
the house.

The following week the royal couple made their first ascent of
Loch-na-Gar.

Saturday, September 16, 1848

At half-past nine o'clock Albert and I set off in a post-chaise,
and drove to the bridge in the wood of *Balloch Buie*, about five
miles from *Balmoral*, where our ponies and people were. Here we
mounted, and were attended by a keeper of Mr. Farquharson's as
guide, Macdonald – who, with his shooting-jacket, and in his
kilt, looked a picture – Grant on a pony, with our luncheon in
two baskets, and Batterbury on another pony. We went through
that beautiful wood for about a mile, and then turned and began
to ascend gradually, the view getting finer and finer; no road,

but not bad ground – moss, heather, and stones. Albert saw some deer when we had been out about three-quarters of an hour, and ran off to stalk them, while I rested; but he arrived just a minute too late. He waited for me on the other side of a stony little burn, which I crossed on my pony, after our faithful Highlanders had moved some stones and made it easier. We then went on a little way and I got off and walked a bit, and afterwards remounted; Macdonald leading my pony. The view of *Ben-na-Bhourd*, and indeed of all around, was very beautiful; but as we rose higher we saw mist over *Loch-na-Gar*. Albert left me to go after ptarmigan, and went on with Grant, while the others remained with me, taking the greatest care of me. Macdonald is a good honest man, and was indefatigable, and poor Batterbury was very anxious also.

I saw ptarmigan get up, and Albert fire – he then disappeared from my sight, and I rode on. It became cold and misty when we were on *Loch-na-Gar*. In half an hour, or rather less, Albert rejoined me with two ptarmigan, having come up by a shorter way. Here it was quite soft, easy walking, and we looked down on two small lochs called *Na Nian*, which were very striking, being so high up in the hills. Albert was tired, and remounted his pony; I had also been walking a little way. The ascent commenced, and with it a very thick fog, and when we had nearly reached the top of *Loch-na-Gar*, the mist drifted in thick clouds so as to hide everything not within one hundred yards of us. Near the peak (the fine point of the mountain which is seen so well from above Grant's house) we got off and walked, and climbed up some steep stones, to a place where we found a seat in a little nook, and had some luncheon. It was just two o'clock, so we had taken four hours going up.

But, alas! nothing whatever to be seen; and it was cold, and wet, and cheerless. At about twenty mintes after two we set off on our way downwards, the wind blowing a hurricane, and the mist being like rain, and everything quite dark with it. Bowman (Mr. Farquharson's keeper) and Macdonald, who preceded us, looked like ghosts. We walked some way till I was quite breathless, and remounted my pony, well wrapped up in plaids; and we came down by the same path that Albert had come up, which is shorter, but steeper; the pony went delightfully; but the mist made me feel cheerless.

Albert kept ahead a little while for ptarmigan, but he gave it up again. When he had gone on about an hour and a quarter, or an hour and a half, the fog disappeared like magic, and all was sunshine below, about one thousand feet from the top I should say. Most provoking! – and yet one felt happy to see sunshine and daylight again.

The view, as one descends, overlooking *Invercauld* and the wood which is called *Balloch Buie*, is most lovely. We saw some deer in the wood below. We rode on till after we passed the burn, and had nearly got to the wood. We came another way down, by a much rougher path; and then, from the road in the wood, we walked up to the *Falls of the Garbhalt*, which are beautiful. The rocks are very grand, and the view from the little bridge, and also from a seat a little lower down, is extremely pretty. We found our carriages in the road, and drove home by six o'clock.[1]

By the late 1840s the Highlands were being used by outsiders for a great many other purposes than the traditional crofters' subsistence farming or sheep runs. The shooting estate became a big attraction to visitors, and the sporting tour was highly fashionable. Charles St John and his friends had an attitude to ospreys on his visit to Sutherland regrettably different from that of the present day. Small wonder they became rare birds.

We were loth to leave our comfortable hostel at Scowrie, particularly without visiting the island of Handa, a great breeding-place of sea-fowl; but being rather pressed for time we got again under weigh for Durness. Our landlord at Scowrie having told us that he had heard that the osprey was building on an island in a loch about a mile from our road, we left the horse and boat under the charge of a bare-legged and bare-headed boy, at the place he mentioned (a small bridge about three miles from Scowrie), and went to a point of rock, from which we could command a view of the loch in question. We immediately through a glass discovered the nest of the osprey, built in exactly a similar situation to the last; that is, on the summit of a rock about eight feet high, shaped like a truncated cone, and standing exposed and alone in the loch. On coming nearer, we could distinguish the white head of the female osprey on the nest. The male bird was not in view. It was determined that I should remain concealed near the loch, while my two companions went for the boat. This plan was adopted for the double reason that I might be at hand to shoot any hooded crow who might attempt to take the eggs while the osprey was off, she having left the nest on our approach, and also that I might have a chance of shooting the old osprey herself in case she came within shot. I must say that I would rather she had escaped this fate; but as her skin was wanted, I agreed to try to kill her.

For some time after the departure of my companions she flew round and round at a great height, occasionally drifting away with the high wind, and then returning to the loch. She passed two or three times, not very far from me, before I shot at her. But at last I fired, and the poor bird, after wheeling blindly about for a few moments, fell far to leeward of me, and down amongst the most precipitous and rocky part of the mountain, quite dead. She was scarcely down behind the cliffs when I heard the cry of an osprey in quite a different direction and on looking that way I saw the male bird flying up from a great distance. As he came nearer, I could distinguish plainly with my glass that he was carrying a fish in his claws. On approaching he redoubled his cries, probably expecting the well-known answer, or signal of gratitude, from his mate; but not hearing her, he flew on till he came immediately over the nest. I could plainly see him turning his head to the right and left, as if looking for her, and as if in astonishment at her unwonted absence. He came lower and lower, still holding the fish in his feet, which were stretched out at full length from his body. Not seeing her, he again ascended and flew to the other end of the lake, the rocks echoing his shrill cry. The poor bird, after making one or two circuits of the lake, then flew away far out of sight, still keeping possession of the fish. He probably went to look for the female at some known and frequented haunt, as he flew rapidly off in a direct line. He soon, however, came over the lake again, and continued his flight to and fro and his loud cries for above an hour, still keeping the fish for his mate. I at length heard the voices of my friends and we soon launched the boat. The osprey became much agitated as we neared the rock where the nest was, and dropped the fish he held into the water. We found two beautiful eggs in the nest, of a roundish shape; the colour white, with numerous spots and marks of a fine rich red brown. As we came away, we still observed the male bird unceasingly calling and seeking for his hen. I was really sorry I had shot her.[2]

Other tourists visited the Highlands with less bloodthirsty intentions, simply to enjoy the mountains, and as this extract from a guidebook of around 1894 shows, the facilities for the visitor were sometimes surprisingly sophisticated (if a Temperance Hotel can be considered sophisticated).

As seen from the Fort William side, Ben Nevis appears a somewhat shapeless mountain, piled shoulder on shoulder, in vast folds of granite into the sky, as if disdaining symmetrical form, and depending on sheer bulk alone to vindicate its grandeur. It is only when it is observed how seldom the summit can be seen free of clouds, that the gigantic height of the Ben is realised (4,406 feet), for it is the highest mountain in the United Kingdom; and it is only when a pedestrian attempts to walk round it, and finds that the base is more than twenty-four miles in circumference, that its colossal bulk is fully grasped. For three-fourths of the ascent the mountain is of red granite, the remaining fourth being of porphyry, "which weathers of a brown colour, but when newly fractured shows bluish and greenish tints, mottled with specks of white felspar." The ascent may be made either from Fort William or from Banavie, about three miles distant, to which there is a branch line of the West Highland Railway, but the feat should not be attempted without a guide, as the densest of mists descend on the mountain without a minute's warning, and render the position of the mountain climber extremely dangerous. It is proposed to build a railway to the summit, similar to that which ascends the Rigi; but it has not yet got beyond the stage of contemplation.

To reach the summit of Ben Nevis means a climb of five miles up a bridle path, on so steep a gradient that in the distance named there is a rise of over 4,000 feet. This is not a task for a weak-lunged or weak-legged man; but the journey may be partly done on a hill-pony, and at the top there is a small Temperance Hotel, with sleeping accommodation for over a dozen guests, where tea, bed, and breakfast may be obtained for half-a-guinea – a small sum to pay for the proud boast in future years that you have slept on the top of Ben Nevis! The view from the summit is a bewildering one, for the eye looks down on nothing but mountain peaks, except where they are broken by the three great sheets of water – Loch Linnhe, Loch Eil and Loch Lochy, or by the sea itself. To take up again a former simile, it is like standing in the "ball" of St. Paul's, and gazing on the endless miles of the roofs of London, for the hill tops below seem interminable, and might almost be called monotonous in their multitude. On a clear day the eye can trace in the north-east the form of Ben MacDhui, the second mountain in Britain, which rises to a height of 4,296 feet in the Baemar Highlands. To the north the vision ranges as far as Ben Wyvis in Ross-shire. Westward, the Cuillin Hills in Skye may be distinguished, and in particularly favourable weather, some of the heights in the Outer Hebrides, ninety miles away. Southward may be distinguished Ben Cruachan, at the head of Loch Awe, lying almost east of Oban. South-west may be seen the Islands, and even a glimpse of Ireland may be caught. It is a prospect astounding in its wide expanse, and he is lucky who reaches the summit of Ben Nevis on a day when the atmosphere permits of a good view. Frequently the hill-top is shrouded in dense mist, giving on the wall of fog an effect as of the well-known Spectre of the Brocken. On the Ben itself there is a magnificent chasm to be inspected – a perpendicular precipice, ranging from 1,500 to 2,000 feet in depth, which Sir Robert Christison has described as the finest precipice in the world.

On the summit of Ben Nevis is the Observatory, where two meteorologists keep watch on the weather day and night, summer and winter, watch and watch about, so that hourly readings of the instruments may be taken, and telegraphed to the low-level Observatory at the base of the hill in Fort William. Tourists should not fail to purchase in Fort William a shilling pamphlet on Ben Nevis and the Observatory, published by John Menzies & Co. (Edinburgh), which will be found more interesting than many novels, so strange is the life in that lonely building, especially in winter.[3]

The tourist trade brought new prosperity to many areas, and transformed some from sleepy villages into bustling holiday resorts. The minister's son at Oban recalled, late in the century, how the 'Charing Cross of the Highlands' had been in his youth:

Oban, as I can myself recall it, in the days of my childhood, was a great contrast in many respects to the big and busy town and tourist centre that it is now. It was a little village, quiet even in the summer time, and far remote from the towns and cities that are now brought so near it by railway and telegraph, swift steamers and daily newspapers – things that, in those far-off years, were unknown and undreamt of.

Any letters from the south had to travel to Oban by way of Inveraray, and I well remember the little red, light-bobbing post-gig that brought the mail-bag to the village, delivering it at the mysterious little office, where an elderly lady, who kept a young ladies' school, was also able to take charge of all the postal business of the district . . .

In the earlier days of my childhood at Oban, the notions we children were able to form of the great world beyond were exceedingly nebulous. But Glasgow was the place of which we oftenest heard. It rose before our young imaginations full of vaguely conceived wonders, like the Bagdad of the Arabian Nights.

The first clear and memorable impression I received of the majesty of Glasgow, I got from my elder brother, when, for the first time, he had been taken there by my father on his way to the Synod, and came back big with the news of the wonderful things that he had seen. Most of these were beyond my power even to grasp. But at last he told me that there was a great street in Glasgow, called Buchanan Street, with big shops, full of things so costly, that you could get nothing in them for a halfpenny. I can still remember the awe that fell upon me at this astounding announcement. Nothing that could be bought for a halfpenny! It was a thought to make my brain reel. For in those days a halfpenny seemed to us a little fortune. Possessed of that valued and coveted coin, we felt an exalted sense of wealth, and sometimes before spending it we made the round of the village shops to see what there was in the windows that looked most tempting, and promised most for the money. We weighed the comparative merits of one of Waddell's "parlies" with Carmichael's big bull's-eyes, or old Granny Stewart's "black man," spread out in dark, glossy fragments on a tin tray, or one of Mrs Rankine's ginger-bread cows, or two of the pale, doughy rabbits, that looked out at us with currant eyes from her little shop window. What could we *not* get for a halfpenny? And now, to think that in Glasgow there were shops so grand that a halfpenny was of no account – could buy nothing at all! It staggered me. It was the first clear revelation I got of the greatness and unapproachable glory of Glasgow.

In those primitive days, moustaches – especially along with a clean-shaven chin – must have been a sight so strange in Oban as to excite suspicion, for I remember my aunt barricading the windows one night, before we retired to rest, because an unknown man with a moustache had made his appearance that day in Oban.

There was no street-lighting of any kind in the village in those days. If any one who sallied forth after dark wanted light he had to carry a lantern with him. Gas had not then been introduced into the village; as for electric lighting, it was a thing unknown and undreamt of, even in Glasgow!

Any shops in the village that kept open after dark burned dingy oil lamps that only made the surrounding gloom more visible. In the humbler houses, and in kitchens, the ancient "cruizie" was employed. I still possess, amongst my family relics, the cruse that burned on our kitchen mantelpiece sixty years ago – used by my brother and myself some years later, to melt lead for the moulding of bullets . . . except at supper, or when there was reading, firelight as a rule was liked better than candles; and most people, when the long nights set in, went earlier to bed.

I remember well the night when gas was first lighted in Oban, how the villagers turned out into the front street, and gathered in groups at MacCaig's & Cumstie's shop-windows to gaze at the new and (as it was then thought) wonderful light.

The only steamers I can remember as coming to Oban in the earlier days of my childhood, were two – the *Skerryvore*, bringing stores for the Lismore lighthouse, and the *Toward Castle*, coming once a week or so from Glasgow, and calling at Oban on her way further north. When this steamer was due, we children used often to go out to the Corran to listen for what was called "the boom of the *Toward*" – a boom that in calm weather sounded from far off – and, also, to watch for her smoke as she left Easdale.

One summer, later on, a new and wonderful source of interest appeared, when a blue coach, driven by a man in a brilliant coat, began to arrive daily in the summer-time from Glasgow, sweeping in splendour down by Dunollie Road to the accompaniment of a bugle horn. We boys used often to go out to meet it, and race alongside, or try to hang on behind, defiant of the occasional lash of the driver's whip.

Some scenes belonging to those years of my childhood recur to my mind in separate pictures, as when one is turning over the leaves of an album.

One such scene was the sight of my father and the village doctors carrying a coffin with a dead man in it from the house in which he had died to a cart that was waiting in the street. The man had died of fever, and such was the awful dread of infection amongst the people that men who would have faced any foe in battle shrank from going into the infected house to coffin or remove the body. Even when my father and the doctor carried the coffin out to the cart, the mourners kept as far from it as possible, and I remember the man whose cart was used standing some yards from the horse with a long rope attached to its head, by which to lead it away to the burial place . . .

Another scene belongs to the time of the Highland famine,

and the picture comes back to my mind of famishing women wandering on the Corran shore at low water, gathering seaweed for food to keep themselves and their children from dying of starvation. It was soon after this that a soup-kitchen was opened in the village, and many lives saved.[4]

Despite all the changes, however, there remained, especially in the Outer Hebrides which by 1900 had become the main centre of surviving Gaelic speech and culture in the Highlands, a strong sense of identity and apartness, of possession of a different scale of values and priorities from the rest of Scotland. This sense is captured by J. S. Grant, brought up on Lewis by English-speaking parents, so both an insider and an outsider, in a chapter in his memoirs called 'Camouflage and a Private World.'

Although I had been to the mainland quite early in life, and knew that my father's parents lived there, it was still remote and separate. I belonged to Lewis and to no where else. Even to this day I belong to Lewis in a way I have never belonged to Britain or even Scotland: in the sense of being possessed by a place, not merely acknowledging, in an objective way, that I was born and nurtured there. Lewis, to me, is not part of Britain. It is not even an island lying off the British coast. It is a community complete in itself, with a neighbour lying across the Minch, often obscured by rain, but sometimes clear along the skyline in blue serrated summits, or snow-capped peaks, glowing apricot or pink in the winter sun. The rest of Britain is an extension of Lewis, the second circle of endlessly recurring and expanding but diminishing waves, which mark the centre where the stone was thrown into the pool. No one who has not lived for a great part of his life on an island can possibly understand the intensity of this love of place.

I have frequently been taken aback, in conversation with intelligent and sensitive people, to hear them express surprise at the parochial attachment to place they have found in small remote communities. It has required a real mental effort for me to adjust to the fact that it is the islander's commitment which is unusual rather than other people's detachment. In our mobile fluent civilisation in which the world has become a single village, and people move rapidly from place to place and from job to job in furtherance of their personal careers, the islander's attachment to his birthplace is an anachronism, an aberration. But that very fact may make it more significant, and, perhaps, more important, than it has ever been. The idea that the future of mankind is best served when the individual's only commitment is to the pursuit of his own career requires the same sort of qualification as the belief that the free play of market forces will produce the best possible world for all. It is a comforting illusion that, if everyone maximises his own personal success, the sum total of success will be greater than if we let ourselves be held back by other considerations. But I doubt it. It is not necessarily true that one man's success is another man's failure, but there is sufficient truth in it to expose the hollow myth that a free-wheeling, competitive society will produce either greater happiness for all, or even greater material prosperity for all, than a society regulated on other principles.

Belonging to an island is very different from belonging to a club, a society, a party, or even a church. All these groupings are based, to some extent at least, on identity of beliefs or interests. They are exclusive of those who do not share them. Attachment to place can be exclusive, too, in the sense that we separate ourselves from other places, but it also means that we accept as members of the same community all who belong to our own place whether we agree with them or not. A fellow islander is a fellow islander even if we hate his guts. As much part of the community as we are ourselves. Indeed in a closely knit community like an island we are as tightly bound to the people we dislike as to the people we love. They, just as surely, help to establish our identity and define our place in the whole. It is this sense of knowing where one fits in that modern man is in danger of losing.

Even absence does not necessarily diminish one's attachment to a place if it is clearly identified to begin with. In fact absence may intensify the attachment because it idealises the object we are attached to. Lewis has benefited greatly from the continuing interest of those who have left, but at times it has suffered. The late Stephen MacLean once commented shrewdly on the damage done, during the Leverhulme era by emigré Lewismen, still interested in the island, articulate and outspoken, but able to take a romantic view. They were fighting to preserve an Eden which had never existed, while those who remained at home had to grapple with the realities of a very imperfect world. I did not choose to remain in Lewis, attached to it though I was. Circumstances held me there, and, at times, I was an unwilling prisoner. But having spent the greater part of my life on the island, I am in no danger of romanticising it. I flatter myself, however, that sitting at my desk in Inverness, looking out on the Moray Firth and the fresh snow on Ben Wyvis, I can write of it with greater objectivity than when I was in Stornoway in the thick of events.

As I have already indicated, I was aware from a very early age that, as part of the Anglicised and Anglicising Stornoway establishment, I was a stranger looking in, rather than myself an integral part of the Lewis community. This unusual and uneasy balance between exclusion and involvement has limited my knowledge of Lewis, in some respects, but has sharpened my understanding. I became aware of my own situation when I moved into the Secondary school and found myself for the first time in a class where the majority of the pupils were Gaelic-speakers, who could withdraw at any moment into a private world to which I had no entry. They never deliberately embarrassed me by using Gaelic to shut me out, and their English was better than my own. But, having thought of rural Lewis up until then, in terms of black houses, and fishermen, barefoot women hawking haddocks from door to door, and gangling youths on Market Day with droves of sheep, I now found myself in the company of boys and girls from these same villages who were in every aspect of life – physical, intellectual and moral – my equals, and often my superiors. In the holidays I sometimes saw the girls of my class, their modest finery set aside, barefoot on the moor with a creel of peats, or the boys, herding the sheep or working the boats, absorbed into their old environment as completely as if they had been camouflaged by nature to conceal the fact that they were no longer part of the egalitarian crofting village, although not yet ready to take wing and leave it for good. The concealment may even have been deliberate, because they had their own loyalty to the closed community of the village to which they belonged, and were slow to separate themselves from the friends who were not graduating with them out of the village and into the professions. Today town and country are almost indistinguishable but sixty years ago it was very different. When I was a child at school, three families out of four in rural Lewis lived in thatched houses, and in the years of unemployment, and crop failure, just after the First World War, Helen Porter, the MOH, commented bitterly, in one of her reports, that in a rural Lewis school you could often pick out the children of war widows from the rest, because they were better shod and clad. It was not that the war widows' pensions were princely, but many other families at that time had even less. Dr Porter's comments were taken up by "John Bull", somewhat distorted and exaggerated. There was great indignation among the good folk of the town who regarded poverty as a stigma, and had no wish to be associated with it. I was aware of the commotion because these things were freely discussed at table, and my father, as the only local journalist, was always at the centre of any conflict between what was actually happening and what people wanted to hear. Piquancy was added to the situation because Dr Porter was then on the point of marrying Hugh Miller, the District Clerk, an apparently confirmed bachelor, a close friend of the family, and the official spokesman of the Council in which the battle between those who wanted to play up the island's poverty for political reasons and those who wanted to play it down for personal pride was raging most fiercely.[5]

The beauty of the Highlands, their dramatic social history and the continuing distinctiveness of the islands will continue to make them a place where insider and outsider collide. What is it to be, a preserved green paradise for the recreation of the descendants of Dr Johnson, Charles St John and the Victorian trippers? Or a reserve for a Gaelic and crofting way of life? Or a region like any other, there to be exploited for money and jobs by those who care to remain within it? The answer will not be a simple one, or without conflict, for these objectives cannot all be attained without collision between them.

References

CHAPTER I: *Changing Times*

1 Thomas Somerville, *My Own Life and Times* (1861).
2 A. Allardyce (ed.), Ramsay of Ochtertyre's *Scotland and Scotsmen of the Eighteenth Century* (1888).
3 Osgood Mackenzie, *A Hundred Years in the Highlands* (1921).

CHAPTER II: *Ordinary Homes*

1 William Cobbett, *Northern Tour* (1832).
2 James Milne, *New Pitsligo Seventy Years Ago* (1956).
3 L. Derwent, *A Breath of Border Air* (1978).
4 *Fraserburgh Police Commissioner's Minutes 1891*.
5 Bert Murray, *Three Score Years and Ten*.
6 Molly Weir, *Shoes Were For Sunday* (1977).
7 In T. Royle (ed.), *Jock Tamson's Bairns* (1977).
8 George Davidson, *Memories of Whiterashes* (1983).

CHAPTER III: *A Comfortable Life*

1 In I. L. Donnachie and I. Macleod, *Old Galloway* (1974).
2 Janet Story, *Mrs Story's Early Reminiscences* (1911).
3 Janet Story, *Mrs Story's Later Reminiscences* (1913).

4 R. Grant, *Strathalder, A Highland Estate* (1978).
5 Ewan Forbes, *The Aul' Days* (1984).
6 Maurice Lindsay (ed.), *As I Remember* (1979).

CHAPTER IV: *At School*

1 Hugh Miller, *My Schools and Schoolmasters* (1907).
2 Amy Stewart Fraser, *The Hills of Home* (1973).
3 In T. Royle (ed.), *Jock Tamson's Bairns* (1977).
4 Pryse Lockhard Gordon, *Personal Memoirs or Reminiscences of Men and Manners* (1830).
5 Janetta Bowie, *Penny Buff, A Clydeside School in the Thirties* (1975).

CHAPTER V: *Starting Work*

1 James Myles, *Chapters in the Life of a Dundee Factory Boy* (1850).
2 Alexander Somerville, *The Autobiography of a Working Man* (1848).
3 David Kirkwood, *My Life of Revolt* (1935).
4 Robert Barclay, *Reminiscences of an Unlettered Man* (Centre for Scottish Studies, Aberdeen, 1985).
5 *Friday Night Was Brasso Night* (Edinburgh WEA, 1987).

6 John Boyd Orr, *As I Recall* (1966).

CHAPTER VI: *Fishing and Farming*

1 Charles St John, *Tour in Sutherlandshire* (1848).
2 Charles Weld, *Two Months in the Highlands* (1860).
3 Janet Story, *Mrs Story's Early Reminiscences* (1911).
4 James Milne, *The Making of a Buchan Farm* (1889).
5 *Royal Commission on Labour*, (Parliamentary Papers, vol. 36, 1893).
6 Essay read to Rhynie Mutual Improvement Club, 22 March, 1849.
7 Joseph Mitchell, *Reminiscences of My Life in the Highlands* (1883).
8 Alexandra Stewart, *Daughters of the Glen*, ed. I. Macbeath (1986).

CHAPTER VII: *Factory and Mine*

1 *Report of Minutes of Evidence Taken by the Select Committee on the State of the Children Employed in the Manufactories of the United Kingdom* (Parliamentary Papers, vol. 3, 1816).
2 William Cobbett, *Northern Tour* (1832).
3 J. Hume (ed.), *William Brown's 'Early Days in a Dundee Mill, 1819–23'* (Abertay Society, 1980).
4 James Myles, *Chapters in the Life of a Dundee Factory Boy* (1850).
5 David Bremner, *The Industries of Scotland* (1869).
6 Robert Bald, *An Inquiry into the Condition of Women Who Carry Coals Underground in Scotland* (1812).
7 Kellog Durland, *Among the Fife Miners* (1904).

8 Charles Brister, *This is My Kingdom* (1972).

CHAPTER VIII: *Religion*

1 James Russell, *Reminiscences of Yarrow* (1894).
2 Ibid.
3 Elizabeth Grant, *Memoirs of a Highland Lady 1797–1827* (1897).
4 Henry Cockburn, *Journal, 1831–1854* (1874).
5 Eleanor Sillar, *Edinburgh's Child* (1961).
6 Thomas Johnston, *Memories* (1952).
7 Harry McShane and Joan Smith, *Harry McShane: No Mean Fighter* (1978).
8 Ibid.
9 John Boyd Orr, *As I Recall* (1966).

CHAPTER IX: *Sex and Courtship*

1 Isabella L. Bird, *Notes on Old Edinburgh* (1869).
2 The *Scotsman*, May 1870.
3 David Daiches, *Two Worlds* (1957).
4 Ralph Glasser, *Growing Up in the Gorbals* (1986).
5 Edwin Muir, *Scottish Journey* (1935).

CHAPTER X: *Drinking*

1 Henry Cockburn, *Memorials of His Time* (1856).
2 'Shadow' (Alexander Brown), *Midnight Scenes and Social Photographs* (1858).
3 James Devon, *The Criminal and the Community* (1913).
4 Sir Archibald Geikie, *Scottish Reminiscences* (1904).
5 Edwin Muir, *Scottish Journey* (1935).

6 Hugh MacDiarmid, *The Uncanny Scot* (1968).

CHAPTER XI: *Celebration*

1 John Firth, *Reminiscences of an Orkney Parish* (1920).
2 Robert Chambers, *Traditions of Edinburgh* (1825).
3 James Taylor, *Journal of Local Events or Annals of Fenwick* (Ayrshire Archaeological and Natural History Society, 1970).
4 Isobel Anderson, *Inverness Before Railways* (1885).
5 Molly Weir, *Best Foot Forward* (1972).
6 Abe Moffat, *My Life With the Miners* (1965).
7 John R. Allan, *Farmer's Boy* (1935).

CHAPTER XII: *Leisure*

1 Pryse Lockhard Gordon, *Personal Memoirs or Reminiscences of Men and Manners* (1830).
2 Henry Cockburn, *Memorials of His Time* (1856).
3 Janet Story, *Mrs Story's Early Reminiscences* (1911).
4 D. M'Ewan, 'Caddie Willie', in E. Dunlop and A. Kamm, *A Book of Old Edinburgh* (1983).
5 William Haddow, *My Seventy Years* (1943).
6 David Daiches, *Two Worlds* (1957).
7 Dove Paterson, 'How I Handle Pictures', in *Kinematograph and Lantern Weekly*, 1908, as recounted in M. Thomson, *Silver Screen in the Silver City* (1988).
8 Michael Thomson, op.cit.
9 Bob Crampsey, *The Young Civilian* (1987).
10 Mary Rose Liverani, *The Winter Sparrows* (1976).

CHAPTER XIII: *Deprivation*

1 Thomas Pennant, *Tour in Scotland* (1772).
2 Edwin Chadwick, *Reports on the Sanitary Conditions of the Labouring Population of Scotland* (Parliamentary Papers, 1842).
3 *Poor Law Inquiry (Scotland)*: Appendix, Part III (Parliamentary Papers, 1844).
4 'Shadow' (A. Brown), *Midnight Scenes and Social Photographs* (1858).
5 Nigel Gray, *The Worst of Times* (1985).

CHAPTER XIV: *Ill-health*

1 S. Burt, *Letters from a Gentleman in the North of Scotland to his friend in London* (1754).
2 James Hall, *Travels in Scotland by an Unusual Route* (1807).
3 Appendix to the *Report of the Royal Lunacy Commissioners for Scotland* 1855.
4 Angus Maclellan, *The Furrow Behind Me* (1962).
5 'Ten Weeks in a Northern Infirmary' by 'A Patient', in the *Aberdeen Free Press*, 9 March, 1895.
6 Molly Weir, *Best Foot Forward* (1972).
7 C. B. Gunn, *Leaves from the Life of a Country Doctor* (1935).
8 G. Gladstone Robertson, *Gorbals Doctor* (1970).

CHAPTER XV: *Crime*

1 S. Burt, *Letters from a Gentleman in the North of Scotland to his Friend in London* (1754).
2 *Courant*, quoted in Owen Dudley Edwards, *Burke and Hare* (1980).
3 Henry Cockburn, *Memorials of His Time* (1856).

4 *Reminiscences of a Clachnacuddin Nonagenarian* (1886).

5 In J. Cameron, *Prisons and Punishment in Scotland* (1983).

6 James McLevy, *The Casebook of a Victorian Detective* (1975).

7 James Devon, *The Criminal and the Community* (1912).

8 Ralph Glasser, *Growing Up in the Gorbals* (1986).

9 Ken Martin, "Anatomy of a Contemporary Gang", *Observer* magazine (12 December, 1968).

CHAPTER XVI: *Travel*

1 Sir J. H. A. Macdonald, *Life Jottings of an Old Edinburgh Citizen* (1918).

2 J. E. Bowman, *The Highlands and Islands: a 19th-Century Tour* (1986).

3 Osgood Mackenzie, *A Hundred Years in the Highlands* (1921).

4 Joseph Mitchell, *Reminiscences of My Life in the Highlands* (1883).

5 W. Roberton, *Sketches of the Highland Character* (1870).

6 Sir J. H. A. Macdonald, op. cit.

7 David Daiches, *Two Worlds* (1957).

8 Molly Weir, *Shoes Were For Sunday* (1977).

9 Alexandra Stewart, *Daughters of the Glen*, ed. I. Macbeath (1986).

10 *Reminiscences of a Clachnacuddin Nonagenarian* (1886).

11 W. S. Speed, *Very Good Sir*.

CHAPTER XVII: *The Highlands and the Clearances*

1 James Boswell, *Journal of a Tour to the Hebrides with Samuel Johnson* (1773).

2 In R. J. Adam (ed.), *Sutherland Estate Management 1811–16* (Scottish History Society, 1972).

3 *Report on the Condition of the Crofters and Cottars in the Highlands and Islands of Scotland* (Parliamentary Papers, 1884).

4 Sir Archibald Geikie, *Scottish Reminiscences* (1904).

5 Norman Maclean, *The Former Days* (1945).

CHAPTER XVIII: *The Outsiders' Highlands*

1 Queen Victoria, *Leaves from the Journal of Our Life in the Highlands* (1868).

2 Charles St John, *Tour in Sutherlandshire* (1848).

3 [Anon.], *Mountain, Moor and Loch, Illustrated by Pen and Pencil on the Route of the West Highland Railway* (1894).

4 D. Macrae, 'Some Reminiscences of Oban', in *The Book of the Bazaar of Dunollie Road United Free Church, Oban* (1902).

5 J. S. Grant, *The Hub of My Universe* (1982).

Index

Patriots and Liberators
Revolution in the Netherlands 1780–1813

Simon Schama

'A rare and magnificent example of total history.'
Richard Cobb, *Times Literary Supplement*

'An outstanding work of historical scholarship . . . Simon Schama writes brilliantly. He can bring a character alive in a sentence . . . This powerful book reads with the ease of a novel. Every page glitters with intelligence and perception. In every way *Patriots and Liberators* is an extraordinary achievement.'
J. H. Plumb

Between 1780 and 1813 the Dutch Republic – a country once rich enough to be called the cash till of Europe and powerful enough to make war with England – was stripped of its colonies, invaded by its enemies, driven to the edge of bankruptcy, and finally reduced to becoming an appendage of the French Empire. Out of these events Simon Schama has constructed a gripping chronicle of revolution and privateering, constitutions and coups, in a tiny nation desperately struggling to stay afloat in the seas of geopolitics. Like his *The Embarrassment of Riches* and *Citizens*, *Patriots and Liberators* combines a mastery of historical sources with an unabashed delight in narrative. The result confirms Schama as one of the most exciting and engaging historians now at work.

'This remarkable book is more than a revision, it is a revelation.'
A. J. P. Taylor, *Observer*

'A dramatic story, full of pathos and true comedy. If any book may be said to inhale without sententiousness the clear, calm and steadying air of a European ideal, this is it.'
Michael Ratcliffe, *The Times*

'Schama's book is written in the grand manner, its sweep as impressive as its erudition and the constant brilliance of its style. He gives the Dutch revolution back to the people to whom it belonged – the Dutch.'
Economist

ISBN 0 00 686156 3

Fontana Press

Landscapes and Memories

An Intermittent Autobiography

John Prebble

'John Prebble's unselfish, compassionate outlook honours the *necessity* of history in all our lives.'   James Malpas, *Observer*

No living writer is more responsible for shaping our picture of Scotland and its past that John Prebble. With his great trilogy, *The Highland Clearances*, *Glencoe* and *Culloden*, he has brought alive some of the central, tragic episodes in Scottish history with an immediacy that their readers will never forget. *Landscapes and Memories* is as close as Prebble will come to writing an autobiography. Like memory itself, it moves backwards and forwards between the distant and the recent past, between Prebble's recollections of his own life and of the lives and history he has written about.

'Some of the writing is as unforgettable as Dr Zhivago's journey across Siberia. His own story is as moving as any of those sagas of Scottish rural and military life on which he has so solidly built his reputation. All who read or write about Scottish history stand permanently indebted to Prebble.'

John Ure, *Times Literary Supplement*

'Along with Christopher Hill and E. P. Thompson, he deserves his place in that great generation of romantic English Marxists of the 1930s who have devoted their lives to celebrating the losing sides of British history.'   Niall Ferguson, *Daily Mail*

'John Prebble . . . has brought Scottish history to a mass audience in his distinguished books . . . the fit between imagination and reality is perfect.'   Frank McLynn, *Independent*

ISBN 0 00 637460 3

Fontana Press